M. M Blake

The siege of Norwich Castle

A story of the last struggle against the Conqueror

M. M Blake

The siege of Norwich Castle
A story of the last struggle against the Conqueror

ISBN/EAN: 9783744723121

Printed in Europe, USA, Canada, Australia, Japan

Cover: Foto ©ninafisch / pixelio.de

More available books at **www.hansebooks.com**

THE SIEGE
OF NORWICH CASTLE

*A STORY OF THE LAST STRUGGLE
AGAINST THE CONQUEROR*

BY

M. M. BLAKE

With Illustrations by the Author

LONDON
SEELEY AND CO. LIMITED
Essex Street, Strand
1893

TO

MY FATHER

THIS STORY

IS

AFFECTIONATELY

INSCRIBED

CONTENTS.

CHAP.		PAGE
I.	THE SUZERAIN'S 'NAY,'	9
II.	LOVE OR LOYALTY,	25
III.	JEST AND EARNEST,	37
IV.	HORSE, HAWK, AND HOUND,	53
V.	NORMAN AND SAXON,	65
VI.	THE BRIDE-ALE,	74
VII.	DELILAH SHEARS SAMSON,	91
VIII.	KNIGHT-ERRANT AND MERCENARY,	100
IX.	NORWICH,	113
X.	LANFRANC,	127
XI.	THE CASTELLAN OF BLAUNCHEFLOUR,	139
XII.	THE STANDARD OF REVOLT,	148
XIII.	ST. NICHOLAS FOR GUADER!	160
XIV.	HOW THE CONQUEROR DEALS WITH REBELS,	173
XV.	'O HIGH AMBITION LOWLY-LAID!'	189
XVI.	WIFE OR WIDOW?	206
XVII.	HOW RALPH CAME HOME,	222
XVIII.	BESIEGED,	234
XIX.	'STONE WALLS DO NOT A PRISON MAKE,'	244

CONTENTS.

CHAP.		PAGE
XX.	À OUTRANCE,	256
XXI.	THE ORDEAL BY FIRE,	272
XXII.	A SUBTERRANEAN CONFLICT,	285
XXIII.	HOW OLIVER DIED,	299
XXIV.	FAMINE,	313
XXV.	BRETAGNE,	327
XXVI.	CONCLUSION,	336
	APPENDIX,	347

LIST OF ILLUSTRATIONS.

	PAGE
HOW THE CONQUEROR DEALS WITH REBELS,	*Frontispiece*
EMMA FITZOSBERN ACCEPTS THE TASSEL-GENTLE,	62
JUDITH WATCHES HER SLEEPING SPOUSE,	92
LANFRANC JESTS WITH THE CONQUEROR,	130
WALTHEOF'S HUMILIATION,	136
BISHOP ODO MEETS DE GUADER,	170
THE TOWER STAIRS,	178
THE RESCUE OF THE EARL,	198
EMMA'S FIRST SIGHT OF THE FOE,	240
THE BIG RAT HAS GONE INTO HIS HOLE,	292
A WARRENNE! A WARRENNE! FOR WILLIAM THE NORMAN!	300
DE GUADER DONS THE CROSS,	342

THE
SIEGE OF NORWICH CASTLE

CHAPTER I.

THE SUZERAIN'S 'NAY.'

IT was towards the close of the year of our Lord 1073. As we now reckon, it would have been some way into 1074, but in those old times they began their twelve-month on March 25th. So, notwithstanding that the daffy-down-dillies were pushing their grey-green blades through the softening earth, and that the partridges had chosen their mates for the season, it was the end of 1073, and just before Easter.

The fair Emma Fitzosbern, sister and ward of Roger, Earl of Hereford, a young damsel of splendid beauty, in whose honour the chivalric champions of Normandy and Bretagne were busy cracking each other's heads, according to the fashion of the times, had followed the example of the partridges, and promised her hand in marriage.

The mate she had chosen was splendid and brave, and, after the king, was equalled in power and wealth but by two other men in all England. Ralph de Guader or Wader had received the earldom of Norfolk and Suffolk, and the post of Constable of Norwich Castle, from the Conqueror, in return for his services at Hastings and his prowess in beating back the Danes from the eastern coast.

His father and grandfather had held lands in England, and he claimed English blood when it suited his purpose, being the only Englishman who bore the rank of earl, save Waltheof Siwardsson, Earl of Huntingdon, Northampton, and Northumberland; but, to his shame be it spoken, he was also the only Englishman against whom it could be told that he fought on William's side at Hastings.

He had been deprived of the lands of his father, Ralph the Staller, the chronicles record not wherefore, but it might well be that the house of Godwin, when they wrought on King Eadward the Confessor, of sainted memory, to drive his Norman favourites from the land, included Ralph amongst them on account of his Breton mother, whose influence, doubtless, inclined the lad to love the folks from over the sea, and who would have taught him to speak French and demean himself in French ways, and, that so, a very bitter and personal feud lay between him and Harold Godwinsson.

He had retired to his mother's estates of Guader and Montfort, in Bretagne, and had returned thence with a proud following of Breton knights and fighting men, under William of Normandy's banner, making the Norman invasion his opportunity to win back his lands at the sword's point, and to gain other broad acres with them.

In 1073, he, and the man whose brother-in-law he wished to become, young Roger Fitzosbern, Earl of Hereford, and Earl Waltheof, nephew-in-law to the king, were the three most powerful nobles in the country. Their estates almost met across England, and, united together, they might have done much as they wished with the kingdom. The Conqueror by no means desired their closer alliance, as we shall see.

But to Ralph de Guader and Roger of Hereford nothing seemed more reasonable and in every way satisfactory than the union of their houses by marriage. The former especially was wildly eager to cement their friendship by this solid bond, for the very good reason that he was deeply in love with the beautiful and high-spirited Emma, and had carried her favour in tilt and tourney with such determination and fury, that champions were shy of accepting his challenge when he took his place in the lists.

A slight hindrance had marred the progress of the *fiançailles*. William, the Conqueror of England, was also Duke of Normandy, and his restless vassals across the straits were apt to get weary of his continued absence in his new kingdom. Robert of Flanders, his ancient enemy, in battle with whom Emma's father, the famous William Fitzosbern, whom Holingshed calls the king's *coosine*, had lost his life, was always ready to foment any little disputes that might arise amongst them, and King Philip of France had now joined the troublesome Frisian hand and glove. So William thought it wise to go in person to Normandy, to keep guard over the movements of the twain.

Of course the marriage could not take place until the king's consent was obtained, and messengers had been despatched to Normandy by the two earls, praying his consent.

Their return was more than due, and was awaited with some anxiety, as Lent was so near at hand, during which, according to the Roman Church, no marriage could take place. However, travelling in those days was very different to what it is in ours. The Channel could not be crossed in all weathers and all winds, and it was supposed that unfavourable breezes detained the messengers. Not for a moment was there any doubt that the answer, when it did come, would be in the affirmative. Permission had been asked merely as a matter of form.

Meanwhile, every effort was made to entertain the guests at Hereford Castle, and to prevent the time of their prolonged sojourn from hanging heavy on their hands.

In Domesday Book there figures a certain Adelina, a female juggler, as having received lands in the county of Hants, having previously enjoyed fee and salary from one Roger, a Norman earl.

The talents of this lady were in requisition, and, a heavy downpour of rain and sleet having rendered out-door sports unpleasant, a large company of knights and ladies were watching her agile movements and ingenious deceptions; shouts and ripples of laughter testifying to their appreciation of her cleverness.

She performed at one end of the great banqueting-hall, and was clad in a scarlet dress made Eastern fashion, having a gold-broidered jacket of the shape we are accustomed to call Zouave, with loose trousers, and slippers turned up at the toes; she wore a turban upon her head, from beneath which her long black hair streamed unconfined to her waist, around which she wore a girdle of snake-skins; her bare arms were covered with bangles, and in her hand she held a wand on which a child's skull took the place of the Punch's head which adorns the staff of a Polichinello.

She had for assistants two brown-skinned, almond-eyed, white-toothed boys, evidently of Moorish origin, and active as the leopards, whose skins they wore, had been when alive in their native jungle; and the bowls, spheres, and other appliances she used were marked with cabalistic signs in the Arabian alphabet. Evidently, whether or no she was herself of Moorish blood, she had learned her trade from the jugglers of the East, whose skill therein still surpasses all others.

In those days the dark-skinned races were identified with Antichrist, and the entertainment therefore afforded that flavour of the forbidden which seems so necessary to the enjoyment of some folks. A gibbering monkey, which perched on her shoulder, and performed strange antics at her bidding, alternately with wild freaks of mischief of its own invention, added to the air of *diablerie* which made the exhibition attractive.

The young Earl of Hereford, his countess, and their two little sons, were foremost among the spectators, the earl laughing heartily at the tricks of his favourite, and rewarding her skill with praise and *largesse* when any special feat called forth the applause of the guests.

Tall and commanding in figure, his face, clean-shaven after the Norman fashion, was both proud and weak, the features handsome, clear-cut, aquiline, but the chin receding too greatly to betoken a strong character. His dress was of the richest, his tunic of tawny samite, sewn thickly with gems, and his long cloak lined with costly furs, his earl's coronet on his brow.

Beside him sat his beautiful sister, in whose honour all the guests were assembled;—like him, yet showing, in spite of all feminine grace and softness, signs of that strength of will in which he was deficient. Her features, like his, were clear-cut and aquiline, but the full round chin stood out boldly from the white, flawless throat, unadorned by any necklace save the delicate crease which Nature had marked on it, and which some folks call Venus' necklace. Her auburn hair was simply braided in two long plaits, and hung below her waist, and was bound by a fillet of goldsmiths' work. Her arched brows were almost black, and the dark-blue eyes beneath them were full of gentleness and fire. Her tightly-fitting green kirtle was rounded at the base of the slender neck and edged with drawn lawn, and showed the graceful contour of her young figure; and her embroidered skirt, which had been 'looted' by her noble father from the house of some rich Saxon in his Hastings campaign, bore witness to the artistic powers of the Saxon ladies, and also to their industry, for its subtly blended hues had taken years of labour to produce, and such skill as was possessed only by the women of their nation.

Standing near her, with his hand upon her chair, was the hero of the occasion. Ralph de Guader's Breton mother had Southern blood in her veins, and he had inherited from her a swart complexion, coal-black hair which curled crisply on his well-formed head, and the hawk nose and pointed chin which is common in Brittany now, though the Bretons of that day had for the most part the characteristics of the red-haired, blue-eyed Celts, who had left Wales but a short time before. From his English father he had inherited a pair of keen grey eyes, hawk-like as the nose between them, and deep set under cavernous brows, black, and somewhat given to frowning.

His figure was firmly knit, broad-shouldered, but not very tall, and his apparel was as brave as that of his brother earl, his tunic being of ivory silk edged with sable and wrought with gold thread, and the baldric blazed with jewels which supported his *miséricorde*, or dagger of mercy,—a weapon always worn by a Norman noble, and serving to put his wounded enemies out of misery,—whence its name,— to protect him from treachery, and to carve his meat and that of the lady he 'took in' to dinner withal.

The deft Adelina had swallowed swords, and made snakes dance to her piping, and produced intact bracelets which had seemed to be utterly crushed to powder before the spectators' eyes, and had danced herself with marvellous agility and grace, and, in short, had performed many feats which have been rivalled before and since by jugglers ancient and modern, when a young baron stood forth and said to Earl Roger,—

'I have heard, my lord, that yonder Paynim witch hath shrewd skill to read the stars. I prithee, command her that she may tell the fates of those who list to know what shall befall them.'

Then Adelina turned round swiftly, so that the gibbering monkey, which sat on her shoulder, sprang down with a screech.

'I prithee, Sir Earl,' she cried, 'give me no such order, for the spirits I summon have a knack of telling the truth, and there are fates in store for some folks they would ill brook to hear. "Enough for the day is the evil thereof."'

'Nay, take not to quoting Scripture, witch; it hath an awkward sound from thy graceless lips,' returned the earl banteringly. ''Tis a left-handed compliment to pay to the valour of any noble gentleman here, that he should shrink to know the worst the devil can do to him. Summon thy spirits! I wager we will face them.'

Adelina's brown face turned yellow as parchment, her knees shook together for fear.

'I beg thee, spare me, Sir Earl!' she entreated in a low voice.

But her opposition only raised the earl's obstinacy, of

which, like most weak people, he had a large share, and he insisted.

So Adelina gave orders to her attendant sprites, who fetched her a big box, and a tripod with a metal mirror above it, and a brazier hung from chains like a censer, and a skull, and a tame raven.

And out of the box she dragged a huge, sluggish snake. The creature rolled and writhed upon the floor in a fashion that caused the ladies to scream and the knights to lay hold of the hilts of their daggers; but after a while it rolled itself in a ring round the tripod, with its tail to its head, and so lay still.

'Whoever hath courage to step within my magic circle may learn the secrets of the future!' cried the sorceress.

But the young baron who had been so eager to learn his fate did not relish the conditions, and made no move.

Ralph de Guader, seeing his hesitation, stepped forward out of sheer bravado, without having any particular desire to know his fate, or belief in Adelina's power to tell it, for he was happy, and all the future appeared to him steeped in rosy hues of hope.

'Oh, Ralph, deal not with the Evil One!' cried Emma, laying a restraining hand on his arm. 'Trust not that horrible beast, I pray thee!'

Ralph gave some careless excuse, and Emma accepted it; for, to say truth, her young head was full of fiery ambition, and her curiosity was great to know what honours her splendid lover would win for her in the days to come. William of Normandy had carved a throne with his sword for Matilda of Flanders; who knew what Ralph de Guader's good blade might carve for her? Everything seemed possible in those days.

So the Earl of the East Angles stepped down from the daïs to the end of the great hall, where the sorceress stood, and stepped across the spotted body of the snake into the charmed circle it enclosed, bidding Adelina summon her allies, be they fair or foul.

But not without remonstrance from the fortune-teller.

'Pause, De Guader and Montfort, Earl of Norfolk and Suffolk! Thy head is heaped with honours, and thy hands are full of fat manors, and—best of all gifts!—the heart of the fairest lady in the hall is openly bestowed on thee! What more canst thou ask of the future? Take what thou hast, and go barefoot to the chapel and thank the white Christ for His bounty! Stay thy questioning, lest what thou hast shall be reft from thee!'

'A brave man defies fortune,' answered De Guader, tossing back his dark head proudly.

'Then if the prophecy be not to thy liking,' returned Adelina, 'if the spirits foretell evil days, I pray thee blame not their mouthpiece.' Her agitation was extreme, which was not surprising, as the fierce nobles of those days were apt to deal harshly with the messengers of unpleasing news.

She chanted a wild incantation, dancing round the tripod and the earl, and swung her censer to and fro till it gave forth strange fumes and clouds of smoke, by which her face and the earl's were veiled from the spectators. Now and again her turbaned head was seen through the vapours, her eyes intently fixed on her mirror, but none could tell what was passing.

Presently the earl returned to the daïs with a somewhat white face. Emma's eyes were bent upon him with anxious inquiry.

'She has promised me that which I covet most, dear lady,' whispered De Guader in answer to her look: 'my bridal with thee is to come to fulfilment. I am to pass my life with thee, and die with thee, near the blessed city of Jerusalem.'

'The Holy Virgin be praised!' answered Emma devoutly; 'and pardon thee for asking the future, if sin be in it.' Then, recognising the admission she had made by acknowledging her joy in the prophecy, she blushed and turned away from De Guader's happy eyes.

'Aha! sister of mine, it seems my sorceress has pleasured thee with her prophecies,' remarked Earl Roger. 'I will see if she can be equally gracious to me.'

'Thou hadst best brace thy nerves for a shock, man,' cried De Guader after him as he left the daïs. 'Those spirits have verily a knack of telling home truths without mincing matters.'

Adelina's agitation increased when she saw her master appearing as the next candidate. She trembled from head to foot.

'I prithee spare me this, Roger Fitzosbern,' she said in a scarce audible voice. But the earl insisted.

Then followed the same preliminaries as before,—the dance, and the chant, and the smoke-wreaths, then the whispered mysteries. But this time sharp, angry interjections and round Norman oaths were mingled with the murmurings of Adelina's voice, and all at once the unhappy fortune-teller threw up her bangled arms and fell backwards fainting, while the Earl of Hereford, with an angry stamp, broke out of the charmed circle and rushed back to his seat.

Adelina's neophytes ran forward to the rescue, for her garments had caught fire from the censer, and all was bustle and confusion. The huge snake lay calmly through it, however, for, to say truth, it was stuffed, and worked with wires.

The Countess of Hereford sprang up to greet her lord, and the two little boys burst out a-wailing, sore frightened at their father's altered face, while Emma also rose to greet her brother with terror in her eyes, trembling at the evidence he gave that evil had been foretold him.

But he soon regained his calmness, and laughed as he saw the reflection of his mood in their agonised faces.

'Pah! it is all nonsense!' he said, wiping the sweat from his brow. 'I believe the witch must be in league with the devil to have so wrought on me.'

He looked round the hall, and gave another forced laugh.

'I am to lose all my lands, to be despoiled of my earldom, and die in prison, she says.'

The ladies exclaimed in horror, and the men laughed derisively; but Earl Ralph's jester, Grillonne, whispered sagely to his neighbour, 'Good nuncle! when they promised me a swishing at school, I made effort to keep it to myself. But I am a fool.'

No one seemed inclined to consult such a fortune-teller for his own part, and the Earl of Hereford ordered a Welsh minstrel, who had been sent him in compliment by one of the Welsh chiefs on the Marches, whom Hereford had lately beaten and made terms with, to regale the company with some of his ballads.

At this juncture a great shout was heard from the castle-yard, and a moment later a servitor announced the return of the messenger who had been sent to the king; and, the Earl of Hereford bidding him enter, a knight and squire, travel-stained and showing signs of a hasty journey, advanced up the hall and bowed before the daïs.

The knight dropped on his knee, and presented the earl with a missive tied with purple silk and sealed with the royal seal.

'How now, Sir Neel! how comest thou so tardily?' demanded the earl, taking the letter from the knight with eager hands and severing the silk with his dagger.

'I was detained, my lord, at Rouen to wait the king's good pleasure.'

The faces of the two earls darkened, and Roger Fitzosbern tore open the king's missive.

Scarce reading it, he flung it to De Guader with a savage oath, stamping his foot upon the ground.

'William shall rue this insult!' he hissed between his

shut teeth, his face scarlet and convulsed with rage; 'and to my father's son.'

De Guader, not less moved, held the parchment with hands that so shook with anger that the dangling seals clattered against each other. His broad chest heaved, and his steel-grey eyes flashed fire as sword strikes fire on helm.

Emma, with pale cheeks and wide eyes, turned from her brother to her lover, and the East Anglian earl, exercising a huge command over himself, kept silence, and returned the letter to Roger Fitzosbern.

Hereford shook it in the air, clenching his fingers, while all the guests hung wonderingly on his actions.

Suddenly he tore the king's letter into fragments.

'Thus has William rent in sunder the ties that bound me to him!' he shouted furiously.

Osbern, Bishop of Exeter, the Earl of Hereford's uncle, who, though he had refused the sanction of his presence to the performances of Adelina, had entered the hall when the king's messenger arrived, made his way through the noble crowd that surrounded his nephew.

'Hist, my Roger! Anger is short madness. Keep a hold over the unruly member, lest words spoken in wrath be thy bane in time of peace. I know not the contents of the missive that hath moved thee so greatly, but I prithee be calm.'

'Calm!' cried Roger. 'Calm! De Guader, art thou calm?'

'Yes,' answered De Guader shortly, his breath breaking in quick pants, and a strange green light not pleasant to witness gleaming in his eyes, so that all who saw him felt that his calmness was more terrible than Roger's fury.

'Then, by the rood! if thou art so calm,' retorted Hereford, 'tell my guests how they have been befooled Tell my sister she has bestowed her hand on one who can resign it "calmly."'

'My son, my son,' remonstrated the bishop, 'thou art unjust to thy noble brother, whose stake in this matter is even greater than thine.'

'Nay, my brother he is forbid to be!' stormed Roger, with another terrific curse.

De Guader turned to the beautiful girl to whom he had come to bind himself in solemn betrothal, and who, having accepted his wooing, had made no secret of her love.

His face was pallid almost as his ivory robe, his lips trembled as he held out his hands to her, but for some moments he was dumb. When at last he compelled speech, his voice was dull with pain and quivering with measureless indignation.

'My lady,' he said, holding one of her hands in each of his, but not trusting himself to look in her face, 'I must bid thee farewell. I have no right to remain longer in this castle. The king has forbidden our marriage. I had hoped to make thee my bride. Bride of my heart thou wilt always be!'

Before the startled, frightened girl could frame a reply, he had stooped and kissed her, sprung from the daïs, and was striding down the hall, with the many barons and bannerets, knights and squires, who formed his *meinie*, following behind him.

The Countess of Hereford led her young sister-in-law from the hall; while the remainder of the noble company, feeling their presence somewhat awkward, as guests at a betrothal which could not be consummated, found excuses to depart, and gathered into clusters, each lord summoning his following and the ladies of his household.

So that goodly company broke up in hurry and confusion and dismay, and the insult the king had inflicted on his two powerful earls was the talk of every mouth.

CHAPTER II.

LOVE OR LOYALTY.

SHORTLY after Easter, on the day that would have been her wedding-day, Emma Fitzosbern sat in her bower in Hereford Castle, looking dreamily at the misty outlines of the distant Welsh hills, behind which the sun was setting in golden splendour. Her favourite bower-maiden sat on a low stool at her feet, and the glory of the sunset poured over the graceful figures of the two girls, and gilded the maundry work of rushes at their feet and the rich tapestry which covered the walls around them, while the gorgeous clouds were piled into battlemented towers, mocking with their vapoury illusion the solid masonry below them.

Emma's companion was looking up at her face with an expression of tender love and sympathy. She was a girl of seventeen, some four years younger than her lady, and wore the Saxon headrail; the little rings of hair which escaped from its close cover were of Saxon gold, while her pale blue robe was made in the fashion of that nation, full and flowing, with large, hanging sleeves. The girdle with which it was bound was ornamented with jewels, and the hems were edged with fur. Her face was less animated and striking than that of the noble Norman, but had a winsome beauty of its own, the blue eyes frank and affectionate, and the rounded features not wanting in character.

An embroidery frame stood before them ; for though Eadgyth of Norwich had lived in a Norman household since she was ten, she had perseveringly acquired the special accomplishment of her countrywomen in spite of difficulties, and Emma fitfully worked at it also under her guidance.

Eadgyth was a cousin in some sort, second or third, perhaps, to Harold Godwinsson, and made it a point of honour to keep his memory green, though she had grown to love dearly the generous Norman maiden, who treated her more as a sister than a dependent.

Many relatives of Harold had property in Norwich, and when Ralph de Guader had received his earldom of Norfolk and Suffolk, which Harold's death on the field of Senlac had rendered vacant, he had taken pity on the forlorn condition of the little damsel, whose male relatives had been slain in the contest, and who was thus left without protection from the insolent conquerors. De Guader had been amused by the patriotic defiance the bereaved maiden of ten had flung at him, rating him as a renegade and a murderer, with other terms of equal politeness which had sounded oddly from her flower-like mouth, and perhaps his conscience smote him, and told him they were not untrue. Her courage moved his admiration and generosity, and, having no womenfolk of his own to whom he could confide her, he had induced William Fitzosbern, the Norman Earl of Hereford, to take her into his castle as a playmate and lady-in-waiting for his daughter Emma. So began a companionship which was to endure for their lives.

The tide of sad reflection was flooding Emma's heart to the brim. Since the cruel day on which the king's mandate had been received, the subject of her interrupted betrothal had been buried in dead silence. Her brother and guardian, the young Earl of Hereford, had set out on a journey a day or two later, but had left even his wife in ignorance of its aim and direction. Emma, on her own part, had shrunk from speech. Her wounds were too sore to bear the probing even of those who loved her. But at length, on this bright May evening, she spoke.

'This was to have been my wedding-day, Eadgyth,' she said.

A cloud of scornful anger passed over the face of the Saxon girl, and her blue eyes flashed.

'So William of Normandy has ruined both our lives!' she said hotly, her young voice quivering with passion. 'I would that the earth had opened and swallowed him up when he first set foot on English ground, instead of only catching him by the ankle, to enable him to make a jest and find a good omen!'

Emma bent down, laughing, that she might not cry.

'Hush!' she said; 'little rebel, thou art talking treason!'

'Nay,' returned Eadgyth, 'for I have never vowed fealty.'

'Ah, well,' answered Emma, sighing, 'my forbears have fought for William's forbears for generations! It is bred in my blood to be obedient to him. He would never have been King of England, had not my father lavished wealth and activity, and roused the barons and the burghers by example and ruse.'

'A fine reason, truly, for making thy father's daughter miserable,' quoth Eadgyth. 'Nevertheless, if thou art bred to obedience, it seemeth not less irksome to thee! Perhaps it is because he owes the keeping of the English crown to the valour with which Ralph de Guader beat back the Danes, that he thwarts *him!* Not that I can spare any pity for Ralph. If he had not played my cousin Harold false, how different all things might have been. He, the grand-nephew of the sainted King Eadward! It seems a just retribution that William should thwart him.'

'On my part, I cannot account it a crime in Ralph to have sided with my countrymen,' Emma said, with a gentle smile; 'but we cannot look on those things with the same eyes.'

'No; I think it is perhaps a good thing that thou sittest here, instead of being Ralph de Guader's bride, though I had lief have gone with thee to my dear old Norwich,' said Eadgyth. 'My dear old Norwich!' she repeated, with a sigh. 'I should scarce know it again, with its fine new castle, and its streets full of Normans and Bretons, and foul, greedy Jews.'

'Oh, Eadgyth! Eadgyth! I will have no more to say to thee, if thou takest part against my knight!' said Emma, withdrawing her hands and folding them on her lap.

'I did not mean to wound thee, Emma!' exclaimed the Saxon, clasping both hands affectionately round Emma's right arm. 'I must needs be grateful to the earl, since I owe to him my happy home with thee. Yet,' she added sadly, 'forgive me if I cannot quite forget that such a refuge would not have been needful to me, if he had been firm to the Dragon standard. Disguise it as thou wilt, I am but thy serving-maiden.'

'When I strive so carefully to disguise it, dost thou think it generous thus to pull it forth to the light of day?' asked Emma, and the tears, which she had till then kept back with difficulty, would no longer be restrained, and rolled rapidly down her cheeks.

'No, it is not generous!' cried Eadgyth, full of ruth. 'And I am not worthy to lace thy shoe latchet! Forgive me, dear Emma!'

As she spoke, the ring of a mailed footstep sounded in the corridor without, and the door was unceremoniously opened, and gave entrance to the young Earl of Hereford, clad in a whole suit of mail, but unhelmed.

'What! sitting in darkness, maidens?' and, turning to a varlet with a torch, who had accompanied him to the door, he took it from the lad's hold, and placed it with his own hands in a sconce beside the hearth. 'I love the light,' he said, laughing. 'Leave darkness to the bats and owls.'

Emma had risen, and ran to him gladly, kissing him on the cheek. 'Oh, Roger!' she said, 'I am so glad of thy return!'

But the joy that had come into her face at his unexpected appearance did not dry the tears which she had forgotten to wipe away in her surprise, and he saw them.

'Tears, Emma, tears? What! is my little sister weeping?' he asked in a tone that was half banter, half tenderness. 'This is a thing that must be inquired into. I can have no weeping damsels in castle of mine.'

'Eadgyth and I were quarrelling,' said Emma gaily, 'because we were so lonely in thine absence, and could find nothing better to do.'

'By the mass! that won't serve thee for an excuse, Emma,' answered the earl; then, taking her hands and looking searchingly in her face, he said somewhat sternly, as if to compel an answer, 'Art thou fretting at the breaking of thy troth with Ralph de Guader?'

Emma turned away blushing from his scrutiny.

'The wound is fresh yet, Roger!' she said. 'It will bleed. Time will perchance heal it.'

'And by all the saints! a very short time too!' said Hereford triumphantly. 'Thou shalt plight a new troth to-night.'

Emma started with apprehension. In those days, damsels of rank were often disposed of in marriage by their male relatives with very little regard to their prejudices or affections, a girl's whimsies appearing of small consequence in their eyes beside the importance of a good political alliance, and Emma feared lest her brother might intend to demand a summary transference of her affections. Hitherto, it was true that the young earl had been tender and indulgent, and had regarded her wishes the more readily perhaps in this matter, that Ralph de Guader, the powerful Earl of East Anglia, was the very man of all others to suit his views of a desirable brother-in-law. But Emma knew him to be both impulsive and obstinate, and visions of a fierce struggle with him, ending in the cloister, the haven of refuge for women in those days, passed through her mind.

The earl, however, took no notice of her trepidation. 'Come,' he said, and led the way down the wide stone staircase. Emma followed trembling, and wondering what ordeal was before her. They entered a small room set apart near the great banqueting-hall, which was the earl's special sanctum.

The next moment she found herself with her two hands clasped in those of Ralph de Guader, while he was looking down at her with a hunger of entreaty in his eyes; and in the minds of both was the unspoken thought, that if all had gone well they would have been husband and wife that day.

The revulsion from apprehension to joy was so great as to be almost a pain.

'Is it thou indeed, Ralph?' she faltered; and the young Earl of Hereford laughed.

'Didst think I had brought home an ogre to be my *beau-frère*,' he asked, 'that thou wast so sore afraid?'

Emma turned anxiously to De Guader.

'The king, then, has relented?' she said quickly. 'In

sooth, I doubted not his heart would soften. He could not be so cruel as to part us!'

De Guader shot a questioning glance at Hereford.

'Plead thine own cause, valiant knight!' said Roger a little sarcastically. 'I was never a maker of speeches, and, by the Holy Virgin! thy eloquence has twisted me round thy little finger. See if thou canst vie with a woman's sharp wits. To say truth, I care not to breathe thy plan to the vagrant air, it has such a treasonable savour.'

Emma looked from one to the other for a solution of the mystery, but she did not see much in De Guader's dark, handsome face to help her to read riddles.

'Thy brother bids me proffer my own petition, dear lady,' he said. 'If I hesitate, be merciful to my unreadiness, for it is no easy boon I come to ask of thee.'

He led her to a carved settle which stood beside the fireplace, and when she was seated, he stood before her silently a moment or two, the firelight scintillating on the rings of the mail in which he was sheathed from head to foot, and sparkling on the jewels of his baldric and the golden hilt of his great two-handed sword, for, like her brother, he was still in his harness.

'Noble Emma, I have come to ask thee to share with me danger and difficulty,' he said. 'The king has not relented. But his mandate is unjust, and I beg thee to disregard it, and to give me once more the sweet promise that thou wilt be my bride.'

'Dost thou mean that thou wouldst ask me to defy the king?' faltered Emma, a great terror chasing away the short-lived joy which had flooded her heart. She turned wide, anxious eyes upon her brother.

'Dost thou not see, Emma, we are sick of spending our lives for William, and getting nothing but kicks and curses from him?' explained the prosaic Roger. 'By the mass! it is hard on Ralph and on me, after so much faithful service, and so maint hard blows given and taken in William's business, that he should mar all our plans and spoil all our pleasure by putting his veto on your marriage. A curse on loyalty! If this is all it brings, we may as well be a little disloyal.'

Roger had better have allowed his friend to plead his own cause as he had bidden him to do. Ralph's appeal to Emma to share danger with him had touched her generous spirit. Her brother's outburst against his sovereign roused all her loyalty.

'I know not what to reply to such converse,' said Emma indignantly; then added, between jest and earnest, the tears trembling on her lashes as she looked at her brother, 'I would fain let it pass as a bad joke, or to think that perchance ye twain have been drinking a little copiously at the wine-cup.'

'Nay, Emma, that is an injustice!' cried Hereford, bursting into laughter, and clapping his hand down upon De Guader's mailed shoulder; 'when this poor love-lorn galliard would not break fast till he had seen thee, albeit he had been in selle all day, so fire-hot was he to mend his broken troth.'

'It may well seem strange converse to the gentle damsel,' said Ralph gravely. 'The earl your father

C

almost worshipped William of Normandy, who, in good sooth, would never have been King of England but for his stalwart aid, and she has never heard whisper of aught against the king. We who have writhed under his imperious tyranny, and groaned in spirit so fiercely,'—here the level brows were knitted and the entreating face grew stern, while the green light shone in the deep-set eyes,—'can scarce conceive the shock she feels at our sudden speech.'

'She will have to get used to it,' said Earl Roger dryly, 'for my patience is at an end. Beshrew me! she will hear a good deal of such talk. William has ever popped upon me like a cat on a mouse whenever any scheme which promised me well was in hand. And what has he given me but ravaged land that the Welsh run over and harry at will? I say he only gives away what he must needs pay a garrison to defend if he kept it himself. What is your earldom of Norwich, Ralph, but sea-washed dunes or waste corn lands? He is ever nibbling at our power. Earls, indeed! Poor earls are we beside Godwin, Leofric, and Siward! But I tell thee he has gone too far this time. I'll not be thwarted in my plan to be thy brother-in-law; no, neither by king-lord or foolish damsel!' He turned to Emma somewhat fiercely. 'Hark ye, sister of mine, by the little finger of St. Nicholas, to whom De Guader has dedicated his castle of Blauncheflour, thou hadst better make no mincing about accepting a man thou hast already pleaded guilty to loving, or I shall have a crow to pluck with thee!'

'Nay, nay!' exclaimed the courteous De Guader, smiling affectionately at the bewildered and somewhat frightened Emma, and not a little pleased by this crude revelation of his lady's favour. 'Thy noble sister must take me of her own free will or not at all. Holy Virgin! her will is my law.'

Emma raised her head with a proud and splendid gesture.

'Ay,' she cried, 'Sir Earl of Norwich! I will have neither thee nor any man else but of my own free will! Did they stretch me on the rack, or persuade me ever so by such-like loving persuasions, I would have none I did not choose!'

The two earls laughed.

'Well crowed, fair hen!' cried her brother, and Ralph regarded her with admiring eyes.

'There spoke the true daughter of William Fitzosbern, eh, Roger?' he exclaimed. 'Methinks if the Lady Emma had felt the Conqueror's heel as heavy as we, her blood would boil as easily. But in sooth, dear lady, the minstrels and romaunt writers fill damsels' heads with fine notions which we poor knights find it hard to carry out in the vulgar battle of everyday life. Thy hero William, our lord-king himself, rebelled when he was ordered to give up the chosen of his heart, the beautiful Matilda of Flanders; and—saints defend us! —it was the Holy Father himself that he disobeyed!' Here the earl crossed himself.

'Thou hast a noble example, Emma; make haste to follow it,' said her brother jestingly.

'Oh,' said Emma, 'your converse brings me to perplexity. Give me till the morning, and let me ponder on your words. They are sudden.'

Ralph raised her hand respectfully to his lips.

'We can do no less, dear lady,' he said.

CHAPTER III.

JEST AND EARNEST.

'THAT means,' said Ralph de Guader thoughtfully, when Emma had left the room, '"Let me consult my ghostly counsellor." Who is the Lady Emma's director, Fitzosbern? Is not Father Theodred of Crowland thine almoner?—he who was the pet of our East Anglian Bishop Æthelmær, and who was recommended to thee by thine English-loving uncle of Exeter?'

'That is so,' assented Hereford; but added impatiently, 'I prithee truce to thy plans and plottings. I am no moonstruck lover, and cannot subsist on air, however well such unsubstantial fare may suit thy humour. Here we have ridden a good thirty miles, and talked a candle to the sconce, and I vow to thee, I had liefer satisfy my hunger than my ambition. What boots a fat earldom to a man if he is to die of starvation before he gets it?'

De Guader glanced rather contemptuously at his companion, but prepared to follow him.

'Let me have speech with thine almoner this night, nevertheless,' he said, 'in my chamber when I retire from the hall. It may make or mar our undertaking.'

'As thou wilt,' answered Roger carelessly; 'but thou canst scarce expect to find the good man in the best of humours if thou hast so little grace as to waken him up in the dead of night. I warrant me he has been snug under his coverlet this two hours.'

'I have that to say which will wake him,' said Ralph grimly. 'But of a truth the hours have sped. It would be better, perhaps, to pray the good father to give me audience with him in the morning, before he sees any other. Wilt thou have such message delivered?'

Earl Roger called a menial and gave the necessary order, and summoned his armourer, whom he bade to attend his guest, and then wait on himself; and they retired to their chambers to be unharnessed of their armour,—a process requiring aid of hammer and tongs,—and to indulge in the refreshment of the bath, a luxury the Normans loved as dearly as the Romans.

The hour was not far past nine, and, to our way of thinking, would not have been late; but the Norman fashion was to begin the day early, dinner being served at nine in the morning, and a second meal only being usual. When a third meal was desired, as on this occasion, it was informal, and consisted usually of cold meats, being called *liverie*.

Accordingly, when the two earls met again, clad in the flowing robes which replaced their military accoutrements, they had no companions at the table save a couple of fine bloodhounds, which were pets of the Earl of Hereford, and had invited themselves when they smelt the good cheer; the Countess of Hereford remaining in her bower, where her husband had visited her, and delighted her by his unexpected return.

The table was covered with fine linen; tall candles, in golden candlesticks handsomely wrought, gave light to the scene; and the dishes of gold and silver containing the meats were presented on the knee by pages, whose tunics were embroidered with the Hereford cognisance, gules, a bend azure and a fesse or.

Before commencing their meal, a silver basin containing scented water was offered to the earls in which to wash their hands. De Guader called for a napkin on which to dry the fingers he had daintily dipped into the scent, whereat the page opened wide eyes, though he obeyed the order, for the Norman fashion was to wave the hands in the air till they were dry, so that the scent might not be lost, and to wipe them on a cloth was considered Saxon and barbaric.

'I am cultivating English ways, thou seest,' observed the Earl of the East Angles. 'It is well to begin at once.' Whereat Hereford laughed.

The fare was dainty rather than bountiful. A cold venison pasty, and a young heron, larded, roasted, and eaten with ginger, forming the most important dishes; with simnel and wastel cakes, and sundry sweetmeats, and wines rejoicing in the strange names of pigment and moral.

The earls carved for themselves with their daggers, and used neither forks nor spoons.

Hereford, although he had declared himself in such a famished condition, showed no great prowess as a trencherman, but seemed more inclined to help himself from the wine-cup. He was obviously in an unsettled and irritable mood, while his companion inclined to the taciturn.

Suddenly Earl Roger exclaimed,—

'By the mass! this meal is not sprightly. Did I not see thy jester Grillonne amongst thy *meinie?* Send for the rogue and for my Marlette, and let the twain hold a tourney of wit. Though I wager thy knave will win.'

'If thy sleepy almoner might not be summoned from his slumber to hold converse on a weighty matter, methinks it is somewhat hard that my poor jester should be called upon to cudgel his wits!' said Ralph. 'But as thou wilt.'

'I'll waken the varlet up with a cup of moral,' answered Hereford; and a few moments later the two fools were introduced, in obedience to his order,—Marlette rubbing his eyes and yawning; Grillonne awake and eager-eyed.

Marlette was a poor imbecile, with a heavy face and clumsy figure, who caused laughter more by the incongruity of his short, puzzle-headed interjections, than by any real humour in his sayings. But the Earl of East Anglia's jester was a born buffoon, who would have made a comfortable living, if not a fortune, in the circus in these days. Little, alert, wiry, his lithe body seemed to be always in motion, and the bells on his peaked cap rarely ceased to jingle. He was nearly sixty, and his scant white hair, straggling from under his whimsical headgear, gave him an elfish look, enhanced by the wizened, wrinkled countenance beneath it, and his oblique, twinkling eyes. He was a Breton, who had come over in the train of Ralph the Staller's Breton bride in good King Eadward's days, and he had loved the gentle lady, who was always kind to him, and well pleased to hear him troll French ballads when she grew weary of hearing the strange Saxon tongue, and felt forlorn and homesick. And he had loved her handsome boy, who inherited her dark face and eagle nose, though not her bright dark eyes, and had followed him back to Brittany, when, for some reason the chroniclers do not report, he had suffered banishment and confiscation of his estates. And he had returned with him when he helped the Conqueror to win England. De Guader knew and valued his fidelity, and took him with him whithersoever he went.

'How now, fool Grillonne!' was the Earl of Hereford's greeting. 'I promised to pour out a full cup of moral to wake thee up withal, but it seems thou art by far too much awake already. I had best give two cups to Marlette here.'

'Nay, good uncle,' cried the jester, 'that would be but sorry sport! I do but walk in my sleep. Give me the wine, and thou wilt see me in my waking state.'

The earl signed to a page to pour out a cup of wine, and handed it to him. He drank it, not hastily, but sipping it, and smacking his lips with the air of a judge;

and when he had drained the cup he turned it bottom upwards. He then performed a series of somersaults from one end of the long banqueting-hall to the other, and finished by springing upon the shoulders of Marlette, standing erect with one foot upon the table, and the other on his brother fool's neck.

'Ha! Good nuncles, I am like our lord King William astride of two kingdoms!' he cried, waving his bauble as if it were a sceptre, and aping an air of majesty, rendered most ridiculous by his effort to keep his balance on his unequal and, on one side, unsteady footing.

Marlette, astonished and quite at a nonplus, sought only to free himself from the weight on his shoulder, and with a yell dropped his half-empty goblet of wine, and dashed away, leaving the saucy Grillonne sprawling on his back on the table, while the pages sprang forward to rescue the dishes, and the bloodhounds snarled in fierce surprise.

'Help, help, good nuncles!' cried the jester. 'Mine island gives me the slip. Ah, well, I'll content myself with the continent! It hath good cheer upon it.' So saying, he began to help himself to the dainties in his reach.

The Earl of Hereford burst into a roar of laughter, but the jester's master, smiling grimly, bade him beware of unseemly subjects. 'Crowned heads are no fit themes for thy cracks, Sir Fool!' he said.

'Chide me not, my Earl of earls!' replied the jester, who saw that his lord was not seriously displeased. 'I meant no damage or irreverence. I have too great a respect for my hide, and would fain save it a tanning!' Wherewith he descended from the table with an air of the most sage gravity, calmly filling his pockets the while with simnels.

'Go to! Thou art an impudent knave!' cried De Guader; and Earl Roger, laughing more heartily than before, pulled out a penny (equal to about seventeen shillings and sixpence of our money) and tossed it to him.

'Thou art the prince of fools!' he exclaimed. 'Would I had thee in my following. Thou art of some worth to drive dull care away.'

In explanation of the fool's dangerous jest, we may relate how William of Normandy dealt with the Angevins when they dared to remind him that his mother was the daughter of a tanner, by ornamenting the walls of Alençon with hides, and shouting '*La Pel! à la Pel!*' in ridicule, when he came to besiege their town. They had formed a *tête-du-pont* to cover the passage of the river, from which William dislodged them by filling up the moat with wood and firing it, so that the unfortunate Angevins were surrounded by flames, through which gleamed the swords of the mocking Normans, barring their passage to the river beyond. The half-roasted garrison fought with unavailing valour, but twenty surviving for a still worse fate from their relentless foe. William ordered their hands and feet to be cut off and their eyes to be put out, and despatched an Angevin soldier, who had previously been made prisoner, and who had witnessed the punishment, to tell the garrison how their comrades had fared, and to promise them a similar fate unless they surrendered before night. That they might not doubt the veracity of the messenger, he had the hands and feet which had been struck from the prisoners put into his mangonels, and shot them on to the walls, which so impressed the townsmen that they surrendered at once.

When the two earls had finished their repast, they retired to their sleeping chambers; but as Ralph de Guader reached his apartment, he was met by the Earl of Hereford's almoner.

'I am come, noble earl, in obedience to thy summons,' he said, 'understanding that thy wish was to have speech of me before any other; and I venture to intrude on thee to-night, because the Lady Emma has desired me to attend her at daybreak.'

'Ha! just as I expected,' said the earl to himself. 'I thank thee, reverend father,' he replied. 'It is courteous and kind, and my wish was to have speech with thee to-night, but that I feared to break in upon thy rest. Take me, I pray thee, to thy sanctum, where we may be together without audience.'

Theodred bowed his assent, and the earl, having dismissed his attendants, followed the almoner to his private apartment, a small but snug room in a recess in one of the towers of the castle. In the centre stood a small table bearing a silver crucifix, covered with parchments and materials for writing and illuminating, a page of an unfinished missal lying on the writing-desk, and showing what the occupant's last business had been.

Father Theodred offered to the earl the carved settle which stood before his writing-desk, and De Guader sank into it with a sigh, and for a time was silent. Theodred, meanwhile, acceding with rare delicacy to his guest's mood, turned to a corner of the room in which was fitted up a small shrine of the Virgin, and busied himself by trimming the little lamp of oil which burned before it perpetually.

He was a man of about fifty years of age, strongly built, and of the very fair complexion characteristic of the Anglo-Danes, the ring of hair upon his tonsured head being lighter in colour than the shaven crown, with a ruddy, healthy face, and kind, frank blue eyes.

'Thine occupation, father, reminds me that I am the guest of a holy man,' said the earl, as the almoner turned to him again. 'I prithee give me thy blessing.'

'Thou hast it, my son,' answered the priest, extending his hands and making the sign of the cross over Ralph's bent head, and murmuring a benediction.

'Thou sayest,' Ralph began, after a time, 'that the Lady Emma has expressed her desire to consult thee. The matter on which she desires thy guidance is one of some weight.'

Theodred seated himself on a wooden stool at a short distance from the earl.

'Doubtless the matter on which the noble Earl of East Anglia would consult me is one of importance also?' he said.

'The matter on which we twain seek thee, father, is one and the same,' said Ralph, with a smile, 'as thy shrewd wits have doubtless already opined.'

'I had some such notion,' answered the almoner gravely.

'Father Theodred,' said Ralph, grave in his turn, 'thou hast the reputation of an honourable man, and I am about to repose in thee a trust that will put the fortunes, and even the lives, of more than one noble personage, including myself, in thy hands.'

Theodred sprang up hastily.

'Stay thy tongue, noble earl!' said he; 'trust neither thy fortune nor thy life in my hands. Thou knowest my English sympathies, and how thou hast outraged them. How can I bear goodwill to the only English noble who fought beside the Norman on the fatal field where Harold Godwinsson—whom God assoilzie!—lost his precious life?'

The powerful De Guader, famed for his pride and haughtiness, and his impatience of all rebuke, even from his royal master, bore this bold speech from the Earl of Hereford's almoner with bent head and dejected mien.

'What if I repent?' he asked softly, his rich voice quavering as he spoke.

Theodred gazed at him with astonished and doubtful eyes, and came back to his stool and sat down again opposite to him.

The earl raised his head and looked the almoner in the face with a keen, appealing glance.

'What if it is to those very English sympathies that I appeal?' he asked.

Theodred, considerably affected, answered, 'Nay then, speak out.'

'And if thou canst not support me, what I say shall be as unspoken?'

'Even so.'

'Swear thou that on the bones of St. Guthlac!'

'The son of Ralph the Staller should know that an Englishman's word is as good as his oath.'

'I will trust thy good faith. A half confidence is but a fool's wisdom. The point on which the Lady Emma will ask thy guidance is as to whether she shall yet deign to be my wife.'

'Ah!' said Theodred, almost involuntarily, in a low tone; 'hast thou ventured so far? Against the king's veto?'

'By St. Eadward, yes!'

Theodred's face darkened. 'Take not the name of that holy saint, who was world-king and heaven-king also, to witness to thy sin! Thinkest thou I will aid thee in treachery to thy liege lord?'

'Sin or no sin, there are those high in the Church who will aid me. Dost thou esteem thyself holier than these?'

The earl leaned forward and whispered in Theodred's ear the names of several high dignitaries of the English Church, including several abbots and bishops.

Theodred betrayed great astonishment.

'What meanest thou?' he asked.

'I mean that there is more in this matter than is at present understanded of thee,' said De Guader. 'Perhaps some insight into my own standpoint would best help thee to the whole question.'

The almoner assumed an attitude of respectful attention.

'Thou dost me great honour, noble earl,' he said. 'Nevertheless I must protest that as a simple priest I had rather keep to matters more within my province.'

'These matters must be within thy province, since thy guidance will be asked by the noble demoiselle whose part in them is of such import,' urged De Guader; and the priest sighed deeply, for he had a great love for the gentle girl whose adviser he must needs be in this the chief step of her young life. He saw nothing but strife before her, and was sorely perplexed as to whether he should forward her happiness, or, still more, her spiritual welfare, by aiding or hindering the suit of the turbulent man who was thus seeking to win him to his side, and whom he scarcely knew whether to abhor for his part at Senlac, or to love as the son of Ralph the Staller. Certes De Guader's show of contrition had strangely moved him, and the bruised and bleeding patriotism which was his strongest passion waked into painful life at the sight.

'Thou knowest,' said Earl Ralph, 'how, when my noble father, Ralph the Staller, died, Earl Godwin, in his hate of the Normans, or any from across the straits, worked with the blessed King Eadward against my Breton mother and myself, her stripling son, or rather, I should say, so wearied him out with complaints against us, made by his daughter Eadgyth, the king's wife, that at last the good king gave ear to a trumped-up story of treasonable practices on our innocent parts, and took my father's lands from his widow and orphan, so that we had to go beyond the sea to my mother's estates in Bretagne.'

'I have heard a version of the matter,' said Theodred —'somewhat differing!' he added, under his breath.

'Canst thou wonder, then, that my love for Harold Godwinsson was not overflowing? the more so as he claimed for himself those dear lands of Norfolk and Suffolk, where my boyhood had been passed. Canst thou wonder that, when he broke his oath to William of Normandy, whom he had sworn not to hinder in his claims to the English throne,—sworn, as thou knowest, on the most sacred relics'—

Theodred groaned. 'Harold knew not that the relics were there till after he had sworn,' he murmured.

'An Englishman's word should be as good as his oath, thou hast said it,' rejoined the earl. 'Canst thou wonder, I ask, that I ranged myself under the banner of the leader whose accolade had given me knighthood to win back those lands of my father's?'

'How couldst thou? How couldst thou fight thy father's countrymen, even to win back thy father's lands?' cried the priest, with irrepressible emotion.

Ralph sprang up and paced about the room. 'Nay, I would give my right hand I had not done it,' he said; 'but,' he added bitterly, 'I am sufficiently punished! After all my valour and manifold services, the haughty

Bastard deems me not good enough to become his kinsman, and insults me by forbidding me the hand of his kinswoman.'

His face was dark with scorn, and the peculiar gleam of green was in his eyes which gave so strange an expression to his anger, while the level brows met above them. Evidently wounded pride had more to do with his repentance than patriotic contrition.

But it was not convenient to admit so much even to himself. 'Blood is stronger than water, in good sooth,' he continued, 'and my father's blood rebels in my veins when I see the hungry Normans ousting staunch English families from their holdings, and revelling in the fat of the land. I had not thought of all that must follow the setting of William on the throne, for I dreamt not that Harold's following had been so strong, or that the tussle would be so bitter. And now that William is away, the curs snuffle and snarl and tear the quarry like hounds without a huntsman, while Hereford and I, through his silly jealousy, have our hands tied, and are powerless to keep order in the land. I tell thee it is galling beyond endurance to see the base churls, whom never a knight would have spoken to in Normandy but to give them an order, ruffling it with the best, and strutting as they had been born nobles, lording it over high-born English dames and damsels, whose fathers and husbands they have slain, and whose fortunes they are wasting in riot!'

'Galling beyond endurance!' repeated Theodred, springing up with a gesture of anguish. 'Christ grant me pardon for the hate that springeth in my heart for the doers of such wrong, for it bids fair to overflow the barriers of my control whenever I let my thoughts wander from the comfort of heavenly things to earthly miseries!'

De Guader's eyes gleamed with triumph as he saw his companion so deeply moved. Stopping in his tiger walk up and down the room, he laid his strong hand upon Theodred's arm.

'Then help me to redress the wrong and repair the mistake!' he said.

Theodred turned on him fiercely. 'Repair the mistake! Canst thou bring then the dead to life, or gather from the soil one drop of the noble blood that has been poured forth upon it like water, the dark stains of which still scare the traveller, and call to Heaven for vengeance?'

'Nay, St. Nicholas defend me!' answered the earl, 'I can do neither of these things. There is that which cannot be undone, and can only be atoned by bitter penance and humble contrition. But there is that which may be restored. Ruined men may have their own again. Prisoners can be set free. Doth not Archbishop Stigand still languish in durance? Is not thine own beloved bishop and Stigand's brother, Æthelmær, living in poverty and shame, since William's tyrannical deprivation of his see on false and scandalous charges?'

'Alas, yes!' admitted the priest.

Then the earl, bending towards him, and fixing his

piercing eyes on the good-humoured and yielding eyes of Theodred, said in a low, clear voice, every syllable of every word thrilling the silent night,—

'An English king may yet fill the throne. Waltheof Siwardsson lives!'

Theodred covered his face with his hands, and staggered into his chair. After a while he murmured, 'And doth the holy Frithic, Abbot of St. Albans, favour this, and Thurstan, Abbot of Ely?'

'Ay; nor is Fitzosbern, Bishop of Exeter, opposed. He groans for the woes of the English people, whose ways he has always loved, and whose manners he has adopted; neither brooks he tamely this insult of William's to his nephew. When such favour me, wilt not thou?'

Theodred extended his palm without uncovering his face. 'I cannot answer thee thus at a moment's notice. The issues are too great.'

'Waltheof, Hereford, and I,' the earl continued, his face lighted with a lofty pride, and his gesture such as might have befitted the Conqueror himself, 'William absent. Who could withstand our combination?'

'I pray thee mercy! This matter needeth meditation and prayer. Leave me. Whether I help or hinder thee, be sure I will not betray thee. The Holy Virgin have both thee and me in her keeping!'

'Amen,' said the earl, and left the apartment. As he walked down the passage, stepping softly lest he should disturb those who had slumbered while he plotted, he heard the strokes of the flagellum with which Father Theodred was lacerating his shoulders

CHAPTER IV.

HORSE, HAWK, AND HOUND.

ON the morrow, a goodly company rode forth over the drawbridges of Hereford Castle, with clatter of prancing horses and barking of dogs and jingle of hawks' jesses; falconers carrying the birds, and huntsmen leading the well-trained dogs, spaniels, cockers, and here and there a wolf or boar hound, in case larger game should be started; a party of men-at-arms to protect them from wild beasts, outlaws, and Welsh, with a few knights in harness to head them, and the ladies and gentlemen of the hunt themselves.

In the place of honour amongst these rode the Earl of East Anglia, mounted on his splendid Spanish barb Oliver, whose fine points had drawn forth praise from that lover of good horse-flesh, William the Conqueror himself, when De Guader had ridden the steed in his presence; a bright red-roan with fox-coloured mane and tail, fine of limb, but of greater strength and endurance than the heavier Norman warhorse, and full of spirit and docility.

By his side ambled Emma Fitzosbern, on a white palfrey, bearing on her wrist a noble 'tassel-gentle,' whose broad shoulders and large nares and long black spurs proclaimed him of the bluest blood of hawk aristocracy.

'Certes, he is a glorious tierce,' said Emma, looking with admiration at the hawk, 'and seemeth well reclaimed, though, knowing me not, he is by nature shy.'

'I hope well he may sustain the reputation accorded him by those from whom I had him,' said the earl, 'and prove his worth by deeds when we reach the waters. He comes straight from Denmark, and is accounted equal to any King Sweyn at present hath in his mews. He will bind a mallard with his beak, nor needeth he any lure save the voice of the falconer. None exceed the Danes for skill in training a hawk.'

The Earl of Hereford, who had been riding ahead with his countess, fell back and reined his horse beside his sister's palfrey, that he might examine and criticise this much-extolled bird. But his criticism also took the form of admiration.

'If he performs as well as he looks,' quoth he, 'I would think him cheap at a hundred marks.'

When they reached the marshy ground to northwest the castle, at which they had been aiming, the spaniels soon put up a heronshaw, and Emma, who had no mean skill at falconry, slipped off the hood from the Danish hawk, and cast him deftly from her little fist into the air at what was called the *jette serré*, that is to say, as quickly after the quarry had taken flight as possible.

The heron soared into the air on his strong wings, with his slender legs stretched straight behind him, till he was almost lost in the clouds, but the tassel-gentle pursued him swiftly, scaling the air by small circles ascending higher and higher like the steps of a spiral staircase.

Emma clapped her hands in delight.

'By the mass! a magnificent mount!' exclaimed Hereford, and his praise was echoed amongst the ladies and gentlemen round, nor did the falconers refuse their meed of honour to the foreign bird, jealous though they might be for the fame of their own particular pets, whom they had tended since they took them from the eyrie at the stage of eyass-down, and lured and reclaimed with daily care and patient skill.

'The tassel-gentle hath the uppermost,' cried Emma, after a few seconds of eager watching.

'Thine eyes are as keen as the hawk's!' cried De Guader. 'At that height I could not tell one from the other.'

But Emma saw truly. In a moment more the tassel-gentle stooped upon his quarry, and the struggling birds came tumbling from the sky together, leaving a long trail of fluttering feathers to mark the course of their passage through the air.

Hereford pressed forward to the spot at which they promised to touch earth, and was ready to despatch the heron ere he could do mischief with his long wings, measuring upwards of five feet from tip to tip. He shook the hawk's hood, and the well-trained bird flew at once upon his wrist. Bravely had he maintained his reputation by deeds.

Other hawks were then flown at various game, mallard and crane and bittern. Sometimes the quarry escaped; on one occasion a falcon failed to win the upper hand, and the heron at which she was cast transfixed her on his long beak and killed her, at which misfortune there was much ado. Others acquitted themselves well, but none rivalled the prowess of the Danish hawk, and when the gay company had turned their horses' heads homewards, and had leisure to discuss the matter, he was acclaimed by all the hero of the day in falcon-world.

'Since thou hast a good opinion of the tassel-gentle,' said De Guader, who had reined his horse again to the side of Emma's palfrey, 'and art pleased to say that I gave no overdrawn picture of his high qualities, I pray thee, noble demoiselle, to pleasure me by taking him for thine own from this day forward; for, in sooth, I obtained him from Denmark for no other purpose, having heard of the death of thy favourite falcon. See, he takes to thee by instinct, and sits thy slender wrist as if he knew it as that of his own lady.'

'Thou art too generous, Sir Earl,' replied Emma, the quick blood flushing check and forehead,—partly through delight, for she was a keen huntress, and appreciated fully the joys of possessing such a bird; but more through confusion, for she felt that she could not accept such a gift from a suitor whom she intended to reject, and that virtually to take the beautiful creature would be to answer Ralph's weighty question of the night before—for in those days a good hawk was of more value than diamonds. To make matters worse, her brother was watching her pitilessly, with a quizzical smile in his eyes, and evident curiosity as to what she would say.

But fortune was kinder than her friends. The company was riding at the moment through a belt of woodland, and, just as Emma was casting about in her mind for an answer to Ralph's speech that might postpone her difficulty, and toying somewhat lovingly with the bird, a lank grey beast trotted silently across the pathway a few yards ahead of the foremost horseman.

The dogs gave tongue and the men also.

'Wolf! wolf!' cried the huntsmen, and half-a-dozen knights of the *meinie* who carried hauberk and lance dashed forward in pursuit.

All was excitement and commotion. Steeds chafed and curveted, and kept their riders from requiring answers to inconvenient questions, and Emma Fitzosbern felt grateful exceedingly to the fiery Oliver for the trouble he gave his master, and the excuse which his antics afforded her to slip behind to the side of her bower-maiden, Eadgyth of Norwich, who was following on a sober-minded brown palfrey, being but an indifferent horsewoman, and always desirous of a quiet mount.

De Guader gave Oliver the rein and galloped forward.

'I am in sore distress, Emma,' said Eadgyth, as she joined her, 'for my foolish Freya has rushed off after the rest of them, as if a gazehound could pull down a wolf, forsooth! I much fear me she will be hurt.'

Almost as she spoke, the knights returned, one holding aloft the wolf's head as a trophy; but another, a young Norman in De Guader's following, Sir Aimand de Sourdeval by name, carried a wounded hound in his arms.

'It is Freya!' exclaimed Eadgyth, and, riding forward towards the knight, she asked if her favourite was much wounded.

'Nothing dangerously, sweet donzelle,' replied Sir Aimand, looking up with a bright smile, and evidently pleased to have so cheerful an answer to give, both for the hound's sake and the lady's. 'A bite in the forearm, nothing worse, though it lames her. I will bind it, with your permission, when we reach the castle; I have a salve reckoned most healing for the wounds of hounds, and I hope it may prove its worth in the healing of thine.'

Eadgyth thanked the young knight for his courtesy with much sincerity, for she had brought up the greyhound to her own hand, and the creature was full of gentle ways and pretty tricks, which her mistress had taught her, besides being exceptionally beautiful, with a satin skin as white as milk and a body as lithe as any eel's.

It was a great relief to Eadgyth also to note how

tenderly Sir Aimand handled her favourite, so that the hound lay quite passive in his hold, and she felt content to leave her to the knight's tender mercies.

When they reached the castle, Emma Fitzosbern found herself still carrying the tassel-gentle on her wrist, and thought with a half sigh that it would be hard to relinquish him, even if she were quite prepared to renounce all that she must take with him. Nor did De Guader give her opportunity to restore the bird to his keeping.

Later in the day, when the May sun was drawing nigh to the summits of the Welsh hills, Emma, her riding garb exchanged for a silken robe of pale blue, embroidered with pearls and silver and edged with vair, very brave to look upon, swept down the long alleys that led from the ladies' bower to the orchard, in company with her young sister-in-law, the Countess of Hereford, and Dame Amicia de Reviers, a venerable lady, who had been Emma's 'guide, philosopher, and governante' since the daughter of Fitzosbern had first opened her grey-blue eyes upon this wicked world, and who now found her aged infirmity soothed by the love and trust of her whilom pupil.

Hereford is, and was, a famous apple country, and in those days it was celebrated for both cider and grape wine. Just then, in the sweet spring weather, the orchard was a pleasant place in which to while away an hour. The insecurity of life making the protection of stone walls imperative, prevented any extensive cultivation of garden flowers, and gardens within castle precincts were necessarily circumscribed. But the orchard was somewhat more free, though lofty walls surrounded it, over which the trained branches of the vines spread in orderly growth, and were putting forth tufts of tender bronze-green leaves at every spur. Gillyflowers bloomed between their roots, and their wild yellow brothers found space for their impudent needs on the crown of the walls. Across the centre of the orchard ran a chattering brook, along the banks of which kingcups made a golden line, and over which a little bridge with toy battlements was built. The pear trees were covered with snow-white flowers and the apples with rosy buds, and under the netted shadows of their straggling boughs the rich green turf was gemmed with primroses and daisies and buttercups; while merles and mavises sat amongst the blossoms, striving which should sing the sweetest songs. From the meadows and pastures beyond the walls came the lowing of cows and the mellow voice of the cuckoo.

Emma carried the tassel-gentle on her wrist, and a page followed her with a lure and dainty morsels wherewith to tempt the proud bird's appetite; and when the countess and Dame Amicia sat down upon a bench in a small arbour near the stream, she went forward to the bridge, and bade the page set down his burden upon the wall. Then, leaning on the parapet, she amused herself by casting off the bird for short flights, and luring him back, teaching him to recognise the sound of her voice. The other ladies, who were in view of the performance, applauded when he obeyed her quickly.

Yet Emma had not fully accepted the gift of the bird, or decided what her course should be. She was in great perplexity. In the morning, jubilant with exercise, the glow and excitement of the chase upon her, all difficulties had seemed light save that of renunciation, and the qualified permission which Father Theodred had given her, to follow her own heart in the matter, seemed to move all obstacles from her path. Now, in cooler mood, her anxious spirit conjured up visions of distress.

To defy the king was both sinful and dangerous. If she dwelt more on the danger than the sin, she must not be judged by the standard of later days. The idea of kingly divinity had scarcely blossomed into flower in the chaos of those dark ages. Every powerful noble was a sovereign on his own estate, and his followers fought his battles with little scruple whether against king or peer. The feudal king-lord was but first among peers, and very few noble houses could display a scutcheon free from the blot of treason.

Vows of fealty and the sanctity of knightly honour notwithstanding, the turbulent barons thought less of it than a modern politician of changing his party. Indeed, they watched all kingly encroachments on the power of their order with jealous eyes, and deemed it a duty to stand by each other. Not till Warwick, 'the Kingmaker,' was laid low on Barnet field, did the kingly ideal become paramount.

So Emma thought more of the blood that would flow if William were defied, than of the heinousness of the defiance. Earl Ralph and her brother would both be involved in trouble and sorrow. And all for her foolish face! Oh, why had she not been born some plain, poor damsel, over whose fate none would concern themselves?

She would not be a centre of strife and confusion! No, she would retire into a convent and lead a life of penitence and prayer; and Ralph would find another bride whom William would not grudge him.

But this pious resolution was accompanied by a deep sigh, and a look of wistful longing at the hawk, as he came fluttering his strong, sharp-pointed wings to her call. Perhaps he typified worldly joys to her at the moment.

Just then two goodly gentlemen came striding across the greensward to the arbour by the bridge, and Emma's heart gave a great leap, for she felt that the time had come when, for weal or woe, she must make her choice.

And the Earl of Hereford went into the arbour and sat down by his wife, but the Earl of East Anglia came straight on to the bridge where Emma stood. 'The tassel-gentle acknowledges the authority of his own liege lady,' Ralph said, with a meaning smile, as he stopped beside her and leaned his arm on the low parapet of the little bridge.

'I fear he learned not his loyalty from his master,' Emma replied, looking in his face with earnest eyes.

'Nay, flout me not, dear lady,' pleaded De Guader. 'Give me an answer to my question of yesternight. It is not like thee to prolong my torture.'

Emma FitzOsbern accepts the Tassel-gentle.

'Indeed, I know not what to answer thee,' said Emma in sad seriousness. 'My heart is torn with doubt. I cannot bear,' she said, laying her hand upon his arm, as if to restrain his eagerness for combat, 'to be the cause of strife. And strife it must mean, if thou shouldst marry me against the king's will. William is not the man to take such defiance smoothly.'

'Nor am I, nor is Hereford, the man to take his insult smoothly,' answered Ralph, with blazing eyes. 'See'st thou not, the strife must be? The insult is given, and can only be wiped out with blood!'

'Ah!'

'See'st thou not, my dove,' asked De Guader, taking the hand she had laid upon his arm in both his own, 'thy decision has nought to do with the strife? Indeed, thy refusal to have me now would but make mine anger against William the more bitter, as I shall in that case owe him the loss of my happiness as well as the affront to mine honour. No, the point is this: I cannot urge thee to share strife and sorrow with me, though,' and his eyes flashed fresh fires, 'the saints might favour me that I won thee but higher honours in the end. If thy heart fails thee, Hereford will send thee over-sea to thy brother in Normandy, where thou canst dwell in peace and safety, while we fight our quarrel out. Fight it out we must! 'Tis not William's first insult, but it shall be his last.'

'Nay, if I cannot stay the strife, I will share it!' cried Emma, touched to the quick. 'Thou dost me wrong to deem, even for an instant, that I shrink for my own welfare's sake! 'Tis not in the nature of a Fitzosbern!' Then, turning to the hawk, she said, 'Thou may'st know me for thy liege lady, my brave tassel-gentle! I take thee, and thy master with thee, but I fear he is by far less well reclaimed than thee!'

CHAPTER V.

SAXON AND NORMAN.

THE little village of Exning in Suffolk was once an important place, the seat of the royal palace of the kings and queens of East Anglia, wherein was born the celebrated St. Etheldreda, who was the foundress of the monastery of Ely; and its state did not entirely disappear till A.D. 1200, when a plague broke out which desolated the population, and a New Market was set up a few miles from it, which still bears that name, and is the well-known racing centre.

Ralph de Guader, as Earl of East Anglia, became the lord of this ancient palace of the East Anglian royal family, and, as it was in his day the fashion for weddings to take place at the house of the bridegroom, it was here that preparations were made for his union with Emma Fitzosbern.

It was in every way convenient for Ralph's purposes. Situated on the extreme verge of his estates, jutting out towards the west, whence his bride must come, it was the very nearest point at which she could enter his domain; near also to Northampton and Huntingdon, over which Waltheof Siwardsson was earl, regarding whom, as we know, De Guader had deep-laid schemes. The celebrity it bore as the time-honoured residence of the East Anglian royalty, and the birthplace of one of the best-beloved of Saxon saints, endeared it to the hearts of the Saxon nobles and thegns, whom it was Ralph's policy to conciliate, and of whom he had invited to the banquet all who still possessed any remnant of their former wealth, and many who had little left but names to conjure with.

Divers Breton nobles and knights also held manors in the neighbourhood, and De Guader had in his own following a strong body of Breton mercenaries, and took care to bid the leading men amongst them, and all he could gather of his mother's countrymen having settlements in England, to the feast. Many Normans also were invited, men who were known to be discontented with their share of the spoil of fair lands and deer forests and riches of various kinds distributed after the Conquest, or who, like De Guader and Hereford, were smarting under William's tyrannous whims. Last, but most important amongst the guests, were the members of the Saxon Church, many of whom came to the bridal, including several of the high positions of bishop and abbot.

Only the highest in rank of such a large assembly could be sheltered under the roof of the palace, built though it had been to suit Anglo-Saxon notions of hospitality, which were on a bounteous scale.

The knights and thegns of humbler degree were encamped in the neighbourhood in every variety of tent and hut that would serve for temporary shelter, while each noble or chief brought with him a goodly train of house-carles, squires, and pages, and a motley following of attendants and grooms, with horses and hounds and sumpter mules laden with baggage. For miles around the air was rent with the neighing of horses and shouting of men, the barking of dogs and clashing of arms, and the braying of trumpets, while above each gay tent floated a silken banner bearing the arms of the occupant, or, at least, tall lances stuck in the ground beside it fluttered their pennoncelles around it. All was merry clamour and confusion, and doubtless Newmarket Heath itself was as gay as it now is on the morning of the Two Thousand Guineas.

The East Anglian earl had elected to have the festivities arranged according to Saxon fashions. Nevertheless, he had endeavoured to satisfy the tastes of all his guests, and a variety of entertainments was provided. A magnificent pavilion had been erected for the many who could not be accommodated with seats in the banqueting-hall of the palace, over which waved richly-coloured flags embroidered with the arms of the three great earls,—the azure lion rampant which Waltheof had assumed as his emblem, the red, blue, and golden arms of Hereford, and De Guader's own cognisance, party per pale or and sable, with a bend vairy.

To one side of it were spacious lists hung with scarlet cloth, one hundred yards long by forty broad, having benches for spectators in tiers along the length of the barriers, and in the centre, on each side, a canopy, one destined for the three earls, who were to be judges of the combat, the other for Emma Fitzosbern,—from whose hands as Queen of Beauty the victors were to receive their prizes,—the noble ladies who were her guests, and the maidens of her train. The tourney was to take place a full day before the wedding, so that the combatants might be rested, and fit for the labour of feasting. The combats were in no case to be *à outrance*, but merely a trial of strength and skill.

On the opposite side of the pavilion a large space of ground was marked out for sports of a less aristocratic character, and set with targets for archery, a quintain,—not the knightly quintain supplied with a full suit of good armour, such as chivalric aspirants tried their skill on, the providing of which was a serious item in the expenses of a feudal castle, but a mere ring and sand-bag,—leaping bars, racecourses both for horse and foot racing, a bear-pit, and other sports to please the various tastes of the soldiery,—the socmen or tenants holding land by service other than knightly,—the bordars or cottagers holding portions of land on condition of supplying the lord of the manor with poultry, eggs, and other small provisions,—and such other freemen as De Guader deemed it well to conciliate.

A richly-decked bower had been prepared for Emma Fitzosbern in the old Anglo-Saxon palace, and in this she sat with her favourite, Eadgyth of Norwich, on the evening of their arrival at Exning. Eadgyth was to be her chief bridemaid, and the policy of the bridegroom was not ill-served by this honour paid to the relative of the great English earl. Emma's face was radiant with happiness, for she loved Ralph de Guader deeply, and her buoyant disposition did not tempt her to meet difficulties half way; so she was able to throw to the winds all foreboding as to sinister results from the bold step she and her bridegroom were about to take in opposing the Conqueror's will.

Eadgyth, however, though evidently trying to be as gay as beseemed the occasion, was unable to hide from Emma's quick eyes the fact that she was herself in low spirits, betrayed by a tinge of sadness in her tone, and half-stifled sighs that would make way between her merry speeches.

'Eadgyth, something hath vexed thee,' said Emma earnestly. 'Be frank with me, and tell me thy sorrow, by the memory of the freedom with which I have reposed my woes with thee.'

'Nay,' replied Eadgyth, with a forced smile, a faint one, it must be said, like December sunshine, 'it would be a sin to talk to thee of sorrow on thy bridal eve.'

Thou canst not hide it, Eadgyth; thou wouldst do more kindly to tell me all.'

'Thou knowest the young knight, Sir Aimand de Sourdeval, who rides in thy bridgeroom's *meinie?*' said Eadgyth in a low hesitating tone.

She had taken Emma's hand in her own, and was twisting the betrothal ring which circled the slender third finger round and round, but, though her face was averted, her white neck and forehead grew pink under Emma's gaze.

'A gallant knight and of good lineage,' said Emma quietly. 'My brother said but the other day that he counted him amongst the best lances he knows.'

'Thou wilt remember he rescued my poor gazehound Freya from the fangs of the wolf the day thy Danish hawk was first flown, and leeched her tenderly after, even using on her a talisman which had been given to him by a holy palmer from the East, nursing the poor beast as gently as if she had been a human child.'

''Tis a good sign in a man to show tenderness to the poor beasts who cannot make their wrongs public,' said Emma. 'He who will suffer inconvenience to save a beast pain, will not do less for weak women or feeble children that come under his charge.'

Eadgyth looked up with sparkling agreement in her eyes, but bent her head again as she continued,—

'This evening, as we drew near the goal of our journey, he took advantage of his duty as escort to ride his destrier close to the side of my palfrey, and asked me what colours I meant to wear at the tourney, and to give him a favour to wear in his helm, with many compliments, saying my good renown was such that the noble Godfrey de Bouillon himself would not disdain to break a lance in my honour.'

'And what was thine answer, sweet friend?' asked Emma. 'I know not what in this can find thee food for grief.'

Eadgyth continued in a grave and measured voice,—

'I thanked him that he should do me such compliment, and said I doubted not his lance and sword would well defend my favour, being plied by a God-fearing knight, and in the cause of a maiden who hath nought to conceal; but I could give no favour, for I had ever held that she who lets a good man risk life and limb in her service, should be ready to guerdon the victor, and that I could not do.'

'Now, Eadgyth, why shouldst thou have given such an answer?' asked Emma vehemently. 'Read me thy riddle, I pray thee, for, in good sooth, I deem not thou hast the knight in ill-favour.'

'Surely the riddle is plain to read,' answered Eadgyth, 'and thou shouldest know enough of my mind to answer it. Is not Sir Aimand a Norman, and am I not the cousin of Harold Godwinsson?'

'I tell thee truly I am sick of thy eternal Harold Godwinsson!' cried Emma, springing up and pacing the room. 'His name is dragged forth in season or out of season. It must be hard for the poor man to rest in his grave! Here are eight years the Normans and the Saxons—if Saxon thou wilt own thyself, sometimes thou wilt correct me that thou art an Anglo-Dane! —have been living in peace, and marrying and giving in marriage, and thou wouldst wake up old quarrels, and part them in sunder again. As well might I refuse to marry Ralph de Guader because of his English blood.'

'But the earl fought with thy people. How know I but that my kinsfolk fell by Sir Aimand's hand? He was at Senlac, though but a young squire. The gulf that yawns between us is impassable!' and Eadgyth's shoulders shook with an irrepressible shudder.

'Even so,' said Emma, 'it was in fair fight on a hardly-contested field, and Sir Aimand would be in no way blood-guilty therefor. When a quarrel is ended, generous foes shake hands.'

'So said Sir Aimand. For he asked me if any reason were behind my answer that he might know, and I told him frankly that my heart still bled for my country's wounds, and that I could not forget that the lance he offered to ply in mine honour had tilted against my countrymen, had perhaps been dyed with the blood of those dear to me. He answered and said, that it had been a fair fight, with no ill blood between the combatants; that God had made the Norman arms prevail, and that I ought to accede to His holy will. But I cannot feel it so,' Eadgyth ended, with a sigh.

'Then I must try to comfort thee some other way,' said Emma, resuming her seat, and taking the face of her friend in both her hands, and turning it up and kissing it, for Eadgyth was sitting on a low stool at her feet, as was her wont. 'Remember thou art on thy way to thy dear Norwich, where some of thy kin may still be found; nay, some may be amongst the invited guests to the banquet, and encamped near thee even now. We know, at least, that more than one noble thegn will be present. Who can say what fate may have in store for thee?'

Eadgyth shook her head.

'Alas, Emma! I shall not find comfort so. There was that in the face of the poor knight as he turned away that I fear me will haunt my memory to my dying day.'

'Nay then, if that be thy mood, I will waste no pity on thee,' said Emma. 'Shame on thee, that thou shouldst send my countryman away with a sad face, and doubtless an aching heart, for such a fantastic whim!'

But the soft tones of her voice somewhat belied her declaration that she would bestow no pity on her wayward friend.

CHAPTER VI.

THE BRIDE-ALE.

THE festivities of the days preceding the wedding had no special incidents to mark them as more worthy of note than a hundred such which have been described in history and romance, but the wedding-day itself left its mark on time, and has been recorded as of woeful bearing on the destinies of the many who partook of its good cheer, by chroniclers contemporary and modern.

The ceremonies observed at the marriage were after the Anglo-Saxon fashions, and Ralph de Guader himself wore the Saxon garb: a tunic of saffron silk reaching to the knee, with a border round the neck and hem of embroidery in gold thread, edged with ermine, and fastened at the waist with a wide belt of highly-wrought goldsmith's work set with jewels; suspended from this a short sword, hilted with gold-inlaid ivory, and a fierce-looking hunting-knife no less richly embellished. On his shoulders a short scarlet cloak lined with ermine, and fastened by a band across the chest of similar work and design to the baldric, having at each extremity a round clasp of Danish filigree, much raised in the centre, where a splendid ruby repeated the red of the cloak. Stockings of scarlet cloth, cross-gartered with golden braid, and short brown leather boots, the heels armed with the golden spurs of knighthood, completed his apparel.

His earl's coronet was embedded in the crisp dark curls of his close-cropped hair, which, to have been in keeping with his dress, should have been long enough to lie upon his shoulders, and the colour of tow; and, to say truth, his swart countenance was still less in character. Yet from an æsthetic point of view the costume was sufficiently becoming, and the personal appearance of the bridegroom drew forth a full share of praise from the noble dames and damsels who graced the day with their presence, for he looked strikingly handsome, flushed as he was with excitement, his face animated, and his keen eyes flashing.

The policy of adopting it was another question. Many of the English nobles and knights, whom it was intended to flatter, rather resented his assumption of their national garb as a mockery and insult, after the part he had borne in helping to crush their cause and help the Conqueror to the throne, while the Normans and Bretons were offended by it.

The guest in whose honour he had chiefly assumed it, Waltheof, Earl of Northumberland, Northampton, and Huntingdon, wore a similar garb with all the ease of custom and grace of habit, and looked in very truth an English prince. Tall, broad-chested, brawny-armed, his long light hair hanging in shining curls upon his shoulders, his strong wrists circled with many bracelets, hands, arms, and neck covered with blue tattoo-marks, he stood by the East Anglian earl with a pleasant smile on his ruddy face and in his sleepy blue eyes. 'This earle Walteof or Waldene,' says Holinshed, 'was sonne (as ye haue heard) to Siward the noble earle of Northumberland, of whose valure in the time of K. Edward the confessor ye haue heard. His son, the aforesaid Walteof, in strength of bodie and hardinesse did not degenerate from his father, for he was tall of personage, in sinews and musculs verie strong and mighty. In the slaughter of the Normans at Yorke, he showed proofe of his prowesse in striking off the heads of manie of them with his owne hands, as they came forth of the gates singlie one by one.'

But this doughty hero, this son of Siward and Æthelflæd, whom the Northern scalds celebrated in their sagas, and who claimed relationship to the kings of Denmark and descent from the Fairy Bear,—the great white bear, the hound of Hrymir, who was credited with twelve men's strength and eleven men's wit by the Norsemen,— was not so strong of mind as of body; the 'eleven men's wit' of his ursine ancestor had not come down to him. He had not the indomitable spirit of Harold Godwinsson or Hereward Leofricsson, and he succumbed to the finer brain of the Norman general. He had done homage to William, and had accepted the hand of William's niece Judith, daughter of the Conqueror's own sister Adelaide, and grand-daughter of Robert the Devil and Arlète of Falaise, and, in return, the earldom which had been wrested from him was restored — the Northumbrian portion of it, at least, a barren waste by fire and sword.

It was whispered that he hated his foreign wife, that she henpecked him cruelly, and was but a spy set to watch all his actions. Some thought the marriage, instead of binding him to William's interest, would prove his strongest incentive to revolt.

However that might be, Judith appeared at Exning with an almost royal following, and was to fill the honourable position of 'bride-woman,' as the matron who in those days gave the bride away was then styled, and whose place is now held by the nearest male relative. Another change has taken place in marriage ceremonial. Then it was the duty of the bridemaids to lead the bridegroom to the altar instead of following the bride, and Ralph de Guader was preceded by a bevy of fair damsels, of whom Eadgyth of Norwich was the chief, while the bride was conducted by a party of handsome young bride-knights, almost as bravely attired as the groom himself.

Emma Fitzosbern still clung to the Norman fashions, and wore a tight-fitting kirtle of pale green samite, embroidered all over with silver thread and pearls; a silver girdle passing diagonally round the hips, richly gemmed with emeralds, from which hung a gipsire of like material. A long underskirt of salmon silk fell to her feet and trailed upon the ground behind her. Her little pointed boots were of green samite, wrought with silver, and a splendid embroidered mantle, in which the colours of the kirtle and skirt were subtly blended, hung from her shoulders, and was held up by two little page boys. Her auburn hair flowed over the mantle, and was bound by a silver fillet, fastened in front with one large emerald. Over face and figure fell a veil of delicate Cyprian crape, flowered with silver thread.

Green signified youth, and salmon or flesh colour typified earthly joy. Her beautiful costume had been designed for her by no less a person than her uncle, the Bishop of Exeter, who was pleased to emulate St. Dunstan by designing a lady's dress.

Judith, her bride-woman, on whose arm she leant, wore a robe of rich red samite heavy with gold, and ostentatiously Norman in style. Her tall, stately figure was as straight as an arrow, and made a splendid foil to the shrinking form of the bride.

Her clear-cut, cold features and sparkling steel-blue eyes wore a sarcastic and critical expression, but she acted her part with a grace and courtesy which the many who longed to pass adverse criticisms on *her* could not but admit to be perfect.

Emma felt a strong repugnance to her kinswoman, the more so perhaps that Judith's features and eyes reminded her of the king she was defying, and every time she met their glance, a thrill of dread and foreboding passed through her heart.

The wedding procession was preceded to the church by a dozen Saxon scops or bards, who sung each to the sound of his cruit, a harp having five strings, yet affording a very sweet music, and by esquires and pages strewing flowers; and the guests were led by Earls Waltheof and Hereford, the latter with his young countess on his arm.

The little church at Exning would not have contained so great a company, but the fashion in those days was for the bride and bridegroom to stand on the threshold till the ceremony was almost concluded. After the wedding ring had been bestowed with due ceremony,—being placed first on the thumb and successively upon the second and fourth finger, where it was allowed to remain, that finger being supposed by the most scientific authorities of the time to be joined to the heart by a small artery,—the couple entered the sacred portal, and advanced to the altar, before which the nuptial benediction was given by the bridegroom, under cover of a square veil, held aloft by four tall knights, and termed a 'carecloth.'

Wine, blessed by the officiating priest, was then poured into a splendid golden bride-cup, in which was placed a sprig of gilded rosemary, supposed to have the gift of strengthening memory and increasing tenderness, and many other good qualities. In this the bride and bridegroom pledged each other, and it was then handed round to all the guests. A wheaten cake, in token of plenty and fruitfulness, was then broken between them, from whence we derive our bride-cake.

On leaving the church, the newly-made husband and wife were crowned with garlands of flowers, and the Earl of Hereford presented his sister with her dower.

The word bridal comes from the Saxon *bryd-eala*, from a custom among that people of the bride selling to each guest a tankard of foaming ale drawn from the tun by her own fair hands, the price being at first paid in kind, and consisting of a contribution to the banquet, by which means the expense of entertaining a great company was lessened for the young couple. For this simple exchange, more costly presents were substituted after a while, a part of the custom which still survives, though the bride no longer offers an equivalent.

This ceremony was magnificently observed at the East Anglian earl's wedding, and Emma de Guader dispensed the favourite Saxon drink in a glorious golden beaker, which was of depth sufficient to try the wind and capacity of the gallants, as they strove to empty it without drawing breath, particularly of the Normans, who were not adepts at the art of copious drinking. Many and rich were the presents offered in payment, with fitting good wishes and compliments, Waltheof bestowing the most superb of all, a pair of Danish torcs of that beautiful gold filigree, the working of which was the special glory of the Danish goldsmiths of that day, and a white bear's skin of rare beauty and value.

A bountiful feast followed, pages and esquires, clad in the colours of the nobles and knights they served, presenting the dishes on the knee, one golden plate being set between each lady and gentleman; it being the duty of the latter to carve choice morsels for his fair charge with his dagger. Peacocks in their feathers, crane, heron, and swan, porpoise, seal, venison, and boar's head, were amongst the delicacies offered, and the united science of Saxon and Norman cooks achieved some triumphs of culinary skill, we may be sure. A receipt for forcemeat which has come down to us from those days, will show they were no novices in the matter. It is to be compounded of pork, figs, and cheese, moistened with ale, seasoned with pepper and salt, and baked in a crust, garnished with powderings of sugar and comfits. All these good things were washed down with rare wines, Gascon and Rhenish, with hippocras and pigment spiced to suit the Saxon palate, with moral and mead, cider, perry, and ale.

In all, Saxon profusion was united to the dainty Norman cookery, and, under the influence of this heavy hospitality, the male portion of the guests grew somewhat boisterous.

When the attendants brought in large Saxon drinking-horns, filled with hydromel and beer, and marked with knobs of brass to indicate to what depth the guests might quaff without fear of intoxication, with cups of spiced wine for those who preferred it, the bride arose from her seat, her Norman delicacy already offended by the copiousness of the potations.

Nevertheless, before she left, she touched her lips to one of the hugest drinking-horns and pledged the guests. Then she withdrew with the ladies of the company, the Countess Judith casting a strange glance of contemptuous malice as she went.

The bride's challenge was, as may be imagined, received with ready enthusiasm, and called forth such lusty cheering, that she had reached her bower ere it died away. Before it had well ceased, the Earl of Hereford rose to his feet, his proud young face full of wayward triumph. 'Noble earls, barons, and knights,' he said, 'who honour this board with your presence, ye have this day pledged the health of the bridegroom, my noble brother-in-law, the Earl of East Anglia, and ye have but now with a noble enthusiasm pledged the bride, my fair sister. I ask of you yet another pledge. Drink to the marriage itself, in token that you, one and all, justify my noble brother and myself in our defiance of the mandate of the tyrant, William the Bastard, who strove to hinder their union!'

Many a jewelled hunting-knife and *miséricorde* flashed in the air to show that their owners accepted the bold pledge; for in those wild days, when every man's hand was against every man, it was the fashion that when two drank together, each should hold up his dagger while the other was in the defenceless position necessitated by the act of drinking.

'By the bones of King Offa, the founder of St. Albans, whose holy Abbot Frithric sits amongst us to-day, ye do well to support me!' said Hereford. 'But I would have your hearts even more closely with me! To that end I ask ye to answer me a question or two, ere ye drain the cup to pledge me. Shall I ask them?'

'Ask them!' shouted every lusty throat around the board.

'I ask ye, then, my countrymen, you Norman barons

and knights, and you noble Bretons, who have fought with us shoulder to shoulder, ay, and you valiant Saxons, who were foemen worthy of his steel, was not my father, William Fitzosbern, a good man and true?'

'*Oui!*' shouted the men of Langued'oui, nor did the Bretons or Saxons gainsay them.

'Did he shed his blood like water in William's cause? Did he fight beside him in the thickest of the fray at Hastings?'

'*Oui!*' shouted Normans and Bretons, and the Saxons assented with muttered curses.

'Could William have conquered his kingdom without my father's aid?'

'*Non!*' cried the Normans.

'Then, I ask, is it fitting and just that William the Bastard should refuse his sanction, when William Fitzosbern's son pleads for it, to the marriage of William Fitzosbern's daughter with a noble English earl?' Here he bowed to Ralph de Guader, who had risen and stood beside him. 'Is it not a threefold affront to the memory of my father, to me his son, and to my noble brother-in-law, the Earl of East Anglia?'

Normans, Bretons, and Saxons joined in a howl of reprobation of William of Normandy's conduct, the Saxons delighting to find fault with the conqueror of their woeful land on any pretext, and boiling with wrath at wrongs of their own. If any dissented, their feeble voices were drowned in the outcry of indignation that stormed round the board. The cups were drained to the last drop.

'William is no rightful Duke of Normandy, still less doth it befit him to style himself a king,' cried a Norman noble. 'He was born in adultery, and God favours not the children of sinful parents.'

'And born of mean blood!' shouted another. 'Who was Arlète of Falaise, the tanner's daughter, that her son should be anointed king, even if he had been born in wedlock?'

'If a natural son might succeed to his father's honours,' said the Earl of Hereford, his face flushed with the success of his appeal, 'Nicholas, Abbé of St. Ouen, had been Duke of Normandy, for he was the son of Duke Robert's elder brother. As Nicholas was set aside on account of his birth, so should William be. Guy of Burgundy is the rightful heir!'

'Nobles and knights of Bretagne!' cried the bridegroom, less fiery than his Norman brother-in-law, but speaking with a calm impressive voice, and flinging out each syllable as if it were a challenge in itself, 'ye who have so faithfully supported me in this land, which is the land of my birth, but not of yours! Men of Guader and Montfort! ye too have shed your blood like water for the sake of this ill-born Norman, who had God's own laws against him, and what reward hath he given you? Lands wasted by the ravages of war, which when you have tilled he hath taken away again to bestow on those who were higher in his favour! Some of your number he hath put to death! Nay more! Bretagne still mourns her glorious Count Conan, whom he slew with the coward's weapon—

poison!—as he poisoned Conan's father Alain before him!'

A low growl of wrath, terrible to hear, answered this appeal. Many of the Bretons sprang from their seats and bent over the table, shouting accusations against William of Normandy; for Ralph's cool determination was inherited from his English father; the men of Lower Britain were characterised generally by the hot-headedness of their Welsh ancestors, which they inherited with their red hair and fiery blue eyes, and Ralph had roused them.

'Ay! he used that coward's weapon too on Walter and his wife Biota in Falaise!' cried a voice above the tumult.

'Remember how he banished William of Mortmain for a single word, and gave his lands to Arlète's son Robert!' cried another. 'He is hateful to all men! His death would give joy to many!'

Roger of Hereford whispered in the ear of the Abbot of St. Albans. The venerable abbot was dearly loved by the English on account of his vigorous opposition to the Norman churchmen, and, in particular, to Lanfranc, the Italian to whom William had given the primacy, and whose untiring adversary he had been. They loved him also for his share in the heroic attempt made by Hereward Leofricsson to beat back the invader.

The turbulent soldiers hushed their outcry as the abbot rose to his feet, and stood waiting to address them, his face seamed and furrowed by age and sorrow, and his sunken eyes gleaming with a lustre that seemed almost supernatural from beneath his snow-white brows. Truly a dignified figure, in his splendid vestments, and a pathetic one also, so worn was he by suffering, so trembling was the thin right hand in which he held out the cross.

'Earls, barons, and knights!' cried the old man in his eloquent preacher's voice, 'the Earl of Hereford, whose health ye have just pledged, has told me grievous news. Know, all present, that he is an excommunicated man!'

Many a cheek that had hitherto been flushed with excitement blanched at that awful word; and a silence that might have been felt succeeded the passionate uproar. Men cast questioning glances at their neighbours, wondering each if the other would have strength of mind either to retract or fulfil his pledges to a man under the anathema of the Church, and which alternative he would choose.

'Yes!' cried Frithric, his voice rising clear as a bell into the silence. 'The Norman Church has cursed him by the mouth of that tool of William the Bastard, that despoiler of saints and robber of sanctuaries, Lanfranc, by the grace of that same William the Bastard, Archbishop of Canterbury! But the English Church blesses him!—the Church of St. Dunstan, St. Eadmund, and St. Cuthberht,—of the blessed martyrs Æthelric and Æthelwine,—whose holy members, Archbishop Stigand, Bishop Æthelmær, and Abbot Wulfric, now languish in the dungeons of the tyrant! In the name of the

English Church, I here pronounce that curse invalid, and give my benediction to the man who has pity on the sufferings of a luckless race, who will help to make its oppressor bite the dust!'

Here he extended his thin hands over Roger's bent head, and repeated the benediction.

The other bishops and abbots present ratified his action, and the tension of the crisis gave way before a fresh burst of cheering, louder than any previous. Then Ralph de Guader turned to Waltheof, who had sat very quietly through all the tumult, but had shown during Abbot Frithric's speech evidence of rising emotion.

'Valiant hero!' he said, 'hast thou no wrongs to complain of at the hands of the man who has conquered thy country, and robbed its princes and nobles of their birthrights? who has murdered or driven into exile the lawful heirs of its broad acres? Hast thou no revenge to take on him who harried thy patrimony, and made it a barren waste, where even the wild beasts starve? Art thou appeased because he gave thee back thy father's lands in such sorry plight?'

Waltheof rose to his feet like a giant newly awakened, magnificent in his slowly aroused wrath, his sinewy chest expanded, the muscles in his splendid neck knotted like whipcord, and his blue eyes sparkling with anger, so that he looked as if he were verily that Thor, God of Battles, whom his Danish forefathers worshipped, come down to earth. He tossed his mantle back from his brawny arms, and his hands worked involuntarily, till the left sought the hilt of the jewelled hunting-knife in his baldric, and the right was extended towards the sky. His long golden moustache bristled till it stood almost straightly from either cheek, and he shook his yellow mane like a lion.

'By St. John of Beverley, no!' he cried. 'The blood of starved women and children cries for justice! The spirits of men whose flesh was eaten by their fellows, after every horse and dog and cat had been devoured, call for vengeance on the harrier of Northumberland! Slaves rattle their chains who through him sold their freedom for food! The sated crows and ravens alone croak his praises from full maws, for they grew fat on the unburied corses of those whose dwellings he had burned and whose homesteads he had laid waste! It would be a sin to hold myself under bond to the tyrant!'

The Saxon thegns received this speech with wild acclaim.

'Ay,' cried one from Hampshire, 'and as in the north so in the south! Other kings have hunted wild beasts that their subjects might not be torn with them. This scourge of God maims and slaughters his subjects that the wild beasts may live for his hunting! May his New Forest prove a bane to him and his children!'

'Noble Waltheof,' cried Ralph, 'the time is come to avenge our wrongs. William is beyond the sea with the flower of his chivalry, and hard beset by rebellions and feuds in the bosom of his family, for such a tyrant is he that his own kinsfolk hate him! It is little likely that he will come back, but if he does, it will be at a disadvantage. Join us, thou whose stalwart arm struck one Norman head after another from its shoulders at the gates of York!—thou who firedst the wood wherein one hundred Normans sheltered, and slew them as they ventured forth like rats from a burning house! Join thy twelve men's strength to ours! We three earls might be again as Siward, Leofric, and Godwin. As if the Norman had not conquered, Godwin's son would have held the throne, so shall Siward's son be king when we in turn have laid the Norman low!'

'Waltheof Cyning! Waes hael! Waes hael!' cried the thegns.

'Call not the Bastard a Norman!' shouted the Earl of Hereford. 'The Normans disown him!'

Then said Frithric, fixing his shining, mournful eyes upon the Earl of Northumberland,—

'Waltheof, son of Siward, let thy words be upheld by deeds! Thy hand was on the plough, and thou didst turn in the furrow and make terms with the spoiler of thy land. See to it, thou failest not thy countrymen again!'

Turning to the Earl of East Anglia, he continued: 'Thou also, son of Ralph the Staller, forget the evil teaching of thy young days, when thy heart was weaned from thy father's land. Give thy manhood in amend for thy youth, and Jesu pardon thee! Join hands, ye two, and tender each a hand to this brave Norman, whose soul revolts at the cruelties of the man whom his father served, alas! for evil as well as good!

Swear a solemn oath, ye three noble earls, to be true to each other, and to right this much-wronged land!'

A huge cheer of assent burst from the followers of the three earls, and they joined hands and swore a great oath that they would unite to oust the tyrant from the throne, and seat thereon in his stead Waltheof Siwardsson.

And they settled it that Waltheof should bring his men from the north, and seek assistance from his old friend Sweyn, King of Denmark, to strengthen his hands; that Hereford should arm the west, and East Anglia the east, and so enclose the forces of William in a deadly triangle of hostile steel.

So ended the fatal bride-ale.[1]

[1] See Appendix, Note A.

CHAPTER VII.

DELILAH SHEARS SAMSON.

ON the morning following the bride-ale, Waltheof should have been early astir, to the end that he might be present at the bride-chamber to witness the presentation of the 'morning gift' from the bridegroom to the bride, according to the fashion of the times.

But alas! the recreant hero lay stretched upon his cushions in the oblivion of slumber, his gigantic limbs outspread in the most complete repose, and his heavy breathing witnessing to the depth of the potations of the night before.

By his couch watched Judith, niece to the man against whom the English hero had raged so potently, when the generous wine had stolen away the caution that was wont to ward his speech.

Her magnificent attire of the previous day was laid aside, and she was dressed in a simple travelling gown of grey cloth.

Her face wore a strange expression of triumphant malice, as she stooped over the sleeping giant, and whenever he stirred or showed any signs of waking, she passed her cool and slender fingers over his heated forehead, and stroked back the thick golden curls that clustered on his brow, mesmerising him to sleep again with her gentle touches.

The day wore on, and the sun was high in the heavens, and Judith's sharp, cold face grew more and more triumphant.

A time came at last, however, when even her deft fingers could no longer bind the wings of sleep, and the earl opened his blue eyes with a mighty yawn, springing into consciousness with an uneasy sense of having undertaken heavy responsibilities. For Waltheof, like most giants, was lazy, and though terrible when roused, had a strong preference for quietness and peace.

Therefore he gave a great sigh when he remembered the vows of the night before, and wished he were well out of his hazardous undertaking. Ambition had small hold of his nature, and he had far rather be an earl in peace, than a monarch who had to fight for his throne. Moreover, his religious sentiments were strong, and inclined to an ascetic renunciation. Judith swept back the curtain from the lattice, and let a flood of noonday light into the hitherto carefully darkened chamber.

Waltheof started.

'It is noon!' he said. 'Why didst thou not wake me? By St. John of Beverley! it was meet that I should have attended the presentation of the morning gift.'

Judith knew that her lord was deeply moved, by his invocation of the Northumbrian saint, whose name was

Judith watches her sleeping Spouse.

connected with all the wrongs that he preferred to forget when he was in an amiable mood. Yet she answered calmly, and with scorn in her voice, 'Who can wake a drunken man?'

And the champion who had struck off the heads of the Norman warriors, one after another, with a single blow of his terrible seax, at the gates of York, was so ignominiously under the rule of his Norman wife, that he swallowed his wrath and made no reply.

Judith made haste to improve her advantage, and to carry the war into the enemy's camp.

'How I hate these Saxon excesses!' she continued; 'only befitting barbarians, lowering men below the level of the brutes, who eat when they are hungry, and drink when they are thirsty, and abstain when want is satisfied. Thou madest not a fair picture, Waltheof, lying sprawled out and insensible in thy tipsy sleep, a prey to any evil creature who had chanced to come thy way. Cyning of the Saxons, indeed! Learn first to be king of thine own appetites!'

Waltheof started, and his brows knitted over his still heavy eyes.

'How knewest thou that, witch of Endor?' he demanded.

'Nay, thou hast experience that the spirits of the air are at my beck, and that my power serves me to gain knowledge of all that concerns my dearly-beloved spouse,' returned Judith, with a sneer.

'Sorceress! I believe, in sooth, thou art leagued with the devil!' quoth Waltheof furiously, and his expression was no metaphor. He was superstitious by nature, and his sharp-witted wife had done her utmost to impress him with the notion that her intellectual gifts were replenished from supernatural sources. Hence her power over him. 'But I tell thee, thou hadst better never have been born than meddle in this concern of thy husband's. For this concern is the concern not of my poor unworthy self, but of my country, of my people! And I tell thee, foreign harridan, I had liefer strangle thee with mine own hands than be frustrated!'

"'Tis pity,' quoth Judith calmly, 'since the matter is marred already.'

'What meanest thou, viper?' shouted Waltheof, fully aroused and springing to his feet, and advancing towards Judith with a threatening gesture, his mighty fist, which could have struck the life from her frail body at a blow, clenched into an iron ball, and the knots in his massive throat working with nervous excitement.

But Judith faced him unmoved, her proud face flashing with scorn. For the blood of Robert the Devil and Arlète of Falaise was hot in her veins, and perhaps she opined, also, that even in his wrath her heroic lord was too generous to hurt her. She did not quail before him but stood looking at him with her defiant, steadfast eyes.

'Slay me if thou wilt,' she said, without a falter in her tone. 'That which is done cannot be undone. My death will not hinder the stout messenger that sped through the night, ere thou hadst reeled from the banquet to thy chamber, from bearing the news of thy treason to Lanfranc. In vain wilt thou seek to overtake him, for he hath nigh a twelve hours' start, and he is mounted on thine own Spanish destrier, the swiftest steed in England—William's gift!'

The oath with which Waltheof answered was too terrible for repetition. He sprang at his wife, and clutched her slender throat with his strong fingers, as if he were in very truth about to execute his threat and strangle her.

She stood like a statue, though the weight of his hands upon her shoulders almost bore her to the ground.

'My people are as dear to me as thine to thee,' she said, expecting the death-grip to follow her bold speech. 'Thou hast sworn fealty to William, nay, thou hast done him homage, and put thy hands between his and vowed to be his man; thou hast married me, his niece! The struggle and the bloodshed are over, the Normans and Saxons should be one, and thou wouldst renew the strife and divide them again!'

With a moan like that of a wounded bull, the son of Siward cast the grand-daughter of Robert the Devil from him, and, covering his face with his hands, threw himself back on his couch in an agony of thwarted and impotent rage.

'Hadst thou been a man!' he muttered,—'hadst thou been a man, that I could do battle with thee hand to hand!'

'Had I been a man, Waltheof,' said Judith softly

kneeling on one knee beside her prostrate warrior,—'had I been a man, Waltheof, I had not been here to save thee, and thy country, and thy people from the consequences of thy drunken folly. Holy Mary be praised that made me a woman! Waltheof, what is thy love for thy people, if thou wouldst plunge them again in blood and fire for the vain hope of satisfying an impossible ambition? Was not the harrying of Northumberland enough, that thou wouldst have the whole country ravaged from north to south?'

No man of many words was the hero of York, and his only reply to this eloquent appeal was to mutter an occasional curse in his beard, nor did he raise his face from the pillows among which he had plunged it.

'I tell thee,' Judith went on, 'William would harry the land from York to Hastings, as he harried it from Durham to York, rather than lose it from his grip. And thinkest thou that he whom Harold Godwinsson could not baulk nor drive from the land ere one Norman castle or stronghold was built in it, though he had the full force of the Saxon chivalry at his back, could be so easily ousted from the saddle into which he has climbed, now the most part of the nation are dead, or ruined and torn by dissensions and rivalry? Thinkest thou I would not gladly be a queen if there were any hope of such an ending to thine exploit? But seeing it not, I have chosen rather to endeavour to save thy life.'

'Save my life? Thou hast rather lost it! Say'st thou not that thou hast betrayed me to Lanfranc?'

He raised his head at last, and looked her in the face.

'Nay, Waltheof!' answered Judith, softly laying her slender hand upon his huge shoulder. 'The foreign harridan loves her husband! I would save thee, not destroy thee. The letter was couched in thy name and sealed with thy seal, and so writ as though thou hadst but seemed to join the plot the better to discomfit the king's enemies.'

'Thou fiend infernal!' cried Waltheof, starting up again in an agony. 'Hast thou so dared to sully my good name?—to paint me so black a traitor?'

'Softly, my husband! The vow that is first made counts most binding. I would save thy name from the foul stain of treachery to thy generous liege-lord, William of Normandy, to whom thou didst homage in person on the banks of the Tees, coming of thine own free will to tender it, and accepting his forgiveness, his friendship, and the hand of his kinswoman. Yes—the hand of thy poor wife Judith, who would fain lead thee back to thy nobler self.'

The logic of this speech bore heavily on Waltheof, who threw himself down again upon the couch with a curse and a moan.

'Would that the sun had never risen on the day I first saw light!' he muttered.

Judith stretched out her hand and raised the golden crucifix which was suspended by a chain from her husband's neck, so that it was on a level with his eyes.

'Though we be of two nations, Waltheof,' she said gently, 'we are servants of one Lord. The abbot who bade thee plunge thy country afresh in blood and fire is no true priest of God. And for my countryman, Roger of Hereford, thinkest thou Lanfranc excommunicated him for nought?—Lanfranc, who loved him as a son. Wouldst thou associate with one accursed? What motive can he have in this save the slaking of his over-weening pride? As for the Breton, or the Englishman, or whatsoever he be called, Ralph of Guader, he who fought against his people at Hastings can have little spur save his own ambition. Wilt thou be the tool of such as these? I tell thee, Waltheof, if thou by timely return to thy sober senses dost frustrate the plottings of these men, thy memory will be green in the pages of the chroniclers, but if thou dost strengthen them in their folly, the ages will curse thee. Without thee they are powerless. It is thy name they conjure with, son of Siward. What Saxon would fight for Roger of Hereford, the son of their mightiest foe, or for the renegade, half-bred Ralph de Guader? Go now to Lanfranc, throw thyself at his feet, and all bloodshed will be stopped.'

And Waltheof groaned, and kissed the crucifix as she held it to his lips, for he was deeply religious after the wild manner of his times; humble in his faith, and little dreaming that the Saxon Church he loved so well would one day account him a martyr, and accord the power of miracle-working to the tomb in which his headless corse would repose, the trysting-place of countless pilgrims,

'I would not willingly bring further suffering on my unhappy country,' he said thoughtfully.

A gleam of triumph passed over the face of Judith, for the fury was gone from his voice, and she knew that she had conquered.

CHAPTER VIII.

KNIGHT-ERRANT AND MERCENARY.

Sir Aimand de Sourdeval, after he had been forbidden by Eadgyth of Norwich to wear her colours openly in his helm at the tourney, had cast about in his mind for some means of so bearing them that she should be aware that he did so, and she alone.

Accordingly, he had a new device blazoned on his shield,—a star shining from a band of blue sky between two barriers of sable cloud, with the motto, '*L'espérance vit dans le bleu,*' blue being the colour most affected by Eadgyth, and to be worn by her, he knew, at the bride-ale.

This shield he bore with brilliant fortune in the joust, and plied his lance so well that the highest prize was awarded to him, a lady's bracelet gleaming with many gems, which Emma Fitzosbern handed to him with a bright smile; while Eadgyth, who stood behind her, thrilled with pleasure and pride that the knight who had placed his valour at her disposal had so worthily acquitted himself, though it was but a painful pleasure, since she deemed that an impassable gulf divided them, and she grieved to see how, without wearing any token openly,

Sir Aimand still contrived to carry her colours. The ingenuity of the homage touched Eadgyth to the quick, for she was no coquette, and had no wish that a gallant youth should waste his breath in vain sighs for her favour.

So, when Emma with a gracious compliment crowned Sir Aimand with laurel, and handed him the prize he had won away from the many dexterous lances and strong arms which had contended for it, Eadgyth's eyes were full of ruth, and Sir Aimand, seeing them, grew suddenly glad at heart.

'Nay, noble Emma,' he said, declining to take the bracelet from her hand. 'Though my lady's eyes are as bright as the jewels that stud this golden circlet, they look not upon me with favour, neither may I wear her token in mine helm, nor place my trophies at her feet. Bestow the prize, therefore, upon one of thy fair damsels whose small wrist, peradventure, it may be of size to suit.'

So saying, he descended into the lists again, mounted his steed, and rode away amid the cheers of the spectators.

Emma turned to the maiden beside her, and bade her hold out her wrist.

'I believe shrewdly the bracelet will fit thee,' she said; and Eadgyth, blushing, was obliged to obey, and saw the jewelled circlet blazing round her arm with strangely mingled feelings of triumph and sorrow.

On the day of the bride-ale, it fell to the lot of Sir Aimand, as the youngest knight in Ralph de Guader's following, to keep ward over the sentries of the camp, and necessarily, therefore, to be absent from the banquet. So, while his chief was pledging his guests with pledges of dire import, and men were feasting and revelling and vowing mad vows to help each other's treason, and follow the three great earls in their wild enterprise, the unconscious Knight of Sourdeval was riding through the starlit night from outpost to outpost, passing the watchword himself had chosen for the night.

'*Corage é bonne conscience*,' he said, as he proved each post.

'*Fait tout homme fort é fier*,' answered each sentry.

For Sir Aimand, it must be admitted, was of a romantic cast of mind, and threw himself heart and soul into the fantastic images of chivalry which were then being evolved by the brightest spirits of the age, and never lost an opportunity of enforcing a good maxim, if it were only in so small a matter as a watchword.

His young head was as full of schemes for the reformation and improvement of the world as that of any modern Socialist; and, having lately met a palmer who had returned from a visit to the Holy Sepulchre, he had fallen a-dreaming on his chances of ever being able to travel thither himself, a project which had haunted him for a long time with more or less persistence, and which had started into prominence again in his mind since Eadgyth had given so discouraging an answer to his suit.

Being profoundly religious, he had been inclined to believe that her answer was guided by Heaven to lead him back to the less worldly scheme which had so filled his heart before he met her, and which he must have laid aside for an indefinite period, if not for ever, if she had consented to wed him; and he found comfort for his wounded love in the thought that he was, perhaps, to attain a higher spiritual life through the denial of earthly joy.

So, as he rode under the sparkling sky, his breast was full of a tender resignation, and the thought that he was guarding the lady of his love caused him a quiet satisfaction. He liked to feel that he was serving her, and vowed to serve her no less zealously that she had forbidden him ever to expect guerdon, and made all manner of silent vows to prove himself worthy of the love he had asked, and to live knight-like and piously, and do his *devoir* to God and man.

So noble a frame of mind might well bring forth fruit of song, and as he rode he hummed snatches of a *lai* which had taken his fancy a few weeks before, when he heard it from the lips of the author, a gallant minstrel, who, like Taillefer the famous, was also a knight of goodly prowess, and was devoted to the nobler branches of the *joyeuse science*.

Sir Aimand sang but snatches to the jingle of scabbard and harness, but this was the poem at length:—

THE WHYTE LADYE.

I.

Sir Bors went riding past a shrine,
And there a mayd her griefe did tyne.
O sweet Marye!

A lilye maid with cheekes all pale,
And garments whyte, and snowy veil,
Shee bitterly did weepe and wail.
     O dear Marye!

II.

Sir Bors beheld, and straight hys brest
For pitye 'gainst his hauberke prest.
     O sweet Marye!
'Ladye,' quod hee, 'I love thee soe,
That I toe Deth wold gladlye goe,
If I might ease thy cruel woe!'
     O dear Marye!

III.

Shee answered, 'In a robber's hold
Lies chained a comlye knight and bold.'
     O sweet Marye!
'Mine herte is fulle of dysmal dred
Lest hee be foully done to dedde,
For I have promised him to wedde!'
     O dear Marye!

IV.

Then grew Sir Bors as white as shee,
And never answer answered hee.
     O sweet Marye!
A cruel stound didde pierce his brest,
Yet soothly laid hee lance in rest,
And parted instant on his quest.
     O dear Marye!

V.

And whilom found the robber's hold,
And freed the comlye knight and bold.
     O sweet Marye!
And sette him on his own good steed
(Though inwardly his wounds did bleed),
And stript his hauberke for his need,
That he might be in knight-like weed.
     O dear Marye!

VI.

And ran before him in the mire,
That hee might fitlye have a squire.
    O sweet Marye!
Then when they reacht the lilye maid,
'Behold thy comlye knight!' he said,
And saw her chaunge from white to redde,
Then, smiling, at her feet fell dedde.
    O dear Marye!

As Sir Aimand hummed his song, a secret joy came to his heart, for he felt that although his plight was sad, being distasteful to his lady for his country's sake, at least no 'comlye knight and bold' of any other nation, Saxon or Breton, had forestalled him in her regard ; of that he felt doubly assured, for, in the first place, if it had been so, he felt convinced that Eadgyth would have frankly avowed it, when he begged her permission to show himself at the tourney as her knight ; and secondly, the expression he had surprised on her face when he had refused to take the prize bracelet.

Suddenly these dreams were interrupted.

The soldier banished the lover.

Sir Aimand checked his horse, and stiffened into rigidity, like a pointer scenting game.

Trot! trot! trot! The beat of a horse's tread leaving the camp at a rapid pace sounded through the darkness.

Sir Aimand struck spurs into his own gallant destrier, and dashed forward in the direction he judged the horseman was taking, endeavouring to intercept him by cutting off an angle.

The trot changed into a gallop, and though the

Norman knight even caught sight of a dark figure hurrying through the gloom, he soon found that his steed was no match for the one he was pursuing; but Judith's messenger had a narrow escape.

Returning to the camp, De Sourdeval questioned the sentries; but, finding that the horseman had issued from the quarter occupied by the Northumbrians in the retinue of Earl Waltheof, over which he had no jurisdiction, he was forced unwillingly to let the matter rest.

Meanwhile the camp had grown quiet. The sounds of revelry and the mighty chorus which from time to time had burst from the palace—Sir Aimand little guessed their dire import—had ceased, and the silence was only broken by the occasional neigh of a horse, or whinny from some of the mules belonging to the ecclesiastical guests, or the clash of a sentinel's spear against his shield and jingle of his harness as he paced his post, or perhaps some wandering owl hooting at the disturbers of his accustomed hunting-grounds.

The east grew red with dawn, and Sir Aimand was relieved from his watch by the knight next on duty, and went towards his own pavilion to rest. As he passed the quarters of the Breton knights in the East Anglian earl's following, he was hailed by a group who were still lingering at the entrance of one of the pavilions, and talking together rather noisily of the events of the evening. Some few of the Bretons were vassals to Ralph de Guader, holding lands under him on his estates of Guader and Montfort, but the greater number were adventurers whom the earl had gathered round him, when he had determined to defy the mandate of William against his marriage. These men were under the leadership of one Alain de Gourin, a bold and reckless soldier of fortune, whose guiding principle was the lining of his own purse and the obtaining a full share of the fat of whatsoever land he might be living in. Between this swashbuckler and De Sourdeval but little love was lost, the Norman deeming the Breton a ruffian, and the Breton despising the Norman as a prig, so a smothered enmity was always between them.

Therefore it was with no great alacrity that Sir Aimand answered De Gourin's hail, especially as he guessed very shrewdly that the Bretons had not returned very steady-headed from the banquet.

'Gramercy, Sir Aimand! Thou hast been out of the world these six hours,' cried De Gourin, who had inherited the physical traits of his Welsh forefathers, having blue, bulging eyes, and light eyelashes, and truly Celtic flaming red hair, and was of a tall, wiry figure, and capable of immense endurance, his age being about fifty. 'Come hither, lad! We have such news for thee as will make thy heart beat faster, if thou hast the love of a true knight for the clash of steel and the hope of glory! Beshrew me! the man who knows how to wield his weapon will have a chance to carve his way to fortune e'er many months are past and gone!'

Here a knight whispered to him rather anxiously.

'Tush! Sir Aimand had been at the banquet save for the need of keeping ward on the camp,' answered Sir Alain. 'I would have the pleasure of seeing his delight!' he added, with a coarse laugh, and half forced the Norman to enter the tent with him, when, pouring out a goblet of Gascon, he challenged Sir Aimand to pledge the enterprise.

'Nay! First I must know what it is,' said the Norman.

'To unseat that upstart and usurper, William the Bastard, from his ill-gotten seat on the throne of England, and to put a better man in his place,' answered Sir Alain in a hectoring tone; 'and to win for ourselves such good shares of the lands as is due to our valorous lances.'

Sir Aimand started back, looking fixedly at the Breton, and his hand instinctively sought his sword-hilt; but in a moment he regained his composure.

'Methinks the earl's somewhat ponderous Saxon hospitality has turned thy hot brains a bit, Sir Alain,' he said contemptuously. 'Neither thou nor I are likely to drink that pledge!'

Sir Alain smiled at him with an evil smile, but he kept his temper. 'St. Nicholas! But every man here has drunk it this evening, and every man who sat at Ralph de Guader's marriage board; and, sooth to say, if thou hadst been present to hear the list of that same William's crimes that were brought up against him, methinks so virtuous a knight as thyself had drunk it too, with a rider to vow that such vermin were best exterminated from the earth.'

'It is true, De Sourdeval! All drank the pledge,— Normans, Bretons, and Saxons,' chorused the knights around. 'We are under oath to pull William from the throne and set up Waltheof in his stead.'

'It cannot be!' cried Sir Aimand, overwhelmed. 'It is treachery! The earl cannot be guilty of such baseness!'

'And who art thou to stigmatise as baseness what so many men as good as thee hold fit and good?' chorused the Bretons.

'By the rood! ye are scarcely fair to the lad,' said one somewhat more sober than his companions. 'The communication is sudden, to say the least. Neither did he hear the eloquent catalogue of William's faults which wrought our blood to the boiling point.'

'Nor would I have listened to a word of it!' cried Sir Aimand fiercely. 'I would have thrown down my gauntlet had it been the earl himself who traduced his liege lord and king! And what were ye for leal knights, fair sirs, that ye gave ear to such treason?'

'Look ye, my galliard,' said Alain de Gourin contemptuously, 'I should advise you to drop that hero of romaunt strain, for it is a little out of fashion here and now. By my halidom, thou wilt scarce find a foot-page in the whole camp that will support thee! The fell-monger's grandson has carried his tyrannies a little too far even for the patient stomachs of his servile Normans at last; and as for us Bretons, we have long bided our time to pay him out for those dishes of Italian soup to which he treated Counts Alain and Conan.'

'I will never drop the strain whilst I have breath in my body!' said Sir Aimand stoutly. 'Perhaps, when the morning comes, it will be you who will pipe to a different tune, fair sirs. Let me pass, gentlemen; I would go to my pavilion.'

'Not so fast!' answered Sir Alain, interposing his bulky person betwixt De Sourdeval and the door of the tent. 'Not until thou hast drunk the pledge! It would be scarce politic to let loose so puissant a knight while he declares himself hostile to our enterprise.'

Sir Alain and the most part of the Bretons were in their banqueting robes, armed only with swords and daggers, but a half-dozen, at least, had prepared for duty, and were in full harness, and these closed round their leader, and barred Sir Aimand's retreat.

'Sirs,' said De Sourdeval, 'ye are six to one, without counting unarmed men. If you stand not at treason to your king-lord, ye will scarce be particular in giving fair play to one who is true to him. But I tell you that ye shall not force *me* into complicity with your traitorous plans if ye hack every limb from my body. And I will sell my life dearly, since every blow I strike will be for my liege as well as for myself.'

'Thou young fool!' returned De Gourin, 'we have no wish to hurt a hair of thy head. Thou needest not drink the pledge if it irks thee, but for our own sakes we must shut thy mouth in one way or other. Resistance to such odds is madness. Yield thyself a prisoner, and the worst that will befall thee is a limited sphere of action till such time as we can honourably exchange thee against any of our members who may get into William's clutches.'

'Honourably!' repeated Sir Aimand furiously. 'When the combat is begun by throwing honour and devoir and all knightly fairness to the winds!'

'By the devil's own horns! thou carriest the matter too far for my patience!' cried De Gourin. 'Fight for it, then, if thou wilt!' Drawing his sword, he made a tremendous blow at Sir Aimand, who parried without returning it.

'I fight not with unarmed men!' said Sir Aimand, and obtained a cheer from the onlookers, who dropped the points of their own swords, as if rather ashamed of the business.

'Nay, if thou likest it better, and none of these men will suit thee, I will go and put on my harness,' said De Gourin.

'It is not I who hesitate!' flung back Sir Aimand, for his blood was up, and he threw prudence to the winds.

'Well crowed, Sir Victor of the Tourney!' cried Sir Alain mockingly. 'Thou hast already unhorsed singly more than one of us, why shouldst thou be awed by our combination? Sir Mordred here cut a shrewdly laughable figure when thy thrust caught his jowl two days agone! Methinks his teeth must chatter yet! No wonder he pauses before attacking so doughty a champion!'

Sir Mordred, stung by the taunt, advanced on De Sourdeval and attacked him fiercely; but the Norman held his own, surpassing him both in strength and skill; and in a few moments Sir Mordred fell to the ground, cured for ever of the toothache or any other ache that flesh is heir to.

His comrades, with a savage howl, closed on Sir Aimand, and, overwhelmed by numbers, he was borne down, and lay senseless and bleeding beside his slain foe.

Meanwhile Judith's messenger was speeding on his way to the Primate, while the unfortunate knight who had striven so hard to stop him was thus foully entreated, lest he should himself be the bearer of some such message.

CHAPTER IX.

NORWICH.

AFTER the bride-ale the splendid company parted, mainly in three great divisions: Earl Waltheof and his following to the north; Earl Roger to the west; Earl Ralph with his bride, his Norman knights, and Breton vassals and mercenaries, his Anglo-Saxon vassals and sympathisers, to the east; a few minor parties of independent barons, knights, and thegns going their several ways.

The Earl of Norfolk and Suffolk and his train rode forth along the old Roman Ikenield Street, which ran then an uninterrupted course from within a few miles of Exning to Norwich.

De Guader rode beside his young countess on a gentle *hacquenée*, which paced quietly beside her palfrey, and did not break in upon their converse by any pranks of his own, his squire leading the fiery Oliver, and an attendant following with a mule carrying his armour, lance, and spear.

It may well be supposed that the noble bridegroom spared no pains to make the time pass pleasantly for his young countess, which, under the circumstances, was no difficult task, for the mid-May weather was delightful, and whether they rode over heaths or through the forests, which then spread over the greater part of the country, they were surrounded with flowers and the song of birds. The yellow gorse was gorgeous in the open, filling the air with its almond scent, and the whin-chats fluttered from bush to bush, trying to lure them away from the spot that hid their nests. Overhead the larks carolled and the sparrow-hawks poised motionless, while round and about them darted the busy swallows.

Where they passed a homestead, fruit-trees were gay with blossom, apple and cherry and pear, and the sweet-breathed kine were standing in the meadows, knee-deep in the flower-jewelled grasses, for was it not *Tri-milki*, the month when cows are milked thrice in the day, according to the quaint old Anglo-Saxon calendar? Now and again they met a shepherd with a flock of ewes and lambs, or, more often, the inevitable Saxon swineherd with his grunting pigs.

But alas! they passed more often the blackened ruins where a homestead had once been, for the curse of war had desolated the land. Over the thatchless rafters hung the white branches of the flowering May, the more like snow, because no girlish fingers had stripped them to deck Maypoles.

They journeyed also through many a mile of forest land, where the great trees interlaced their boughs into the beautiful arches which the Gothic architect imitated so well in stone, and the wild birds thronged in undisturbed security, countless in kind and number, and the antlered stags trotted nimbly down the glades.

The greenwood in those days, however, had its dangers as well as its delights. Wolves and boars and wild cattle shared its shelter with the feathered songsters; and more formidable still were the indomitable Saxons, who had sought refuge in the wilderness, and made war without mercy on such of the conquering race as trespassed on their domain. Many a Saxon thegn, who had lost house and land in the great struggle against the Norman invader, had retired into the woods, and there lived the life of a freebooter, some taking with them not only their families, but their vassals and retainers. To be an outlaw was accounted an honour by these men, who would not acknowledge the right of the law-makers to command. They swarmed even under the walls of the Norman castles, and harassed the conquerors continually. Retaliation was sanguinary, and the unarmed peasants were punished under pretext that they harboured the outlaws. In return, the kings of the forest attacked the English households who favoured the Normans, and every house was fortified to resist a siege, and stores of arms and food were laid in; at night the head of the family read aloud the form of prayer then used at sea in a storm, praying 'The Lord bless and help us,' to which all present answered 'Amen.'

But the strong and well-armed retinue that accompanied the Earl of East Anglia's party assured safety, and the most timid amongst the ladies could fear no harm while surrounded by so many gallant knights in all the pride and panoply of glorious war! They made a goodly sight as they moved along, the sunshine flashing on their mail hauberks and high-peaked steel saddles, and the wind fluttering the gonfalons on their lances, their well-appointed horses snorting and curvetting, a strong body of men-at-arms, bowmen, and slingers following afoot.

Doubtless many a Saxon serf and bordar cursed them as they passed, not knowing that the powerful earl who led them had avowed himself champion of the Saxon cause, and meant once more to raise the standard of revolt.

Doubtless many a stout forester peered at them from behind the shelter of .green leaves, and raged with impotent anger at their strength.

Perhaps others greeted them with courtesy and proffers of friendship and offerings of game, for the outlaws contrived to be wonderfully well informed of the march of events, and De Guader was keenly alive to the desirability of making all possible allies amongst the scattered English, and did not neglect the brave spirits who had taken to the wilds rather than submit, and who wielded so strong a weapon in possessing the love of the common people.

However that might have been, they journeyed safely through wood and wold, going slowly to suit the comfort of the ladies, and the capacity of the sumpter mules, and revelling in the bright spring weather.

Amongst the knights who pressed round them Eadgyth looked in vain for the figure of Sir Aimand de Sourdeval. Emma, happy with her bridegroom, took no notice of his absence, till, on the second day of their journey, the earl having left her side to give some necessary orders to his train, she saw that Eadgyth was sad and silent, and remembered that the hero of the tourney had not appeared in the ranks of their escort. She surmised that it was likely he had purposely avoided companionship which could only lead to pain, and had contrived to fulfil some other duty; so, when the earl rode up to her side again, she put some light question to him regarding the knight, and was surprised to see his face grow dark as thunder. He answered briefly, however, that Sir Aimand was detained on business of weight, and Emma, rather perplexed, did not venture to question him further. At the moment the jester Grillonne ambled up, mounted on a piebald nag with a chuckle-head and goose-rump, and cut capers which made both earl and countess laugh, so that the poor Knight of Sourdeval was banished from Emma's thoughts.

On the evening of the fourth day they came in sight of the churches and trees of Norwich, with the newly-built Castle Blauncheflour rising in stately strength above them (for no cathedral spire dwarfed it then), the brilliant beams of the setting sun gilding its snowy towers, and lighting the square mass of the lofty keep, which still, after eight hundred years of war and weather, stands firm and solid on its throne above the city.[1]

Emma exclaimed in delight when she first came in

[1] See Appendix, Note B.

sight of this goodly castle, which brought home to her pleasantly the power and wealth of her noble husband.

'A garrison of five hundred might hold it for ever!' cried Ralph enthusiastically, 'if only manna would fall from the skies to feed them, or that they might be fed by a San Graal. That reminds me, sweet, thou wilt like to hear my minstrel tell the story of Blaunchefiour, who was the betrothed of Percivale, the searcher for the Graal. The fair white walls, faced with goodly Caen stone, seemed to me in their invincible dignity to resemble a pure maiden, so I named them after her.'

Norwich in those days was surrounded by broad and deep streams, at least five times as wide as its present modest rivers, and the chroniclers of Edward the Confessor's day record that the fisher-folk suffered terribly through the receding of the waters. A sandbank some distance out at sea was just emerging where Yarmouth now stands, and sea-going vessels could make their way past the walls of Blaunchefiour.

The level of the water was many feet above its present mark, and the castle was surrounded, and rendered very strong, by deep ditches of early British construction, on a similar scheme to those traced at Rising, Castleacre, and many other places, where Norman architects had availed themselves of the earthworks constructed by earlier peoples. The castle was surrounded by the circular moat which still exists, while a large horseshoe fosse extended to the south, covering the great gate of the castle, which was at the foot of the existing bridge, which is of Saxon construction, and measures forty feet in the span, being the largest remaining arch raised by that people.

The great gate was a strong and imposing structure, and had four towers, two at the base and two at the top of the bridge, and was the only entrance to the upper ballium, which was guarded by eleven strong towers, and contained various halls and lodgings, beside the great keep, which is all that remains to us.

The fortress might well look imposing, with its moats and earthworks, strengthened by strong palisadings of wood, its formidable walls and gate-houses dominated by the great square tower, with many a pennon waving from the topmost points, and warders marching to and fro on the battlements, their glittering mail shining in the sun.

Norwich was not a city then, the see of the Bishop of East Anglia being at Elmham, but there was a monastic church called Christ's Church where the present cathedral stands, and the bishop had a palace on the site of the well-known Maid's Head Inn of the present, the walls of which were lapped by the river.

Herfast, who held the see from 1070 to 1076, had been chaplain to William the Conqueror when he was Duke of Normandy. It may be that he somewhat favoured Ralph de Guader, or chose to be blind to the doings of the turbulent earl, for, though Norman of the Normans, he bitterly hated Lanfranc, who had once exposed his ignorance to pitiless scorn, and who unsparingly denounced his vices, bidding him 'to give over dice-playing, not to speak of graver misconduct, in which you are said to waste the whole day;' and bade him 'study theology and the decrees of the Roman Pontiffs, and to give especial attention to the sacred canons.' Also to 'dismiss certain monks of evil reputation.' At all events, he does not appear to have been an active opponent to the East Anglian earl, and it may be that he was not sorry that the archbishop he so much disliked should have a little trouble during his time of temporal power.

In the Domesday survey, made eleven years later, 1086, fifty-four churches are recorded, and 1565 burgesses and 480 bordars were among the inhabitants. The town was probably larger in 1075, as it suffered much during the subsequent siege, and many an entry of '*Wasta*,' '*wasta*,' '*wasta*,' bears testimony to the sorrow Ralph de Guader brought upon the place.

Where the busy market-place is now, spread broad meadows for the castle use, called the Magna Crofta or castle fee, and through them ran a stream, having its rise on All Saints' Green, and flowing across the present site of Davey Place to the river. The quiet Quaker burial ground occupies the Jousting Acre, or Gilden Croft, where many a noble knight gave or received a broken head in sheer good fellowship and amiable love of fighting; and many a fair lady encouraged the giver with smiles, or wept for the receiver. So the lovers of peace sleep calmly under the sod that once was trampled by the eager steeds of the men-at-arms.

Such was the Norwich to which Ralph de Guader

brought home his bride; and, as they entered it, the knights in their retinue pricked their jaded steeds and stirred their mettle, that they might prance sufficiently gaily. The trumpeters flourished their trumpets, to give notice to the good people that their earl and his bride were approaching, and, though travel-stained and weary, the cavalcade made a brave appearance.

Rich and poor, Normans, Saxons, Danes, Flemings, and Jews, all of which nations were represented in the town,—the last-named having made their first appearance therein at the heels of the Norman invaders, and being hated accordingly,—crowded into the streets to welcome and admire the bride and bridegroom, or, at the least, to render that homage which circumstances rendered politic.

For it must be remembered that the dignity of the powerful Earl of East Anglia was almost royal. The feudal king was 'first among peers,' and the earls came next to him; even so late as the reign of Queen Elizabeth the parliamentary formula of royal speeches was, 'My right loving Lords, and you, my right faithful and obedient subjects.'

The 'Ykenilde weie' entered Norwich where afterwards stood the Brazen Doors, passing by All Saints' Green to the Castle Hill; the cavalcade so entering what was called the New Burg, consisting of Norman dwellings erected since the Conquest, which, then as now, took its name from the Chapel in the Field, and included the parishes of St. Giles and St. Stephen's. Here the enthusiasm was effusive, and a well-dressed populace waved caps of rich fur in the air, while silken hangings and gay banners waved from the windows.

It was with mingled feelings that Eadgyth of Norwich re-entered her birthplace in the train of the Norman lady. All her loving recollections were embittered by the sight of changes that reminded her of the sufferings of her people and the ruin of their cause, and the tears came into her eyes when she compared the welcoming crowd of foreigners that shouted around her with the scenes stamped on her childish memory, when she had seen the stalwart Danes and Saxons gather to greet Harold Godwinsson, and heard their loud 'Waes hael!'

Storms of anger and jealous misery moved her as she passed through the New Burg, for the smart dwellings on each side of the street had all been built since the Conquest, and showed the wealth of the invader. As they approached the castle, her heart sank more and more. It seemed to her as if its heavy foundations had been laid upon her breast, so cruelly did it bring home to her the strength of the yoke which was riveted upon the necks of her people. For in architecture more than in any art did the Normans excel the people they conquered, and though the moats had been there when Harold was earl, the fortress within them was but a rude structure.

When they reached the castle gate, a lively scene was enacted. The garrison marched down to salute the earl and his bride, led by the castellan on a prancing charger, and forming in glittering lines on either side the Bale. There were companies of archers clad in mail coats reaching halfway to the knee, over which they wore jerkins of stout leather, their ell-long shafts stuck through their belts, and their bows of yew, ash, witch-hazel, or elm, held in their right hands, and capable of despatching the arrows to a distance of from 200 to 300 yards, with little steel-caps on their heads shaped much like the prim head-coverings worn by the Puritan maidens of later times; and men-at-arms, shining from head to foot in chain mail, or with little steel rings sewn thickly upon leather, armed with straight swords about a yard in length, and wearing helms like upset saucers; others less heavily armed, bearing oval shields and long lances, their shoulders and chests protected by glittering capes of scale armour; and others again, still more slightly armed, with lighter lances, and small round shields not larger than dinner-plates, with which to baulk a lance thrust; slingers, with light tunics reaching to the knee, and little or no armour, their weapon a long pole provided with a loop, from which the practised hand could sling stones with great force and precision. A good two-thirds of the archers and slingers were Bretons; for the men of Bretagne were famed bowmen, and furnished the chief contingent of the archers who did so much execution at Senlac.

Besides these there were the engineers, who worked the mangonels and catapults, and a large troop of smiths and armourers, whose duty it was to repair with hammer and anvil the damage done by wear and war to the accoutrements of these various gentry,—in all some two to three hundred men.

They rent the air with a great cheer, as they formed in line before the earl and countess and their retinue; and the castellan, Sir Hoël de St. Brice, a knight who had grown grey in the service of the Lords of Guader and Montfort, and who had fought under the father of Ralph's Breton mother, gave the cue, with a compliment to the bride.

'Long live the daughter of William Fitzosbern!' he cried, whereat the soldiers cheered again.

Emma smiled and bowed, and tried to pay them equal compliments in return.

'With such a castle, and such gallant defenders,' she said, 'fear would be impossible, even if the blood of the veriest coward ran in her veins instead of that of a hero.'

Whereat they gave still louder cheers, and vowed that they would spend every drop of their blood to defend her if need were.

Then the earl treated them to a little harangue.

'He knew they meant what they said,' he told them, 'for he had seen them fight, not only from behind stone walls, but hand to hand on the field of Hastings;' and added, 'that he was glad he knew their metal, for perhaps it would be rung sooner than they looked for.' An announcement received with vociferous delight by the wild men of war, who scarce thought life worth living in time of peace, and looked to the giving and taking of shrewd blows both for amusement and fortune, caring little in what cause they were bestowed.

While this took place, Eadgyth had turned her eyes to the south-east, the old portion of the town looking over to the Thorpe marshes, where the bright Mary buds 'had oped their golden eyes,' and the willows were white with catkins, and the Thorpe woods were in their fresh verdure. An overwhelming sense of desolation came upon her as she marked the old familiar objects among which her childhood had been passed—and more forcibly as she noted the absence of others. She drew her veil across her face, lest it should be seen that she was weeping.

The cavalcade moved on again, Sir Hoël riding by the earl's side. They passed into the northern end of King Street, and so to the ancient palace of the East Anglian earls, which stood where the St. Ethelbert Gate is now, and had a chapel dedicated to that saint, who had been a king of the East Angles. He was murdered by Offa, King of Mercia, at the instigation of his wife Quendrida. The head of the victimised prince rolled down as his body was being carried away; a blind man stumbled over it, and, accidentally touching his eyeballs with the blood, received his sight again. A well sprang up where the head fell. So runs the legend.

At the palace they were received by a gaily-clad host of servants and retainers. Brave squires and smart pages, portly bursar and anxious steward, cellarers, cooks, and scullions; stately dames and pretty bower-maidens, tirewomen, dairy and grinding-maids (for in those days windmills had not been invented, so 'woman's sphere' included the grinding of flour in a hand-mill),—these, and many more, stood waiting in order of their rank, and dressed in their bravest apparel.

Behind the earl's household was a still larger company of socmen and slaves from the nine manors which William of Normandy had bestowed on Ralph de Guader when he gave him the East Anglian earldom, making altogether a goodly crowd of retainers; and we may guess how they all strained forward to catch the first glimpse of the noble young bride their lord was bringing home, and how Emma, though well used to homage, was glad to bow her fair head under excuse of courtesy, and so hide her glowing face from so many curious eyes.

On the plain before the palace, opposite St. Michael's Chapel (Tombland), six fine beeves were roasting whole for the entertainment of the populace, and a tun of wine and several fat barrels of ale were broached, wherewith throats that had grown hoarse with shouting welcome should be refreshed.

So came Emma, Countess of Norfolk and Suffolk, to her new home in Norwich, where she was to spend but a few short months full of terror, suffering, and sorrow, and by her bearing under misfortune to prove herself the worthy daughter of her noble sire, and to be known in the pages of history as the heroine of the most romantic incident in the annals of Norwich Castle.

CHAPTER X.

LANFRANC, PRIMATE OF ALL ENGLAND.

WALTHEOF, instead of continuing his journey northward, left his retinue privily, and, with as small a following as the state of the country rendered imperative, made his way to Canterbury and craved audience of the Primate, appealing to him in the double capacity of a spiritual father, and, for the time, while King William should be absent, as a temporal superior also, the archbishop having been appointed justiciary of the kingdom in conjunction with Robert, Earl of Morton, and Geoffry, Bishop of Coutances.

After certain ceremonious delays, he was received. Lanfranc, Archbishop of Canterbury and Primate of all England, was a man of high character and subtle intellect, uniting the business capacities and breadth of view of the man of the world, to the piety and earnestness of a sincere churchman.

A Lombard by birth, he had attained eminence in his youth as a law student at Pavia. His birth was not noble, but his parents were said to have been of senatorial rank, which indicated a good social position. His eloquence as a lawyer was so great, that he triumphed over veteran opponents, and soon became famous. Italy, however, was at that time torn by dissensions, and he was early involved in political quarrels, so that he deemed it wise to quit the arena of his forensic triumphs, and to seek the less genial but safer climate of Normandy. Here he soon attained high eminence, and opened a school at Avranches, to which scholars came in crowds; but suddenly the illustrious advocate disappeared, and no one knew whither.

He was discovered, some three years later, living the life of a penitent in the secluded monastery of Bec, a small establishment founded by his countryman Herluin, but which afterwards became famous through having supplied Canterbury with three archbishops. After a time, Lanfranc became the prior of Bec, and was as much sought as a religious teacher as he had hitherto been as a lawyer.

In his newly-awakened zeal, Lanfranc took it upon him to denounce the intended marriage of the Duke of Normandy with Matilda of Flanders; the Pope having threatened excommunication, as the couple were within the prohibited degrees of relationship.

One fine day, the quiet monks of Bec, working in their garden amongst their cabbages and onions, were surprised by the advent of a gay company of knights in holiday attire, surrounding an ecclesiastic who rode pompously upon a fine white mule. The excitement increased to boiling point when the visitor was found to be the duke's chaplain Herfast, whom we have already introduced to the reader as holding the Bishopric of Elmham in 1075, and that his retinue was composed of nobles high in favour at the court; and the much-impressed monks hastened to tell their prior of the honour shown him. But the prior was giving audience to a beggar, and made the duke's emissaries wait till his conference was leisurely concluded. He understood perfectly well that William wished to bribe him, by this display of favour, into giving his assent to the wedding, and he had a mind to assert his independence.

Herfast was as ignorant as he was pompous, and the accomplished prior took every opportunity of exposing his guest's ignorance, even placing in his hands an abcdarium, or spelling-book, to the great amusement of the spectators and the huge wrath of Herfast, who rode back to his royal master with a fine tale of the insolence of the Lombard upstart.

William was so incensed, that he fell into a paroxysm of rage, ordered Lanfranc out of the country, and sent a band of soldiers to burn one of the granges of the monastery to the ground, as a practical witness to his anger at the way in which his courtiers had been treated.

Imagine the consternation amongst the monks of Bec. Lanfranc, however, was equal to the occasion. William had ordered him to quit the country. But the brethren of Bec were poor, and there were no parliamentary trains in those dark ages to carry passengers from one end of a country to the other for a penny a mile. They must travel in the saddle or on foot. Churchmen, for the most part, patronised mules of considerable size and high breeding, and journeyed in no small state. But the only animal the stables of Bec could boast was a sorry steed, angular of joint and far from sound. None the less the prior mounted it, and set off for Rouen, where he had been bidden to appear before the duke ere he quitted the country.

William came forth to meet the haughty churchman, who had dared to thwart and condemn him, and to make fun of his chaplain, accompanied by a gallant train of knights and squires. He expected to meet a cavalcade almost as numerous and magnificent as his own.

His face was dark with anger, and he wrapped himself in thoughtful taciturnity, meditating a rebuke befitting the insolence with which his condescension and favour had been met.

He grew impatient when along the straight level road nothing could be seen but a single horseman on a lame jade, whose nose almost touched the ground at every step, and whose pace was easily kept up with by a follower on foot.

As this sorry trio approached, however, he saw that the men were habited as monks, and Herfast, who rode beside his royal master on his sleek white mule, flushed deeply red.

''Tis Lanfranc himself!' he exclaimed.

'What new mummery is this?' demanded William, his keen eyes straying over the comical figure of the prior and his wretched mount, and a smile gleaming over his stern face, brief but irrepressible, for William was a

Lanfranc jests with the Conqueror.

lover of horseflesh, and spared no pains or expense in the importation of fine horses from Spain for his own use. The creature he bestrode was a splendid animal, and the strongest of contrasts to the prior's pitiful nag.

Slight as the smile was, and hastily repressed, Lanfranc saw it, and took instant advantage.

'By your commands,' said the audacious prior airily, 'I am leaving your dominions, but it is only at a foot's pace that I can proceed on such a wretched beast as this; give me a better horse, and I shall be better able to obey your commands.'

William had a keen sense of humour, and perhaps felt that the clever Lombard would be a formidable foe.

He laughed a royal laugh of magnificent amusement. 'Who ever heard before,' he asked, 'of an offender venturing to ask a donation from the very judge he has offended?'

Herfast grew redder than ever with chagrin and mortification, for he saw very plainly that the subtle prior had mollified the duke by his intrepid joke. And so it was, and from this strange meeting resulted no less a matter than the establishment of a friendship which lasted till William's death.

Not long afterwards, Lanfranc went to Rome to plead with the Pope, and urge him to give his sanction to that marriage which the prior had hitherto opposed so bitterly. And this he did without inconsistency, for his opposition had been based upon William's defiance of the Holy See; when, therefore, he persuaded the haughty duke to humble himself, and plead meekly for a dispensation, with promises that he and his bride would bind themselves to many duties in return, amongst others, to endow each an abbey and two hospitals, the seeming submission of Lanfranc was really a triumph.

After a while, though much against his will, Lanfranc was induced to leave Normandy, and assume the onerous post of Primate of William's newly-conquered kingdom of England. He even appealed to Pope Alexander II. to extricate him from the difficulties of such high office, and to permit him to return to the monastic life, which above all things delighted him. But the Pope refused to interfere, and Lanfranc accepted the inevitable, and set to work with courageous zeal to make the best of his manifold duties. And he acquitted himself like a brave and good man, steering a wise course amongst the jealous Normans and aggrieved Saxons, selecting virtuous men to fill the posts which became vacant; and though, no doubt, partaking the prejudices of the conquerors, yet securing good men amongst the Saxon clergy as friends. The Church of England owes much to him, for he was distinctly an imperialist, and stoutly resisted papal aggression, laying the seeds of that nationality which has saved us from so many evils.

It may be imagined that the simple-minded and gentle Waltheof, much more adept at wielding a seax than at chopping logic, and who was as wax in the hands of his clever wife, was as water under the treatment of this subtle Lombard, who could mould to his wishes even the self-willed and astute William.

The archbishop received the Earl of Northumberland with much pomp and circumstance, giving him the ceremonious honour due to his high rank and his position as husband of the king's niece, so that Waltheof had to beg for a private interview.

This being granted, the unhappy hero knew not how to begin his forced confession, and the keen black eyes with which Lanfranc searched his face did not lessen his confusion.

But the archbishop had no intent to deal harshly with his illustrious penitent.

His features softened with a winning smile. 'What hast thou to say to me, my son?' he asked in a gentle voice. 'Why hesitate? Dost thou not know me for a true friend?'

'Alas, father! I have a sad tale of sin and weakness to reveal to thine ears,' said the son of Siward at length. 'But I pray thee advise me. I have taken an oath, and since then, heated with wine, and somewhat overawed by numbers, I have taken a second contrary thereto. By which am I bound? Am I forsworn in that, notwithstanding this second oath, I sent the messenger to thee, who, if nought mischanced, reached Canterbury some four days agone?'

'Thou hast sinned, my son, answered the archbishop gravely; 'but not so heavily but that, after due penance, the offence may be pardoned. An unwilling oath, taken under the compulsion of an excited crowd, can scarce bind as that which was the fruit of calm reflection and sober judgment. Rather must it be accounted evil in thee, that thou didst consort with a man who was anathema of the Holy Church.' His mobile face grew stern, but it was a sternness not unmixed with sorrow.

'Nay,' answered Waltheof eagerly, 'I knew not of that till the banquet was well-nigh ended, when it was impossible to turn back.'

He was relieved at the tone of the archbishop, yet could not keep reflecting bitterly in his heart, that this light treatment of a forced oath when taken by the son of Siward *against* William, was very different to the view taken of that made by the son of Godwin *for* William. Harold had been branded a perjurer for abjuring a forced oath.

'Nevertheless,' said the archbishop, not yet relaxing his face, 'thou hadst knowledge that the men whose bread was broken for thee were acting in direct opposition to the mandate of thy king-lord and kinsman, whose clemency had pardoned thy former misdeeds against him, whose hand had been reached to thee in fellowship, and whose niece had been given to thee to be bone of thy bone, flesh of thy flesh.'

'In good sooth, father,' replied Waltheof reluctantly, and with the air of a schoolboy repeating a lesson by rote, 'I thought mine uncle and king-lord was playing a somewhat tyrannical part in dividing two true lovers. I see now that he had reasons which I little suspected.'

This defence had been suggested by Judith.

Lanfranc's fine sensitive face grew sad. Speaking in a low, sorrowful voice, as though the subject caused him inexpressible pain, he said, 'My son, it was not for light or frivolous reasons that William our king-lord interfered to thwart the wishes of his earls. Nor was it without cause, or, in truth, without grievous necessity, that I declared the anathema of the Holy Church against the son of the man who did more than any other to crown our Norman duke an English king. Had it been but a question of a marriage,' the archbishop continued in the same strain, but in a still softer tone, and rather as if speaking to himself than to the earl, 'God forbid that I should have parted whom He had elected in His all-seeing wisdom to unite!' He sighed deeply, for in his youth he had been the husband of a much-loved wife, whose death had taken all flavour from earthly joy for him, and had been the cause of his precipitate retreat from a position of wealth and fame, to seek consolation in the cloister. 'I have loved Roger Fitzosbern as a son! I have striven with him in affection! But, alas! in vain. One folly was added to another, until at last foolishness swelled into crime. He denied justice to the injured. He invaded the property of his king-lord, and of his peers; and now he has crowned all by this attempted treason, brought to the light at the unholy banquet at which thou wert thyself tempted to evil, Waltheof! Ah! I have wept tears of blood over this lost sheep. Would that my efforts had recalled him to the fold! But the time is past.'

He stretched out his thin, transparent hands before him, his dark eyes fixed upon space, as if contemplating a vision of the bloodshed to come.

He was silent, and Waltheof, being a man of few words, was silent also.

Suddenly the Lombard turned his gleaming eyes upon the Northumbrian earl. Waltheof started, for in his heart was no repentance for having attended the banquet, nor for any of his treasonable designs, but only a fierce wrath against the Norman wife who had defeated his plans, and brought him more tightly under the yoke he hated, and it seemed to him as if those dark eyes could read his most secret thoughts. He shifted his huge frame uneasily, so that the bracelets which ringed his tattooed arms almost to the elbow, clanged together, and his large fingers sought the jewelled haft of the hunting-knife which hung at his baldric, not threateningly, but from habit.

Yet if his thoughts were read, they were ignored.

'But thou at least art here!' Lanfranc exclaimed, his mobile features lighted by a brilliant smile. 'Thy better angel has prevailed, and, by the mercy of Our Lady, has brought thee back to the fold at the eleventh hour.'

Waltheof looked relieved, and he lifted his head and tossed back the yellow mane which had fallen over his face.

'I pray thee, father,' he said earnestly, encouraged by the Primate's smile; 'stand by me in my trouble, and plead my cause with William of Normandy. *Thou* hast the power to influence him. Advise me how I may best act to win his pardon for my transgression; how best assure him of the sincerity of my return to allegiance.'

Waltheof's Humiliation.

'I will stand by thee, my son,' replied the archbishop, clasping Waltheof's great hand in his slender fingers. And he fulfilled his promise with unswerving fidelity, even to the last, when the unfortunate son of Siward lay doomed to death in prison; nor, if Lanfranc could have prevented it, would William have consummated that greatest blot upon his reign, the execution of the Northumbrian earl. 'Thou art impulsive, my son, and simple-minded, and therefore easily snared. But I believe not that thy heart is evil, or that thou wouldst be other than a pious son of our Holy Mother Church.'

'No, indeed!' said Waltheof, much affected by the appeal, which roused all the natural piety and humility of his nature. He crossed himself with much fervour. 'Tell me what to do, father. Whatever thou wilt command I will perform.'

'My son, I would bid thee cross the sea to Normandy and seek William in person, confessing all frankly, and throwing thyself on his mercy. Nor would it be detrimental to thy suit if thy hands bore somewhat of the produce of the lands and honours he has bestowed upon thee with so lavish a generosity.'

Waltheof shuddered. It was no pleasant prospect to the powerful earl, whose head had of late been so filled with schemes of ambition, thus to humble himself a second time to the conqueror of his people.

But Waltheof's courage was more of the physical order than the moral. He was, besides, of gentle disposition, and sincerely desired to avert bloodshed, and he thought that his defection from the ranks of the conspirators would prevent any attempt to meet William in the field.

Therefore he bowed his head. 'Thine advice is meet, father,' he said; 'I will cross the seas and seek William, bearing rich presents to testify my regret for the past, and present goodwill.'

CHAPTER XI.

THE CASTELLAN OF BLAUNCHEFLOUR.

RALPH DE GUADER had said little to his bride of the proceedings at the marriage festivities, but a time came when it was necessary for him to break in upon their brief honeymoon with rumours of war, for it was not possible to hide the fact that he must take the field in defence of life and liberty.

The defection of Waltheof had been a great blow to the conspirators; his untimely betrayal of their plans was more serious still, as their chance of success lay chiefly in the hope of taking the king's forces by surprise.

Waltheof himself had supposed that his course would altogether put a stop to the undertaking, seeing that his two brother earls had represented that to place him on the throne was its chief object.

But De Guader and Fitzosbern were too proud to give up their hopes of aggrandisement so easily, and, moreover, their case was desperate. If they submitted at once and unconditionally, they could only look forward to disgrace and imprisonment, whereas the chances of battle might still be in their favour. It was not wonderful, therefore, that they elected to fight it out, notwithstanding the odds against them.

The Earl of Norfolk and Suffolk had assembled his forces, and held all in readiness for departure on the morrow. The dreaded moment had come, and he sought his wife's bower, feeling that he would much liefer meet William's men-at-arms.

It was a sunny little room on the east side of the palace, looking over the marshes of the low holme which then bordered the Wensum with a wilderness of sedges and white water-lilies, and upon which, some eleven years later, Herbert de Losinga erected the cathedral which is our present pride and joy.

Emma loved to watch the high-prowed galleys passing to and fro upon the river, with sails spread, and oars flashing, and stout rowers bending to their work; and to see them lading and unlading at Lovelly's Staithe, a wharf situated about a third of the distance between the present ferry and Foundry Bridge.

Here Eadgyth would entertain her with stories of her girlhood, and tell how she had seen her cousin, Harold Godwinsson, land at that wharf, when he came to Norwich after his imprisonment in Normandy; and how Leofric, Earl of Mercia, to whom the sainted King Eadward had given the East Anglian earldom in Harold's absence, met him with all honour; and of the magnanimous strife between the two, when Leofric would give back the earldom, and Harold would fain have had him keep it; and how Harold took it for a time, but returned it on ascending the throne.

And when the white swans came sailing amongst the reeds, bending their long necks from side to side, the Saxon maiden would tell her friend of Harold's beloved, her namesake Eadgyth Swannehals, the most beautiful woman in Norfolk, or, for the matter of that, in all England, and would burst into tears when she thought of the sad ending of that fair romance.

And Emma would smile at her enthusiasm, but yet grew in sympathy with this English people, the smoke of whose dwellings was rising around her, and almost found it in her heart to wish that her hero William had been a little less successful, and to question whether it had not been more virtuous of him to stay at home in his native Normandy. Somehow she had never admired him so freely since he had endeavoured to part her from her betrothed.

In such a mood as this was Emma when her husband sought her, with the intention of telling her the secret of his bold enterprise, but he little guessed how much her sympathies had turned against William, for, as is often the case when convictions are changing, she had made up for her coldness of feeling by warmth of speech, and had sought so to atone for her act of rebellion in marrying Ralph against the king's mandate.

Therefore the earl knew not how to begin his explanation, and sat before her embroidery frame almost as deeply embarrassed as Waltheof had been before the archbishop. 'Tis true he had told her ere their wedding that the quarrel must needs be fought out, yet it seemed not the easier to say, ' My standard is lifted.'

His face was ashy pale, for it was to him cruel as death to leave his young bride before a month had passed, although he had known that the parting must come.

Emma, looking at him, dropped her silks in horror, and, throwing her arms round his neck, asked coaxingly what ailed him.

And Ralph turned his head away without speaking.

'Can it be that I have offended thee in aught?' asked the young countess anxiously.

'Nay, Emma, I am the offender, if offender there be. Methinks the worst of all ailments is mine, for I must leave thee, and perchance anger thee also.'

'Leave me?' Her breath caught in a sob of terror.

Ralph faced her desperately. 'My love, thou knowest our wedding was against the express mandate of the king. Lanfranc, the king's man, whom he made Primate of all England,—in place of the holy Stigand, whom he unjustly deprived, and who yet languishes in prison,—hath turned bitterly against thy brother of Hereford, whom whilom he was wont to treat as a son, and has set a ban of excommunication upon him.'

A low cry of horror escaped from Emma.

Ralph's eyes flashed fire. He caught his wife's white hands as they were sliding down from his neck, half withdrawn at the fear that her love had led her into deadly sin, since the brother who had countenanced her marriage, and urged her to its fulfilment, was cast out by the Church.

He understood the loosening of her clasp, and caught her hands as a protest.

'Emma,' he cried, 'thou hast taken me for better or worse. I hoped to have made thee the second lady in the land. But alas! I must fight to hold mine own, nay, for dear life,—life which is precious for thy sake.'

'I do not regret my choice,' said Emma, meeting his gaze with her frank eyes, her proud Fitzosbern spirit rising to the test. 'Only I fear lest I have sinned in taking thee against the will of my king-lord and the voice of the Holy Church.'

'Say rather the voice of William's creature,—a Lombard upstart, without a drop of noble blood in his veins. Dost thou forget the holy men who blessed our union and gave it the sanction of the Church? They blessed thy brother for taking up the cause of an oppressed people. Shall the curses of the wily Italian have more weight than their benedictions? Dost thou throw over thy brother so easily to his untender mercies?'

'Alas! I am bewildered amid so many conflicting counsels,' Emma sighed.

'This poor land and all who are in it are so bewildered, my sweet lady,' Ralph answered, kissing the hands he still held. 'None can see the right clearly. William—the Conqueror, as he proudly styles himself—hath gone mad with his success, and the luckless people groan under his tyranny. Would I had never helped him to leave his duchy of Normandy! But it is useless to groan over the past, nor can I stop to chop logic over the present. The point is this: The king's men are marching to attack me. My only course is to fight for it, and, if possible, make a junction with thy brother Roger, when it may be that the oppressed Saxons will strike a blow to regain their freedom, and, with my trusty Bretons, I may still gain the day.'

Emma clasped her hands in sore distress.

'Is it in good sooth come to this, that thou must go forth against the king? Alas! my foolish face tempted thee to wrong. 'Tis I that am to blame.'

Ralph caught her to him and kissed her. 'Nay, by the heart of Our Lady. 'Tis William's mad pride that is to blame, and that alone. Speak no slander against my wife, or it will go ill with thee, for I will not brook to hear it.'

Emma drooped her head against his shoulder, smiling through her tears. 'Oh, Ralph,' she said, 'if thou wert but going in a good cause, the parting would not be so bitter.'

Ralph, having no good argument to proffer in reply, lost his temper. He sprang up and paced the room, making his golden spurs jingle at each impatient stride.

'I thought when I wedded a Fitzosbern I should escape the lot of most men, to be wept and wailed over at every crinkle in the rose-leaves of fate. But it seems thou art but of the same stuff as other women, after all.'

Emma flushed over neck and brow. She drew herself

proudly erect, and hastily wiped away the tears that were rolling down her cheeks.

'Naught but dread of guilt and a too fond love could have drawn tears from a Fitzosbern,' she answered haughtily. 'Thou shalt not need to complain again, my lord.'

'Nay, my sweet lady, pardon me,' pleaded the earl, turning to her with entreating eyes. 'In good sooth, I am well-nigh distracted, and the sight of thy tears makes me too bitterly conscious of my own lack of worth. But what wouldst thou have me do? If it were but a question of my own poor life, I would submit, and let William do his worst, if such a course would pleasure thee; but I cannot desert thy brother, nor my own poor Bretons, and the Saxons who have thrown in their lot with mine. Thou knowest William is not gentle with such as cross his will. It would mean loss of lands and lifelong imprisonment to thy brother and myself, and the lopping off a hand and a foot for each of my Bretons, at the least, while hanging would be too mild a measure in his eyes for the Saxons.'

Emma's hands were tightly clenched together. The momentary flush had faded from her face, and it was pale as death, but she neither sobbed nor flinched.

'I have made my choice, and I will abide by it,' she said in a low, firm voice. 'Nor will I quail before the consequences of our deed. We have chosen each other against the whole world. Perhaps if thou hadst trusted me more fully, thou hadst not been vexed with tears. Thy announcement was somewhat sudden.'

K

'Let that ill-grained speech rest in its grave, dear love. Thou hast spoken like a Fitzosbern now,' said the earl, taking her hands again in his and drawing her back to his shoulder. 'I want thee to be of good courage, for I have treated thee as a hero's daughter, and appointed thee Castellan of Blaunchefour in my absence. I have vested in thee the supreme and sole command. Thine it shall be, in case of siege while I am away,—which God forfend,—to surrender or defend the castle on whatsoever terms may seem good to thee. Sir Alain de Gourin and Sir Hoël de St. Brice will act under thine orders and be thine advisers. Wilt thou take the office?'

'Yes, I will take it,' answered Emma, without a moment's hesitation, although her whole soul trembled within her at the prospect of being left in her young feebleness to command the turbulent De Gourin, for whom she had a strong aversion, and the veteran Sir Hoël, who was a total stranger to her, albeit he had been so long in her husband's train.

'Thou art indeed a fit bride for a warrior,' cried Ralph, gazing with admiration at her determined face.

Emma longed to throw her arms around his neck and sob, but conquered the impulse, answering only with a smile.

'Thou saidest I was sudden, sweet,' resumed Ralph. 'Methinks an agony that must be sharp had best be short. To that end I would not poison for thee the brief time we had together with the shadow of parting.

That is why I told thee naught till now, upon the eve of my going forth.'

Emma could not repress a slight start.

'Dost go so soon? To-morrow?' she said.

'To-morrow thou wilt enter on thy new office,' answered the earl gaily, kissing her forehead. And then he slipped from the apartment, congratulating himself that the mischief was out, and full of admiration for his bride, in that she had borne the tidings so bravely.

Emma listened to his footfall as he strode down the long corridor till its echo was lost in the distance. Then the emotion she had violently repressed had its way.

She stretched out her arms after him as if to call him back, and threw herself on her knees near the door.

'Oh, Ralph!' she sobbed,—'oh, Ralph, my husband! Saints and angels protect thee! Guard him, St. Nicholas, thou under whose patronage he has placed himself. I vow seven candlesticks of pure gold to thine altar in Blauncheflour.'

Her voice died away, a strange sensation of numb oppression succeeded her violent anguish, and she sank in a dead faint by the door her husband had just passed through.

CHAPTER XII.

THE STANDARD OF REVOLT.

The day which was to part Emma de Guader from her bridegroom dawned clear and bright, and the summer sunshine sparkled upon the broad reaches of the Yare, and gleamed amidst the pale green rushes and brown osier beds of the Cowholme, shining with impartial equality, not only upon the just and the unjust, but upon the joyous and the sad.

In nooks and corners amongst the reeds and water weeds, the coots and water-hens were tending their nestlings.

On the site of the busy railway station, the tall heron poised gracefully on one leg, as his descendants do to this day, some ten or fifteen miles nearer the sea.

The yellow water-lilies were pushing their golden buds to the surface, and the reeds were growing dusky at the top, while the hot sunshine brought out the fragrance of the sweet-gale, or bog-myrtle, which covered many an acre, now built over, with its dark green bushes.

Westward the broad woodlands were in the young

beauty of their summer dress, wearing still somewhat of the rich variety of spring. Mountainous white clouds cast purple shadows over the sea of their close-packed crowns, in the shelter of which sang merles and mavises, and the fitful nightingale; while above marsh and woodland many a hawk and bustard hung poised on motionless wings, for in those days the gamekeepers had no quarrel with them.

The sentinels on the keep of Blauncheflour had a fair panorama to look upon as they marched to and fro upon the walls; but they did not pay much heed to the beauties of nature, they were far too much engrossed in the doings in the courtyard of the castle below, and their eyes only left the knights who were gathered there, for an occasional glance at the armed host assembled within the circle of the barbican.

Truly the cluster of gallant warriors before the grand portal of the castle, glittering from head to foot with shining steel, lavishly ornamented with gold and silver, were a goodly sight to see; though perhaps Roger Bigod may have gathered a still gayer company round him a century later, when gaudy plumes and surcoats embroidered with the coats of arms of the wearers were the fashion of the day. In William the Conqueror's time, military finery had trenched little on the strictly useful, and the richness of these cavaliers consisted more in fine inlay of precious metals than in feathers and embroidery, or fantastic helms or armour. Their heads were covered with small conical steel-caps, having a nasal to protect them from a transverse cut across the face, or were encased in huge cylinders of steel, having narrow apertures for the necessities of sight and breathing; their long hauberks were of linked mail, or leather sewn all over with little rings of steel; their straight cross-hilted swords measured three and a half to four feet in length, and were encased in richly-chased and jewelled scabbards, and suspended from baldrics ablaze with gold and gems. Each wore in his belt the *miséricorde*, and at the saddle-bows of some hung the battle-axe or mace. Their oval or heart-shaped shields were from four to five feet long, richly embossed, and often bearing a raised spike in the centre. Their long lances were adorned with square or swallow-tailed pennons, according to their rank, for, when a knight obtained the rank of banneret, or leader of a troop, the points were shorn off his pennon. Their saddles and horse furniture were studded with steel bosses, and often the reins were steel chains plentifully enriched with gold, and the heavy steeds they bestrode had need of all their sturdy strength to carry their burdens of man and metal at a gallop, even at the prompting of golden spurs.

Before the portal stood De Guader's magnificent barb Oliver, champing his bit, and with difficulty restrained by the squire who held his bridle-rein, the white foam flying from his heavy curb upon his gilded trappings, and his fox-coloured mane tossing in the breeze.

A few words of the great portal itself, before which this brave company was assembled. The vestibule on the eastern side of the keep, now known as Bigod's Tower, was not built, but the very beautiful early Norman archway was certainly a part of the original structure, and opened upon a raised platform of stone, from which sprang a drawbridge connecting it with a flight of twenty-eight steps, ended by a gate to the south.

Beneath this drawbridge was the sally-port, a narrow postern strongly fortified, which in case of siege could, by raising the drawbridge of the main doorway, be made the only entrance to the keep.[1]

At a signal from a sentinel who stood upon this platform, the trumpeters executed a lively *fanfare* on their instruments. A moment later the portal was thrown open, and the earl came forth, clad in complete armour, and leading the young countess, who was very gallantly apparelled in crimson cloth, broidered over with jewels and silver; she wore a small gorget of blue Milan steel, and had on her head a little cap of the same, damascened with gold; round her waist a jewelled belt, from which were suspended a little *miséricorde* and a short steel chain.

Behind the earl and countess followed Sir Hoël de St. Brice and Sir Alain de Gourin, both in full harness, attended by several squires and pages. As they came upon the platform, the greater part of the garrison—all that were not actually on duty as sentries, warders, and like offices—filed into the courtyard, and took up their places behind the group of knights.

---

[1] Some idea of the arrangement here described is given by the figure of the ruins of Hedingham Castle in Strutt: *Manners and Customs of the English*, vol. i. plate xxix.

'A Guader! a Guader!' shouted knights and soldiers. 'Long live the earl and countess!'

The noble couple bowed courteously, and the earl, who held in his hands the keys of the castle, turned to his consort, and then cast a proud glance along the ranks of his retainers.

'Knights and soldiers,' he said, in clear trumpet tones which could be heard even by the sentinels on the battlements, 'before I go forth to battle, it is meet that I should appoint a Castellan to have charge of my castle of Blauncheflour, and this I do now before ye all assembled, in the person of my dear lady and countess, Emma, daughter of the valiant William Fitzosbern. I appoint her to the sole and supreme command, and to have as deputies under her, and as military advisers,— but under her pleasure, and to be dismissed if she think fit,—Sir Hoël de St. Brice and Sir Alain de Gourin. Knights and gentlemen, you who are about to go forth to battle with me, and to share my dangers, and, I hope, my successes, I make you witnesses of the fact of this appointment, so that if I fall in the chances of the field, you may hurry to my lady's standard and reinforce it with your strength. Knights and soldiers of the garrison, I charge ye to serve your Castellan and liege lady with faithfulness and fervour; to render her humble obedience, and to defend her as ye would defend your own lady-loves, wives, and children. I commit her and my castle, and with them my joy and my honour, to your care. Justify my trust!'

As he spoke he handed the keys of the castle to

Emma, who took them with trembling fingers and attached them to her girdle, looking at the ranks of steel-clad men around her with a brave though blanched face.

A great roar of cheering rolled round the spacious courtyard, such as Emma had never heard in her life before, though she was to hear its like in the coming months. Asseverations and vows and battle-cries mingled in wild confusion, shouted from stentorian lungs in more than one language. 'Dex aie!' cried the Normans; and the Bretons cried 'Guader et Montfort!' 'Aoie!' 'Heysaa!' and 'The Holy Rood!' from English of varying types; while the knights shook their lances, and cried to God to shield their lady in their absence. Arms clashed, and horses stamped, and it seemed as if all the dogs in Norwich were barking.

When the tumult had somewhat subsided, and the startled pigeons were circling back to their favourite perches on the battlements, Emma, with a beating heart, made her little speech in answer. Turning first to the garrison, she said,—

'I thank ye all for your devotion, good sirs and soldiers!' and her clear, flute-like voice was to the full as distinct as that of the earl. 'Nor do I doubt that ye will do your duty to God, to your earl, and to me, his deputy, in whatsoever sore straits may befall. To you, noble knights,' she continued, turning to the group who were about to depart with the earl, 'I return thanks for your courtesy, and beg you to bear in mind that my lord's fortunes and fair fame, nay, even his life, do in some measure depend upon the sharpness of your swords, and your promptness to use them in his behalf, and therefore every blow ye strike will be struck in my defence, for, in sooth, I should die if ill or dishonour came to him!'

The cheers of the garrison and the vows of the knights to do their *devoir* by their lord burst forth more tumultuously than before; but the countess, turning to her husband, said in a low voice,—

'I can bear no more, Ralph. Farewell! May Our Lady and St. Nicholas guard thee and bring thee shortly home!'

She held out her hands to him appealingly, and he, pressing them, bent forward hastily and kissed her on the forehead.

'*A Dieu*, dear lady!' he said, with a voice less steady than her own. 'Forget not to name me in thine orisons!'

He stepped forward and mounted his impatient destrier, which, excited almost to madness by the cheering of men and the clash of arms, pranced and curveted proudly as he felt his master's hand. The trumpets blared, the portcullis creaked upon its hinges, and the drawbridge clanked upon its chains.

The gay cavalcade set forth on their adventures, none knowing how, or when, or if ever, they should return. The armed heels of the steeds clattered upon the pavement and thundered over the drawbridge, and lusty cheers rent the air before and behind them, from the waiting host upon the plain, and from the garrison in the courtyard of the castle.

Emma, with a heavy heart, ascended the circular staircase in the north-eastern angle of the keep, her ladies following, and went round to the southern side of the battlements, whence they commanded a view of the country for many miles around, and could see the earl's army in glittering array upon the space within the barbican, and also the road by which they would march away, that same broad Ikenield way by which the young countess had entered the town such a short time before, happy in her bridegroom's society.

The troops assembled in order of march. A cloud of archers and slingers in the van, chiefly Bretons; after them the bills and battle-axes, and the Anglo-Saxon contingent with their round red shields and great two-edged seaxes—the weapon from which they got their name of Saxons, though it was modified from the ancient scythe-shaped blade to a straight, double-edged sword; next in order, the javelins and pikemen, and men of various arms, many only wielding stout clubs of oak and ash, or carrying long staves. Then, glittering and shining, the body of knights headed by the earl. Near him rode Sir Guy de Landerneau, the richest and most powerful of De Guader's Breton vassals, to whom was accorded the honour of bearing the gold and black standard of the earl—the standard of revolt.

Next after Sir Guy rode his body-squire, young Stephen le Hareau, the handsomest and most promising of all the aspirants for knighthood who rode in Ralph de Guader's train, the darling of the ladies' bower, after whom more than one fair face looked wistfully as he went away, full of high hopes and visions of glory, bent on 'winning his spurs,' and wearing till he had done so, as the custom was, a golden chain around his right arm. Laughing and fearless as he rode away, with the blue summer sky reflected in his blue Norseman's eyes, little did they who watched him dream in what plight they would see him return. After them followed pages leading *hacquenées* which their masters might ride when the weight of their armour had fatigued them and their fiery war-steeds. Next the baggage on sumpter mules, and a second body of archers and slingers to protect the rear.

So they rode away on the bright summer morning, and Emma and her ladies watched their slow progress from the battlements till the last glimmer of the glittering armour was lost in the distance, her eyes following them by wood and mere, now hidden by thickets, now crossing the open moorland covered with golden gorse, now startling a solitary heron from his post amongst the marshes, now a skein of wild fowl from some shining pool.

Eadgyth watched beside the countess with eager eyes, and a great hope in her bosom that her countrymen might yet come by their own again. A delusive hope, and one she would scarcely have held if she had known more of the facts of the case. The English hated their conqueror, and found his yoke oppressive. If Eadgar Ætheling had been man enough to stand against William, and lead them in revolt, they might have struggled to overturn the Norman;—even Waltheof they might have welcomed as a national chieftain;—but they saw too clearly that Ralph de Guader and Roger of Hereford were bent only on their own advancement, to rally in numbers to their banners. Small gain would it be to them to pull William from the throne only to place one of his turbulent barons in his stead.

But the patriotic talk which the Earl of East Anglia had affected, with the hope of gaining Saxon aid, had been as honey to the listening ears of Eadgyth, and had helped her to bear the trial of seeing strangers in the palace which had been Harold's aforetime. She had almost forgiven Ralph his part at Senlac, and was building the most noble castles in the air as she watched the rebel army marching away.

But the young countess, torn with doubts, in bitter anguish for both husband and brother, watched with clasped hands and a set, pale face, and spoke not a word; but at last, when even her anxious gaze could no longer discern a vestige of the moving force, she turned to Eadgyth.

'Let us to our bower amid stone walls, sweet,' she said. 'I had hoped to have done with such when I left the stormy borders of Wales, and came hither to peaceful Norfolk. At least, I had thought that their shelter would be needed only for protection against the wild Danish Vikings, not to guard me from my own folks.'

She sighed deeply, and Eadgyth scarce could think of consolation. Like most other people in all days and all places, it seemed to them that their times were sadly out of joint.

So they descended from their post of observation, and, crossing the courtyard, entered the Constable's Lodge, which was to be their home till the war-engines of the royal forces compelled them to shelter behind the solid walls of the keep.

The bower De Guader had prepared for his bride was as magnificent and comfortable as the resources of the times permitted; and here Dame Amicia de Reviers sat awaiting them, her infirmities having prevented her from climbing the steep newel staircase of the great tower.

The pretty bower-maidens clustered round the venerable old lady, and chattered to her gaily of all that had taken place, vying with each other in recalling all the details of the stirring sight they had just witnessed, and in conveying them to her dull ears.

But Dame Amicia felt keenly that what was but a pleasant excitement to most of them must have been acute anguish to her darling.

'Where is your lady, children?' asked she; but only Eadgyth had noticed that before they left the great tower, the countess had slipped quietly away from them.

She had gone to the oratory, that little oratory which is still shown to those who visit the remains of Norwich Castle.

The archway by which she had entered was supported by two columns with ornamental capitals. At the angle were carved pelicans, in their piety vulning their breasts.

'Ah!' thought Emma as she passed them, 'if I could strip my own breast, and so make soft the beds of those

I love! Brother and husband! Ah me, what sufferings may await them! The warrior's lonely death on the cold, pitiless earth, or worse, that of the prisoner on the colder flags of the dungeon of their foe! William is without mercy. St. Nicholas, make my Ralph prevail!'

She shook from head to foot with a shudder of dread, as she threw herself upon her knees before the altar; but the tears she had so long repressed would not now come to her relief. Dry-eyed, with a dull, persistent pain at her heart that made each breath a sigh, she stretched up her arms in mute supplication to the Help of the helpless for aid.

CHAPTER XIII.

ST. NICHOLAS FOR GUADER!

THE original plan of campaign drawn out by the Earls of East Anglia and Hereford had been sadly marred by the defection of Waltheof, whose counties of Huntingdon and Northampton lay between them, so that, instead of being a bond of union, they had now become adverse territory.

With Waltheof assisting them, only Worcestershire and Warwickshire would have divided them, but since he had left them in the lurch, they must needs fight half across England to effect a junction. They had this comfort, however, that Waltheof had left the country in order to make his peace with the king, and would not personally encounter them, while their positions at the extremes of east and west exposed any force attacking either of them to be itself attacked in the rear by the other. Further, the unsettled state of the Welsh border, and the readiness of the Celts to seize any excuse for invasion, rendered Hereford's movement doubly formidable for the king's lieutenants.

De Guader hoped that, for this reason, the main force of the opponents might be turned towards Hereford, and that he might be upon them before they were aware that he had taken the field. The hope proved delusive.

When he reached his manors at Swaffham, of which place he was lord, he found that the royal army was almost upon him, and that he must give battle there and then.

Ralph had need to put forth his best powers of generalship, for the force against him was led by four of William's most brilliant officers:—

Earl William de Warrenne and Surrey, the husband of the king's stepdaughter Gundred, to whom had been given twenty-eight manors in Yorkshire, and one hundred and thirty-nine lordships in Norfolk, and who was building a fine castle at Acre near Swaffham, so that he was Ralph's neighbour, and probably no very cordial one. The Norman earl had won experience of Fenland fighting in the campaign against Hereward a few seasons previously, and had never forgiven the English for killing his brother, who was leading the king's men through the terrible quagmires of the Isle of Ely; so he ground his teeth and swore strange oaths, as was the way of the Normans, that now the time for retribution had come.

Next there was Robert Malet, son of the brave old Sir William, who had helped to bear the corse of Harold Godwinsson to its first burial, and who took with him to his own grave the love and respect of Normans and English alike, leaving his son an inheritance of lands in Norfolk and Suffolk.

L

Besides were two warlike bishops: Odo of Bayeux, the king's half-brother, and Geoffrey of Coutances, warriors whose prestige was itself equal to a large body of troops.

After the death of Robert the Devil, Arlète of Falaise, the mother of William the Conqueror, married a knight named Herluin de Conteville, and bore him two sons, Robert, Count of Mortain, and Odo, Bishop of Bayeux.

Odo had a large share of the military genius of his great half-brother; nevertheless the chronicles say: 'He was no instigator to war, nor could he be drawn thereto, and therefore much feared by the soldiers. But upon great necessity, his counsels in military affairs were of special avail, so far as might consist with the safety of religion. To the king, whose brother he was by the mother, his affections were so great that he could not be severed from him, no, not in the camp.' He equipped one hundred ships of war as his contribution to the invasion of England, and fought in person at Hastings, for which he was rewarded by the earldom of Kent, one hundred and eighty-four lordships in that county, and two hundred and fifty in other parts of England, including Rising, in Norfolk, where he built a fine castle.

Affluence did not improve his character. He grew rapacious and greedy, and degraded his sacred office by flagrant immoralities.

The followers of these four redoubtable leaders far out-numbered De Guader's, and were better drilled and equipped; moreover, the defection of Waltheof had caused many of the Saxon and Anglo-Danish nobles to join the Norman camp, seeing a good opportunity to curry favour with the Conqueror.

Ralph's naturally dauntless spirit was, however, strung by the impossibility of turning back, and he formed his troops in the strongest position he could, taking advantage of the great Saxon fosse and rampart known as the Devil's Dyke, which runs from Eastmore to Narborough, lining the steep vallum with his archers and slingers and javelin men, and massing his cavalry on the firm open ground of Beachamwell Heath, with the hope of forcing his foe into the morasses that lay around Foulden; for in those days the Bedford level was undrained, and there were no old and new Bedford rivers to gather the waters, no Denver sluice to carry them off; the sweltering fens stretched far and wide, and miles and miles of land that is now fertile pasturage was haunted only by wildfowl and fishes.

Before commencing the attack, the leaders on the king's side sent forward a knight with a herald carrying the royal standard, and accompanied by trumpets to sound a parley. This being acceded to by De Guader, and a knight bearing his standard sent forth to meet them, the royal envoy, who was no less a person than the Bishop of Bayeux himself, rode forward, and delivered his charge in so loud and clear a voice, that it was audible to the cluster of knights who gathered round De Guader, before the herald officially repeated it.

Ralph was not ill-pleased to see the Bishop of Bayeux come forward, for the cruelties he had perpetrated while sharing the vice-regency of England with William Fitzosbern had won him the hatred of the Saxons, and the Normans regarded him with jealousy and distrust; so that of all William's leaders he was least likely to win Ralph's followers to his side by personal influence.

Yet the warlike bishop was well fitted to grace the saddle of a knight. Tall, robust, and handsome, in the prime of youthful manhood, he looked indeed a noble cavalier, and any who saw him might well deem that the feats by which he had made himself famous at Hastings might be eclipsed by his prowess on the field before him.

His eyes sparkled with the excitement of the coming struggle, and his upright and muscular form was armed *cap-à-pie* in all the trappings of knightly harness. Only in one particular did his equipment differ from that of the warriors around him. He bore neither lance nor sword, but only, hanging from his saddle-bow, a huge mace with iron spikes, a weapon more deadly than either, be it said, though less like to spill blood; by this subterfuge professing to obey the law of the Church which forbade his order to shed blood.

He now came as a messenger of peace—on conditions. But what conditions!

'Noble barons and knights,' he shouted, 'here present in contumacious assembly! In the name of our king-lord, William of Normandy, supreme sovereign of these realms, by the will of the sainted Eadward the Confessor, and the election of the Witanagemót'—('No!' thundered some of the Anglo-Saxons who followed Ralph de Guader)—' By the will of the sainted Eadward the Confessor, and the election of the Witanagemót!' repeated the bishop in still louder tones, 'we, his representatives, do here demand of you that ye deliver up the body of the vile and audacious traitor, Ralph de Guader, sometime Earl of Norfolk and Suffolk, but now under attainder for high treason; and the persons of his Breton followers, here arranged in blank rebellion against their liege lord and sovereign, William the Norman, upon which deliverance and your immediate return to allegiance, your past misdeeds will receive free pardon, be ye Norman or Saxon.'

Ralph de Guader's dark visage was convulsed with passion when he heard himself and his countrymen thus singled out and excepted from all hope of pardon; and he vowed within his throat that if his Norman and Saxon vassals and allies accepted the terms, himself and his bold Bretons would forthwith turn upon them, and so entreat them that few should live to profit by their delinquency.

But the doubt was short-lived. Ralph was a brave leader and a generous master, and, moreover, well skilled in raising the ambitions of such as had embarked in his boat. A shout of derision hailed the bishop's harangue before the herald had time to repeat it formally, rising first from a dozen or so of lusty throats in Ralph's near neighbourhood, and spreading afterwards through the whole host. Ralph himself flung back the answer.

'Tell your base-born usurper,' he shouted, 'that the Normans have tired of his ingratitude, and deem his offers of pardon as little like to be fulfilled, as the fair promises of lands and honours he made them before Hastings. Tell him that the Saxons have yet to avenge Harold Godwinsson, and win back their broad acres, and that the Bretons are not yet within the power of the murderer of Count Alain and Count Conan.'

'It is well!' replied the bishop, who, notwithstanding the elasticity of his ecclesiastical conscience, preferred honest fighting to the chopping off the hands, ears, and noses of prisoners which must needs have followed the acceptance of his terms. 'After such a message, we need have no compunction in striking the first blow.'

The day was overcast, and heavy masses of grey cloud were scudding up from the south-west, shedding blinding gushes of rain at intervals, and a gusty, whistling wind swept the open heath. As Bishop Odo withdrew to the ranks of the king's men, a wilder whistle shrilled through the air, and sharp cries of pain startled the larks and the whin-chats from their nests among the gorse.

The battle had commenced with an almost simultaneous flight of arrows on each side. For a long time De Guader acted stubbornly on the defensive. His only chance was to keep the king's forces at bay along the Devil's Dyke. But the line to be guarded was very long, and the number of the foe enabled them to attack many points at once.

He stood with his standard and his cavalry on the high ground towards Beachamwell, where alone they had any chance to manœuvre; but down in the fens towards Fouldon the fierce clashing of axe on spear, the clang of swords on buckler and mail, the whiz of arrows and the sharp twanging of bows mingled strangely with the shrill screaming of frightened waterfowl; and the wild shouts of the combatants frightened many a skein of mallards and plovers in their reedy haunts, from which they rose on whirring wings, with clamorous shrieks of fear.

Alike on the heath and in the fen, Normans were striving with Normans, and Saxons with Saxons, while the Bretons fought with the courage of desperation, well knowing that not only ruin, but the most terrible tortures and mutilation awaited their defeat.

Time after time the assailants strove to throw bridges across the dyke, and more than once succeeded in fixing their grappling-irons upon the rampart.

Time after time they were beaten back, leaving so many dead and dying behind them that the bodies of their friends might almost have served for a bridge.

But numbers prevailed at length. There came an hour when De Guader's archers and slingers, thinned by the continuous iron hail of arrows and quarrels to which they had been unceasingly exposed, no longer sufficed to guard the extended line of the rampart. While they were defending one hotly-contested point, the enemy forced another, and before they were well aware of their misfortune, a large body of knights had gained the eastern side of the dyke.

De Guader instantly formed his cavalry and led them to the charge, with the cry of 'St. Nicholas for Guader!' and the ground shook beneath the thundering feet of the destriers.

'*Dex Aie et Notre Dame!*' shouted the warlike bishop, who led the foe, and the mailed hosts closed with a crash that was heard by the warders on the walls of the new castle that William de Warrenne was building at Castle Acre.

But when De Guader and his followers had hewn their way through the thick squadron that met them, a fresh body stood ready for them, and further hosts were pouring across the dyke.

The odds were so overwhelming, that the East Anglian earl was forced to fall back; an awful retreat, for his troops were harassed in the rear by the remnant of the band they had just charged.

The royalist knights pressed after them, driving them back and back off the firm heath towards the morasses near Fouldon; many a gallant horseman floundering into the quagmires and stifling in the black ooze. Carnage grew fierce round the East Anglian banner, and anxious eyes followed the waving gold and black plumes upon De Guader's helm, for many felt that to lose their leader would be to lose the day. In those times individual prowess often turned the fortune of a field. It was the era of single combats, and a thrill passed through all the host, when, after long seeking, Ralph and Odo met at length. It was as if the whole field paused to watch.

They had fought side by side at Hastings, these two splendid warriors, to Ralph's shame be it spoken! They had sat side by side at many a festive board, and had tried their strength and dexterity in the friendly struggle of the tourney. Now they met as mortal foes, hurling insult at each other.

'Pitiful renegade, twice told a traitor!' cried Odo, 'how darest thou draw good steel to defend thine unknightly carcase?'

'Nay! My sword has better cause than ever hath thy mace, unsanctified shaveling!' retorted Ralph 'the cause of a fell-monger's grandson!'

The taunt struck home, since it included Odo with William.

Striking the rowels into their horses, they flew at each other like tigers.

The head of Ralph's lance had been chopped off a few moments before by a blow from a Saxon seax, so he had but his sword to oppose to the bishop's awful mace.

A gleam of steel, and a dull, horrible crash! A wild yell of execration and triumph from a hundred throats! For both the champions were down. Each party closed up to protect its leader, and a fearful conflict began around the fallen heroes.

But though Odo was down, Geoffrey of Coutances, William de Warrenne, and Robert Malet were ready to take his place, and shrewd blows were given and taken in the neighbourhood of each of these redoubtable champions, while, although the East Anglian earl had many brave knights in his following, the insurgents were virtually without a leader.

Ralph's fall decided the fate of the day, if it had ever been doubtful. The flight of his army was only delayed by the frantic valour of the Bretons, who were bent on selling their lives as dearly as possible.

The tide of battle rolled eastwards, gradually degenerating into a pursuit and butchery, and the original site of the struggle was left to the dead and the dying.

The wind had risen, shaking the white tassels of the cotton-grass which covered acres of the marshes, and bending the aspens till the white undersides of their leaves alone were visible, as if it were preparing white shrouds for the dead. As the clouds parted, the red sun shone forth between their scudding masses, flushing them to vivid crimson, and shedding a lurid light upon the ensanguined field of fight, glittering redly on the harness of the fallen, and painting the pale faces of the dying with a hue as bright as the life-blood that welled from their wounds. But no wind could shake yonder tuft of reeds as it is shaken! Behold a motley figure comes cautiously forth and advances along the field, peering curiously into the faces of the fallen as it comes.

It is Grillonne, the Earl of East Anglia's jester. Grim jests he must make if he would suit his wit to his surroundings!

And grim jests he does make; for often, when, after

Bishop Odo meets De Guader.

considerable toil, he has gained sight of the face of a dead or wounded man, half buried under fallen friends and foes, he expresses his disgust and abhorrence at recognising one of William of Normandy's supporters, by pulling his nose or moustachios ;—not very violently, it is true, and usually following up the indignity by placing the victim's head in as comfortable a position as the circumstances allowed.

But at last he found a face which he treated otherwise.

'Ah, my dear lord!' he cried, placing his hands tenderly under the senseless head; he could do no more, for a heap of slain and the hoof of a dead charger were piled above the earl.

'Oh, sweet nuncle, open thine eyes, thy dear eyes, and glad the heart of thy poor faithful fool. God forbid! Thou canst not be dead! For thy lady's sake thou canst not be dead!' He took from his breast a small flask containing a strong cordial, and poured a portion of its contents down the earl's throat, tenderly wiping away the blood which oozed from a contused wound in his forehead; and after a time Ralph's eyes opened languidly,—opened and closed again almost instantly.

'Good lad! Good lad!' exclaimed the old jester cheerfully. 'There is life in thee yet, I well see, and we will have thee all safe and sound yet, Holy Mary be praised! But I cannot do the job single-handed, valiant hero as I am, and I like not to leave thee, lest thine enemies return. Hist! I have a notion!'

He took off his little parti-coloured cape, and got it upon the earl's shoulders; and he drew from his pocket his jester's cap, which he had thrust therein to still the noise of the bells, and decorated therewith the earl's stately head; and he took the earl's battered helm, which had rolled off, and lay near by, with its gold and black plumes mightily draggled, and fastened it upon the head of a dead Breton knight, Sir Guy de Landerneau, who had fallen at a little distance from his leader, and not long afterwards. Next, he armed himself with the mail jerkin and steel-cap of one of the slain archers, added thereto a short sword, then fled precipitately to find help to extricate the earl.

And he was but just in time.

Scarcely had he disappeared, when a searching party of the king's men came to that quarter of the field, and carried off triumphantly the dead knight upon whom Grillonne had fixed the earl's helmet.[1]

[1] See Appendix, Note C.

CHAPTER XIV.

HOW THE CONQUEROR DEALS WITH REBELS.

THE days passed drearily for the Countess of East Anglia, mewed up within the protecting walls of Norwich Castle, and the anxiety she felt on behalf of her husband and brother made the hours seem unutterably long.

Her office of Castellan was no unusual one for women in those days. The annals of chivalry teem with stories of noble ladies who held castles for their male relatives or feudal superiors, but as no enemy was, at present, near the castle, it did not afford her much occupation.

An occasional hawking or fishing party was organised for her entertainment, but the disturbed state of the country, the fear of treachery, and the uncertainty of the whereabouts of the king's forces, rendered so large an escort necessary, and entailed so much trouble and preparation, that the sport was robbed of all zest. If orders were given in the evening, it most frequently happened that the morning would be wet and uninviting; if left till a suitable morning had dawned, all freshness had vanished before the advancing sun ere so large a party could be put in motion.

Moreover, Emma had little heart for such entertainment, which chiefly served to bring back memories of happier days, when Earl Roger and Ralph de Guader had been beside her; and all the prowess of her Danish hawk did but remind her of her husband and his dangers. Soar, and stoop, and chancelier as he might, he failed to move her enthusiasm, and did but render her more sad, while the encomiums of Sir Alain De Gourin, who made a point of attending her on these expeditions, irked rather than pleased her. His criticisms, admiring as they were, seemed to her impertinent when passed on a bird which Ralph de Guader had pronounced as one of the most perfect he had ever seen.

So she strove to cheat the hours by embroidering a magnificent mantle for her absent lord, using all the most elaborate Saxon stitches, which she had learned from Eadgyth, who sat ever at her elbow to help her, if she forgot her lesson. Such gorgeous mantles were much in fashion among the Norman exquisites.

Eadgyth herself was busy, by Emma's desire, making an altar-cloth for the chapel of the castle, in which the De Guader and East Anglian arms were mingled somewhat incongruously with pictorial illustrations of the life of St. Nicholas. The chaplain of the aforesaid chapel had drawn the designs, being a very clever limner and illuminator, and he took great interest in the progress of the pious work, losing no opportunity to visit the fair embroideress when she was engaged upon it.

He was a young Breton of good family, but had sunk his patronymic for the priestly 'Father Pierre,' the venerable title being rather incongruous to his boyish face and shy, shrinking ways. He was an ascetic enthusiast, believing sternly in the mortification of the flesh, and his young cheeks were sunken, his large dark eyes hollow and glittering, and his tall figure painfully emaciated. But his sternness was all for himself; to his flock he was the kindest of pastors, and in his humility he did not venture to enter upon political matters, accepting the judgment of his feudal superior as paramount, and not to be questioned.

Emma did not feel drawn to him. Her practical nature could not comprehend or draw comfort from his mystic and dreamy ecstasies, and she needed a strong, clear-headed guide, to advise her on the tangible and imminent perplexities that encircled her.

'Oh for an hour of Father Theodred!' she sighed one day, when Father Pierre had left the apartment, after making a vague reply to a question she had addressed to him, touching some small urgent duty of the hour. 'Our good chaplain hath more anxiety regarding the ordering of thy needlework warriors for the adornment of his chapel, than for the bodies of the living men who are defending it, methinks! In good sooth, Eadgyth, I feel tired of this stitchery. I would the wind blew not so keenly on the battlements. I could be ever watching the horizon like some sea-rover's deserted mate, looking out for the glint of sun on a steel headpiece, as such an one would watch for a sail. The stone walls well-nigh stifle me! I feel entombed sitting here, where I cannot see if any approach to bring tidings of my dear lord! Fetch me mantle and head-rail, sweet damsel. Methinks, if I sit here longer, chewing the cud of bitter reflection, I shall go stark staring mad. Let us go to the battlements and fight the wind!'

Eadgyth, whose more phlegmatic temperament did not seek relief from mental pain in physical exercise, smiled at the restlessness of her friend, but instantly laid aside her needlework, aud sought her lady's tire-woman, who brought the wished-for garments.

In a few moments Emma and Eadgyth had left the lodge, ascended the spiral staircase in the great tower, and were pacing upon the battlements. It was one of those grey chilly days, frequent in the Eastern counties, when the north-west wind brings haze from the Fenlands, and the Wash, and the North Sea; covering the sky with a leaden pall, and bringing winter into summer's heart. Columns of dust rose along the roadways, but the wind swept away all mist and fog, and the country showed bleak and naked to the horizon.

The sentinels saluted their countess and her lady-in-waiting with a deep reverence, but they were accustomed to see their fair Castellan scanning the distance, as if distrusting that any eyes could be so keen and faithful as her own.

They paced the circuit of the battlements some five or six times, and played with the pigeons that crowded upon the merlons, and greeted them with soft cooing and much fluttering of soft-coloured pinions, for they knew well that Emma's gipsire was generally stored with peas for them.

Suddenly Emma caught her bower-maiden by the wrist.

'See!' she cried. 'My sail is in sight! Dost thou not catch the glint of a morion over yonder?'

They were on the southern side of the keep, and she indicated a far speck upon the course of the Ikenield way.

'Nay,' replied Eadgyth, 'mine eyes reach not so far, the more especially as this stinging wind brings unbidden tears into them.'

'I am right, Eadgyth—it is a horseman approaching! Ho, sentinel! thy vigil is no very keen one!'

'In sooth, lady, I can see naught,' answered the sentinel, with a respectful salutation.

It had been a favourite amusement with Emma, when a girl at Clifford Castle, to challenge her maidens and squires, and any noble visitor who might chance to be present, to a trial of sight, from the walls of that goodly fortress, and seldom had she found any who could rival her for length of vision. She proved to be right on this occasion. A horseman was approaching, and at a gallop, and the sentinels soon acknowledged his coming and gave the fitting signal.

A while later, and the traveller had reached the

barbican, and, after a short parley, the portcullis was raised, the drawbridge lowered, and he rode forward into the courtyard of the castle.

Emma descended full of tremulous excitement. Sir Alain de Gourin met her, on his way to the courtyard, to question the new-comer.

'I will send word at once, if he prove to be one of the earl's men, or brings any message or news,' said Sir Alain.

'Nay,' replied Emma, 'I will myself go down. Each moment of waiting will prove a year.'

So, with Eadgyth beside her, and her train of ladies following, she went down to the great portal on the east side of the keep, whence a short time before she had bidden 'God Speed' to her noble spouse and his army.

The horseman was surrounded by a curious crowd of soldiers and domestics. Archers and men-at-arms of all sorts and conditions from the guard-room, pages, squires, cooks, and scullions, had all come forth to see. Certain of the garrison who had been trying their strength for pastime in a wrestling bout, had left their sport, and stood with brawny arms akimbo, and mouths agape. Even the pale face of the chaplain was amongst the group, his dark eyes gazing with pity and awe upon the man who formed its centre.

He was in sorry plight! His horse, flecked with foam and bloody with spurring, head down, nostrils red, and limbs trembling with fatigue, looked as though another mile had been utterly beyond his spent

The Tower Stairs.

powers. The casque of the rider was battered, and his countenance so gashed with wounds as to be beyond recognition, nor did his surcoat or harness in any way help to show his identity, so stained and torn were they. Shield he had none, and his right arm hung straightly at his side.

He took no heed of the crowd buzzing round him, nor of the countess standing at the portal of the keep, with Sir Alain de Gourin at her right, and Sir Hoël de St. Brice on her left, and her train of ladies and squires behind her, but sat on his panting steed, with his chin sunk on his breast.

Suddenly one from the circle around him cried, '*Mort de ma vie!* He has lost a foot as well as a hand!'

A murmur of surprise burst round him.

'Those are no gashes gained in fair fighting! His nose is slit! Saints and angels! He has been in the hands of the Bastard's men! We all know how William serves his prisoners!'

'Speak, Sir Fugitive, or Sir Messenger, or whatever your name is,' thundered De Gourin, 'and speedily! Is it so? Who art thou? For thy beauty is so spoiled we are at a loss by what title to greet thee! By the rood! his own mother would not know him!'

The countess hastily bade her leech be called, and shuddered, not only with pity, but with a dread presentiment of evil, as the ghastly witness of men's merciless cruelty turned his maimed face towards them, his bloodshot eyes staring vacantly, half dazed with terror and pain.

'It is all over!' he muttered hoarsely, forcing his swollen lips to utter the words with difficulty. 'The earl is slain, and my master; and the army is scattered like a flock of sheep! Flee, flee! They are coming after me to storm the castle!'

He raised his right arm, from which the hand had been riven, the stump black with the searing of red-hot irons with which the flow of blood had been staunched, in a gesture of entreaty.

A fearful witness truly as to what might be expected to follow on defeat.

A howl of fierce anger ran around the courtyard, and many a strong breast heaved with an indignant sob of impotent rage; curses loud and deep were showered on the heads of William of Normandy and his vicegerents.

'Heed him not, noble Emma!' cried Sir Hoël de St. Brice hastily. 'By the Holy Virgin! 'tis but a recreant who has let himself be made prisoner, and now repeats the story they have stuffed him with! Out of his wits with their rough treatment, and small wonder! May the Foul Fiend seize them for their barbarity!'

'Christ be my witness, I speak sooth!' cried the unfortunate fugitive. 'I am Stephen le Hareau, squire of the body to Sir Guy de Landerneau, and I swear by the Holy Cross, I saw the earl fall with mine own eyes!'

'Thou Stephen le Hareau? Thou?' shouted Sir Alain de Gourin, startled out of his equanimity as he looked at the pitiful object before his eyes, and remembered the handsome gallant he had seen ride from the castle gates a few weeks before.

A fresh hiss of execration burst from the bystanders, as the cruelty of the young man's fate came home to them.

Stephen le Hareau! The handsomest and most popular squire in the earl's following! They knew him, too, for a brave and dauntless soldier.

Sir Hoël looked towards the countess, wondering how she would bear the blow, for the difficulty with which she had maintained her self-control when she had parted with her noble bridegroom had been manifest to all, and now the worst fears she could then have entertained were declared to have come to pass.

But Emma, who had shrunk from the approach of evil, stood firm to meet its actual contact. Her face was white as marble, and her lips quivered, but she said in a firm voice,—

'The cruelty this poor gentleman has undergone may well nerve our hearts to resistance. St. Nicholas grant thou art in the right, Sir Hoël. He may well deem things blacker than they are! I prithee, keep him no longer answering our vain queries. Let him be lifted from his horse and carried to the spital. I will tend him with my own hands. His poor steed also, let it be cared for.'

Eadgyth and several of the ladies were sobbing hysterically behind her. She turned to them.

'Courage, dames and damsels!' she said, with a

simple dignity that shamed them into self-control. 'I have heard as evil tales as this, and found them vanish like dreams at the breaking of the morn.'

She gathered her robes around her and swept back into the keep, and, calling her tirewoman, ordered her to bring sundry essences and simples, which, like every noble lady of the time, she kept by her, the science of medicine being chiefly in feminine hands in those days. Then, bidding Eadgyth to attend her, she proceeded at once to the spital, to leech the unfortunate squire.

She stopped a few moments in the chapel, to direct the chaplain to offer masses for the souls of those who had fallen in the battle. A sob caught her breath as she remembered the earnest repetition with which Stephen le Hareau had declared that the earl was amongst them.

But she dare not think, and went on hurriedly to direct that others should be offered for the safety of those who had escaped, and for the success of their undertaking.

Her ministrations to the wounded man kept at bay the fierce troop of agonising thoughts that were thronging down upon her like a pack of hungry wolves. Rolling bandages, and preparing salves and unguents, she had scarce time to speculate upon the probability of the truth of her patient's direful news. True, no doubt, it was as far as his knowledge went, but there was hope, as Sir Hoël had suggested, that his report of the battle had been supplied by their opponents, and himself sent off by them, as a messenger of evil tidings, with the express intent of demoralising the garrison of Blauncheflour.

The physical sufferings of the poor squire were so terrible to witness, that Emma almost forgot the awful shadow of death and impending peril that hung over her own head, and the hours flew past without her noticing their flight. All that she and her leech and her ladies could do to lessen his pain was done, but it was not much.

Even in these days little could be done for such a case, with all the skill of advanced science.

Presently a page came to the countess with a message from the two knights, St. Brice and De Gourin, begging her to give them audience in the council-chamber.

'Watch over my sufferer, Eadgyth,' said Emma.

When she entered the apartment in which the two knights were awaiting her, she quivered with apprehension as she saw their grave faces. Sir Hoël's kindly visage was white as his silver hair, and even Sir Alain's inflamed countenance was a shade less purple-red than usual, while his expression was distinctly anxious.

They both hesitated to speak, but the countess broke the pause.

'Tell me the worst, gentle sirs, I pray you. Suspense is ever hardest to bear, and I see you have ill news.'

Sir Hoël advanced and took her hand in both his own, a little forgetting the ceremony due to her rank, in his huge pity for her youth and the forlorn fate that he feared too surely had befallen her.

'Alas, dear lady, the news is ill indeed! Sir Walter

Deresfort, and the Saxon thegn, Alfnoth of Walsham, with some dozen men-at-arms, have ridden in from Cambridgeshire, and confirm'—a sob broke his voice—'in every item the dire tidings brought by poor Stephen le Hareau.'

'Do they say, then, that I am a widow?' asked Emma in a strange, hard voice, with so awful a calm in it, that the thick-skinned Sir Alain, who was little wont to heed the tears or shrieks of women, or to spare them in any respect if they stood in his way, shuddered as he heard it. He thought the countess was going mad.

'I fear,' answered Sir Hoël, 'there is no doubt the earl is slain, St. Nicholas rest his soul!'

'Then, gentlemen,' asked Emma in the same strange tone, 'what is to be done?'

'God knows!' exclaimed Sir Hoël, the great tears running down his furrowed face, and dripping upon his hauberk.

'Noble lady,' said Sir Alain eagerly, speaking for the first time, 'it is well known that the wrath of the Primate, and of his master, William the Norman, is principally enkindled against the countrymen of the late earl. Thy safety, most noble countess, is, of course, what every man in the garrison would give his life to insure, therefore my humble counsel, for what it may be worth, is that thou shouldest at once take ship with the trusty Bretons under my command, and make for Bretagne, and thy late husband's estates of Guader and Montfort.'

'What is thy counsel, Sir Hoël?' demanded Emma, still with the same unnatural calm.

'Dear lady, I would advise thee as doth Sir Alain.'

'But would not the garrison, thus bereft of half their numbers, fall an instant prey to the enemy?' asked Emma.

'It is not William's policy to provoke the Saxons, and to his own countrymen he is ever complacent,' urged De Gourin, with the same eagerness. 'Therefore my meaning is, that the castle be surrendered at once, in which case the garrison would probably be softly dealt with, we Bretons being out of the way; whereas further resistance will be useless, and will but further provoke their vengeance, the style of which we have seen.'

'Art thou of this advice also, Sir Hoël?' demanded Emma.

Sir Hoël bowed his head. 'Dear lady,' he said, 'there is no doubt that the Primate hath animosity against us Bretons, and may prove kinder to Normans and Saxons; yet methinks I will stand by them, and advise them not to try his mercy sooner than is needful. I counsel, therefore, that thou shouldest so far follow Sir Alain's advice, as to take ship with himself and his band for Bretagne. For my part, I will fight for it with the garrison remaining to me. Blaunchefleur has been built to stand a siege, and we may well victual it before supplies can be cut off. We may yet make good terms.'

'There spoke the spirit of a true knight!' cried Emma, turning on De Gourin with so fierce a flash in her eyes, that he started, so great a change was it from the stony indifference of her former manner.

'Go, fair sir, if it suits thee! Take all thy faint-hearted mercenaries with thee to their native Bretagne! I will stay with Sir Hoël and defend this castle, which the earl gave into my charge. The *late* earl, thou said'st? Methinks thou art wondrous quick to make so certain of his death! Methinks all these gallant gentlemen who have galloped back to the safe walls of Blauncheflour in such hot haste, scarce waited to see if he was wounded or slain! For *me* he will never be the *late* earl. On earth or in heaven he is my husband still, and I will hold his castle, hoping, perhaps selfishly, that he will come to claim it. I will hold it if only to have vengeance on his foes!'

Sir Hoël watched her in delighted surprise. Sir Alain flushed hotly under her attack, but could not but admire the high-spirited beauty as she hurled her indignant taunts at his head.

'Now, by all the saints! thou art unjust to me and my poor following, noble lady!' he exclaimed. 'My object was but to secure thy safety.'

'If the earl be indeed slain,' said Emma, with a tremor in her voice, 'my safety boots me but little; if he be not, it is important that Blauncheflour hold out to the last gasp. Besides, ye know not how it fares with my brother of Hereford; his arms have perchance prevailed, and he may be able to relieve us.'

'A slender hope,' said Sir Alain impatiently. 'But our lives are at thy disposal, noble Emma.'

He accompanied this speech with a smile of homage, which he meant to be irresistibly touching and pathetic; for a new idea had come into the adventurer's bullet-head, which somewhat gilded the pill of hard fighting without hope of plunder, which the countess's decision forced him to swallow. He remembered that if, as he fully believed, De Guader was slain, the beautiful Emma had become a widow with a goodly dower! for even if, as was probable, her late husband's possessions in England were forfeit through his treason, and all English and Norman property of her own, the estates of Guader and Montfort were beyond William's jurisdiction, and she would doubtless draw rich rents from them. This rich prize was here under his hand, and, to a great extent, in his power. If he played his cards well, he might secure her for himself, albeit she was William of Normandy's kinswoman.

But the good old Sir Hoël looked at her fair, flushed face with very different thoughts. 'God bless thee, dear young lady,' he said, with a husky voice. 'He would be a coward indeed who grudged to give his life for thee! Though, for that matter, we must needs fight for our own sakes, so we need not try to make out that all our valour is on thy behalf!'

Emma met his kind eyes, and scarce bore their sympathy.

She turned away hastily. 'There must be more wounded in the spital,' she said; 'I must tend them. Make what preparation needs for holding out under a long siege.'

And so saying she quitted the apartment.

'Alas!' Sir Hoël murmured, more to himself than to De Gourin, when she was gone, 'I doubt she is buoying herself with a false hope, and that our noble De Guader will glad her eyes no more.'

'By the rood!' answered Sir Alain, 'I doubt so too. But methinks so fair a widow, and so well-dowered and youthful withal, may find consolation on this side the grave. Holy Mary! A dame of spirit! If our motley garrison, Saxons, Danes, Flemings, and other, were of metal that would ring to the same tune, our case would not look so desperate.'

'Methinks the mercenaries under thy hand are the most doubtful metal within the walls, good sir,' answered Sir Hoël gravely, eyeing his companion somewhat keenly. 'If thou canst get the right ring out of *them*, I think I can answer for the rest!'

CHAPTER XV.

'O HIGH AMBITION LOWLY LAID!'

THE choughs and ravens which had flapped lazily away, with noisy wings and harsh croaking, when the Royalists had come to search amongst the dead and wounded for Ralph de Guader, had settled down to their banquet again as soon as their disturbers had departed, mistakenly laden with the body of the Breton knight whom Grillonne had decorated with the earl's helmet. Their foul beaks were busy with the flesh of the dead and the eyes of the living.

The harsh clamour of these noisy revellers pierced at length to the fainting ears of the fallen earl, who was in some measure revived by the cordial which Grillonne had poured down his throat. Consciousness came back to him, a poor exchange, under such circumstances, for kind oblivion. For he could move neither hand nor foot, and the weight upon his chest was as the oppression of a fearful nightmare—a nightmare from which there was no awaking. He lay helpless—the living under the dead!

Above him stretched the twilight sky, still flushed with fleeting, blood-red clouds, beyond which, from pale green pools of infinite depth, glimmered, here and there, a silvery star. To the right stretched the sombre heath, its rising hills crested with fantastic figures of contorted slain, men and horses stiffened into uncouth and terrible forms; while groaning wounded were heaped between them, their panting anguish not less awful than the silence of the dead.

To his left also were witnesses of battle, but not so many, for on that side the hungry morasses had swallowed them up. To the south and west the measureless fen stretched to the horizon, crimson to its farthest verge with the ensanguined glow of the sun, the tall reeds reddened like warrior's lances that had been dipped in the life-blood of the foe.

The air was full of the awful scent of wounds and blood, and the weird, dank odours of the decaying sedges, while the wailing wind piped and moaned over the wold, swaying the rushes, though scarcely making a ripple on the protected surfaces of the bottomless lagoons.

Mallard and teal and plover came circling back to their haunts in the lonely swamps, now that the din of battle, which had frightened them, was over and done; and, as the twilight deepened, bats and owls came forth with silent wings to hunt their night-roaming prey.

Ralph's open eyes looked only into the sky, and at the wild, wind-driven clouds fleeting across the calm, immutable heavens beyond, as the struggling hosts of mortals fleet over the face of eternity.

His soul was filled with an overwhelming sense of

desolation and guilt. He had brought his fate upon himself, and he must face the Shadow of the Valley of Death, all forsworn and blood-stained as he was; alone, helpless. No wife to comfort him, no priest to absolve him,

> 'Cut off even in the blossoms of his sin,
> Unhousel'd, disappointed, unanel'd.'

Against the clear spaces of the sky, he saw, high up, almost above the clouds, an ordered flight of wild swans passing swiftly westward into the sunset glow.

Oh, that he were free as they, winged as the wind! His spirit writhed in fierce rebellion. He put forth all his force in a wild struggle to drag his limbs from the prisoning mass that detained them, but he could not lift the ghastly burden that weighted him to earth an inch.

'Mary in heaven, help me!' he groaned. 'I am scarce wounded, and so strong! It will take me hours to die, and these foul birds will perish mine eyes!'

The cold sweat burst from his brow, and, as he writhed again, he somewhat shook his head, and the bells on the jester's cap tinkled.

He quivered with astonishment, and contrived so far to lift his head as to catch a glimpse of the points of the cape which covered his shoulders. At first the idea seized him that he was no longer on earth at all, but in purgatory, and dressed in a jester's garb, in that his sin had been through the folly of pride and mad ambition. Then, with a flash, came the joyous thought of Grillonne, the faithful, the ready of wit, the fertile of resource.

A wild gladness came to him, but as the sky grew dark, and the stars were obscured by clouds, hope left him again.

'If it were he indeed, he has forgotten me, or has met his death in trying to save me.'

Then all the joys of earth passed before him in a fair pageant, and he thought of his young bride with her clear, loving eyes that he might never see again, and to whom he had been united with such magnificence scarcely a month before, and who was but a few short miles from the scene of his present suffering; and at the thought, burning tears welled from beneath his closed lids and rolled down his bronzed cheeks, moistening the parti-coloured edges of Grillonne's cape.

'Ah, it is bitter!' he groaned.

'Not more bitter for thee than for the scores and tens of scores thou hast led into like misery,' said awakened conscience grimly.

'*Mea culpa! mea culpa!*' murmured the unfortunate warrior in his anguish. 'My days have been evil in the land. I have sought not the will of Heaven, but mine own vain-glory. But oh, Mary Mother, let not my sins be visited on the head of my sweet lady! as thou wert a woman, protect her from all harm! Sure William will be merciful to his kinswoman.'

Dismal indeed were the thoughts that chased each other across his restless brain, which seemed to make up by its activity for the enforced stillness of his body. Visions crowded upon him of his castle of Blaunche-flour in flames, and his lady in the power of insulting or — and it was little less terrible to his ambitious, jealous spirit—too-courteous conquerors, some one of whom might, perchance, find favour in her eyes and drive his memory from her heart.

At length, however, as the stillness of the night fell over the plain, broken only by the moaning wind or the agonised groan of some fellow-sufferer, he grew calmer, and a deep resignation flooded his breast.

'*Mea culpa!*' he murmured again. Death seemed inevitable, and he bowed his spirit humbly to accept it.

Hark!—

The mingled anguish and joy of hope awaked once more. For the silence was broken by a sound so faint that his listening ears could scarce detect its repetition, distracted as they were by the tumultuous pulses which throbbed at the possibility of escape. Yet why hope rather than fear? Why should the sound of approaching steps mean friends rather than foes?

The fact grew certain. Steps were approaching, and were accompanied by a clash of arms that betokened soldiery.

How he strained to catch every faint sound that might indicate the direction in which these, his fellow-men, alive and strong and capable of help, were moving!

'St. Nicholas befriend me! If the miracle is wrought that I be rescued from this living tomb, I vow to make pilgrimage to the Holy Sepulchre before my days are done!'

Then he shuddered in sick misery lest the band

should pass him by! Better a blow from the *miséricorde* of an enemy, than the languishing torture of his present position.

Others thought so too, for he heard more than one piteous cry for help.

Then he, the proud earl, lifted up a feeble voice and craved deliverance, even by death!—

And it came.

'Here! here! This way, my lads, this way!' cried the familiar voice of the faithful jester. 'Look you, galliards, there is my famous cap and cape! Saints be praised! He wears them still. The Lord grant there is a living skull in the cap. I shrewdly thought I heard him squeak!'

'Ay, Grillonne, thou didst, sure enough!' cried the earl; and the revulsion of feeling from despair to hope was so great that he fainted again.

When he revived, his head was in Grillonne's arms, and the intolerable weight of the slain who had fallen above him was removed from his limbs, which, however, were so numbed that he could not move them. Half-a-dozen stout fellows, archers, slingers, and spearmen, were bustling about him, dimly visible by the light of a horn lantern which one of them carried.

Grillonne, seeing his eyes open, instantly held a flask to his lips, and when the draught had helped his revival, nodded sagely.

''Tis well to be taken for a fool sometimes, nuncle,' he remarked, twitching his tinkling cap from the earl's head. 'Thy fine helmet has been carried off in triumph to the enemy's camp on the corse of poor Sir Guy de Landerneau, whom I bedecked with it; seeing that, as they had already killed him as dead as a Norwich red herring, they could do him no further hurt. 'Twill have given us time even if they discover the cheat, as most like they will, for so many of them are full well acquainted with thy noble hawk nose.'

'Ah, Grillonne ready-wit,' said the earl, 'St. Nicholas reward thee! That prince of hypocrisy, Lanfranc, may say that jesters have no hope, and are doomed without fail to the worm that dieth not and the fire that knows no quenching![1] But I tell thee, Grillonne, he in hell shall pray to thee in heaven as Dives to Lazarus!' and the groaning noble kissed the hand that lay upon his breast, albeit the member belonged to one of that despised class, for death is a greater leveller than any democrat or republican of them all, and Ralph de Guader had held long converse with him.

Grillonne raised the hand which had been so honoured to his own lips and added some hearty smacks to the aristocratic salute it had received.

'Nay, my dear lord,' he said in a rather husky voice, 'I would fain lay that hand up in lavender and take it to heaven with me when I die, since thou thinkest I have hope to get there. But alack! we have rough work before us to prevent thee from getting thither before thy

---

[1] 'D. Have jesters hope? M. None. In their whole design they are the ministers of Satan. Of them it is said : "They have not known God, therefore God hath despised them, and the Lord shall have them in derision, for mockers shall be mocked."'—Lanfranc's *Elucidarium*, p. 256, quoted by Hook, *Lives of the Archbishops of Canterbury*.

palace is prepared for thee. Thou art not saved yet by a very long chalk. If St. Nicholas is half so generous as thou deemest, he will give me my reward at once, like a free-handed gentleman, in the shape of success to the safe ending of my undertaking; nor must we spend further time in palaver.'

He beckoned to the men who were with him, and four of them came forward with a litter roughly woven of osiers, of which a plentiful supply was near at hand. Grillonne and another lifted the earl into it, and they set off at a rapid pace, the jester guiding them along the smoothest path; and watching over his charge with tender care.

To De Guader it seemed as if he were couched on pillows of softest down, notwithstanding his wounds and the pain the motion caused him, for the joy of being rescued from his horrible entombment, and of having yet a chance of life and love, was so intense that he seemed to be in a dream of bliss.

His eyes filled with grateful tears each time that a gleam from the lantern gave him a fitful glimpse of Grillonne's face. Never had he thought to be so glad to look on that wizened, whimsical countenance, with its oblique eyes twinkling with mingled malice and affection, and which seemed almost quainter under the conical steel-cap with the nasal, in which he had ensconced it on giving up his cap to the earl, than in that strange headgear itself.

The way was no flowery one either. Slain men and horses encumbered the bearers at every step, and more than one pitiful voice from some wounded wretch, in such plight as the earl had just been rescued from, besought them in mercy to stop and give aid, for the sake of Mary Mother and the saints in heaven. Most pitiful of all was the cry for 'Water, for the love of Christ!' from men whose limbs were actually immersed in the rippling edges of the meres or engulfed in the slimy ooze, and who were so faint from wounds, or so set fast by the slain above them, that they could reach no drop wherewith to moisten their parched lips and slake the burning death-thirst which tormented them. But they cried to deaf ears; nay, when entreating arms were thrown around the limbs of the litter-bearers, a sharp cut across the knuckles with dagger or anlace speedily unclasped the detaining fingers, whether they belonged to friend or foe.

It was rough treatment, but the men were risking their lives in their endeavour to save that of the earl, and delay would have been fatal both to him and to themselves. The fact that the body of Sir Guy de Landerneau had been removed by the enemy proved that they desired to make certain of De Guader's fate, and on finding their mistake they might at any time return to rectify it.

The moon had risen by this, and shone between the swift fleeting clouds that sped across the sky. By her light and the uncertain glimmer of the lantern, Ralph saw that two of his rescuers wore the winged helms and long moustaches and golden torcs distinguishing the costume of the Danes. His heart leapt with hope that the messengers he had despatched to the court of King Sweyn had moved the warlike monarch to seize the opportunity of striking a blow at his ancient enemy, William of Normandy, and had sent him timely reinforcements. But their progress was too rapid for speech, and whatever might be his curiosity, he had to lie passive in his litter and allow himself to be borne whithersoever his rescuers pleased.

And by what a weird and desolate pathway did they bear him!

Heading, apparently, for the very heart of the fen that stretched westward as far as eye could reach, its level surface unbroken by tree or hill, and only varied by beds of tall reeds and snake-like pools of still, dark water, the surfaces of which were scarcely rippled by the gusty breeze, they advanced steadily for the better part of an hour.

The fitful light of the half shrouded moon cast ghastly gleams upon the waving plumes of the flowering sedges and white tufts of the meadow-sweet, whose strong and somewhat sickly perfume mingled, strangely luscious, with the dank odours of peat and decaying rushes and grasses. Now and again some frightened bird flew screaming from its roosting-place, or dusky water-rat glided hastily into thicker cover, or plunged with a flop into the water, while the pipe of the curlew, or boom of the bittern, sounded from afar off in the melancholy marshes. The loneliness was intense, and seemed but accentuated by the presence of bird and beast.

The Rescue of the Earl.

In the dimness of the cloudy night, with the uncertain bursts of moonlight, that seemed to make the chaos of scarce divided earth and water but more difficult to distinguish, the men who bore the earl threaded their way through the bewildering maze, with an unerring celerity and absence of hesitation that proved them to be no strangers to its mysterious solitude.

At length they halted, beside a channel less overgrown with weeds and rushes than the many they had passed, and which was, in fact, the Great Ouse River.

One of the party put a horn to his lips and sounded a couple of mots. His summons was answered from the water, and in a few seconds a boat impelled by eight sturdy oarsmen shot forth from a bend in the river and drew to the bank. The earl was speedily put on board, with the faithful Grillonne at his head, and his bearers embarked, some with him, some in a second boat which had come in the wake of the first.

De Guader confided himself utterly to the safe keeping of his jester, and the rhythmic sound of the oars, which he believed were every moment bringing him nearer to liberty, soothed him inexpressibly. He fell into a drowsy sleep of exhaustion, never really losing consciousness, but devoid of all impatience, and almost of all curiosity as to whither he was being taken.

But the splash of the oars ceased at length, and the keel of the boat grated on the shore of a small island, raising a modest crown a little above the level of the surrounding fen. It was protected by an earthwork somewhat similar in construction to the great dykes with which Cambridge is seamed, the Devil's Dyke, Fleamdyke, and others, and, had the light served, the low turrets of a long, rambling, two-storied house might have been seen behind its shelter.

A summons was given by a few mots on the horn, and in answer a deep voice threw a challenge across the sullen surface of the waters,—

'Who goes there?'

'St. Nicholas for Guader!'

A rattle of chains and hoarse creaking of bolts and hinges followed, and a heavy gate was slowly lifted, which admitted the boats into an inner moat. They glided in and moored their vessels at a small landing stage on the opposite side, the gate closing instantly behind them.

As they did so, the sentry asked anxiously, in a low voice and in the Saxon tongue, 'What cheer?'

'All's well!' was the answer.

'St. Eadmund be praised!' ejaculated the sentry fervently; and the earl's heart leapt with a thrill of joy and gratitude to the poor unknown soldier who cared about his safety, so infinitely precious had the humblest human sympathy become to him since those dreadful hours when he had thought himself doomed to quit the cheerful earth and the faces of his fellow-men for evermore!

Inside the enclosure a party of wild-looking ceorls surrounded them, with shaggy locks and rude jerkins of sheepskin, armed with pikes and staves for the most part, but some few better clad, and bearing the terrible seax ; their brawny necks half hidden by their unshorn beards, which hung in tow-coloured elf-locks round their weather-beaten and scarred faces. Amongst them were one or two tall fellows, dressed, like those in the party of rescuers who had attracted De Guader's attention, in Danish mode.

This much he gathered by the fitful moonlight and the feeble light of lanterns carried by the men. Question and answer followed quick between his bearers and their rough colleagues, but he could comprehend little of what they said, for they spoke in all manner of tongues and dialects.

'Thou hast had a harsh ride, I fear me, good nuncle,' said Grillonne, bending over his beloved master with tender solicitude. 'Gramercy! 'Tis a God-forsaken hole we have brought thee to ; but beggars must not be choosers, and let us hope that the archbishop's people will keep their pious noses from sniffing thee out in it! Troth ! if they venture them here, I parry, some of these stout carles will slit them for them parlous quick ! '

'Methinks any corner of the earth is better than being quite out of it, Grillonne,' returned the earl, with a gentle smile. 'I am not like to be critical ; but in good sooth I would fain know the title of my host?'

'I scarce know it myself, good my lord,' replied the jester. ''Tis a Saxon, or more properly Anglo-Danish thegn, whose son went shares in thy escapade, and has got a maimed foot for his share of the booty, they tell me. The father and son have had a price on their heads since Hereward Leofricsson's downfall, and have a natural fellow-feeling for thy discomfiture, sweet nuncle.'

Meanwhile they had reached the entrance of the house, and the earl was borne into a long barnlike hall, very sparsely furnitured, with a table running almost from one end of it to the other, and rude settles and stools placed against it, as in preparation for a meal. At one end was an archway leading into another apartment, which seemed, to judge by the heat and the savoury odours, the noises of pots and kettles and other indications which came from it, to be a kitchen; while at the other end was a cheerful fire of peat, beside which sat an aged warrior wearing the Anglo-Danish tunic and cross-gartered hose, his white hair flowing back over his shoulders and his grizzled beard growing close up his cheeks, so that it seemed almost to meet the bushy white eyebrows that shaded his bright blue eyes. His baldric was richly worked with gold, and he wore massive gold bracelets on his arms.

Beside him stood a broad-shouldered, athletic young man in similar garb; his thick fair hair surrounding his head like a lion's mane, and his long moustaches and golden beard showing lighter than the bronzed skin of his cheeks and chest; his eyes as bright and blue as those of his father, and his neck and sinewy arms covered with tattoo marks. But the linen tunic he wore was drabbled with mud and gore, and one of his feet was swathed in bandages, through which the crimson stains would force their way, and his muscular hand grasped the arm of his father's carved oak chair to ease his weight somewhat from the wounded foot.

On the opposite side of the large open fireplace sat a monk in the habit of the Black Friars, and near by a stately lady, wearing the headrail and flowing robes which had been the fashion in the time of the Confessor; while a bevy of damsels waited behind her, looking towards the wounded earl with curious eyes.

The old thegn rose as the bearers brought their noble burden forward, advanced to the litter, and, bowing with great dignity, said in his own tongue,—

'By the Holy Cross! my heart is glad to see thee safe beneath my roof, oh, valorous earl! Would that Ealdred Godwinsson had means to offer fitting hospitality to the son of Ralph the Staller, in whose hand his own has been placed and under whose standard he has fought in many a hard field! Alas! the glory of his house has faded! Barely can he save his last days from the fury of his foes by hiding in this wilderness of the meres! But to such as he possesses, thrice welcome, noble earl! Had not age and infirmity clogged his steps as securely as chains of iron, he had sallied forth to thy rescue himself. Had not a spear-thrust in the instep, got this morn while fighting in thy ranks, crippled Leofric his son, that son had gone forth to seek thee.' Here the younger man bowed deeply in token of assent and reverence. 'It boots not! His followers have been true, and thou art here.'

'Brave thegn,' returned De Guader, raising himself as far as possible in his litter, 'I thank thee for thy fidelity to a ruined and defeated man! The saints forefend that my presence bring evil to thy retreat!'

'Nay,' answered Ealdred, 'had those who would harm us the wit to track us, we had perished long since. But thou art sore wounded! Berwine, the widow of mine eldest-born, shall leech thy hurts.'

A couch was prepared in a recess near the fireplace, and the earl was placed thereon. Cordials and delicate soups, with omelettes of plovers' eggs, were brought to tempt his appetite, and the young thegn's widow examined his wounds, pansed and dressed them with soothing unguents, and finally bound them up in linen of her own weaving, and with the greatest tenderness and skill.

Meanwhile the stalwart fellows who had borne the stricken noble so far upon their strong shoulders,—no light burden, sheathed as he was in all his mail!—with Grillonne and others, were regaled with the savoury messes whose odours had assailed them with such enticing welcome through the kitchen door as they entered, and, in sooth, they had a *ménu* fit for a king.

Stewed and fried eel, pike and lampreys in pasties, roast gossander, curlew, and snipe!—fare fit for an epicure, and by no means cavilled at by the hungry men before whom it was served—add thereto good cider and ale.

For this island in the meres was the home of innumerable wildfowl, and fish as many crowded the waters around it. 'Wild swannes, gossanders, watercrows, hernes, hernshaws, cranes, curlewes, mallard, tecle, bytters, knotts, styntes, godwytts, widgeons, smeaths, puffins, and many sorts of gulls; eels, pike, pickerel, perch, roach, barbel, lampreys, and sometimes a royal-fish' (turbot or sturgeon?); so that, as the chronicler relates of Hereward's refuge in the neighbouring Isle of Ely, foemen might sit blockading the place for seven years without 'making one hunter cease to set his nets or one fowler to deceive the birds with springe and snare.'

In this asylum we will leave the earl, and see how it fares with Blaaunoureflour.

CHAPTER XVI.

WIFE OR WIDOW?

THE Castellan of Blaunchefleur swept hastily from the chamber where she had held council with the two knights, doubting lest her power of self-control should fail her, and that the desperate grief which was gnawing at her heart should gain the upper hand, and mar the stately boldness of mien which she saw affected them not a little, by bringing the weak tears which are accounted a woman's privilege.

She remembered bitterly that almost the last day which she had spent with her dear lord had been clouded for him by her weeping, and she felt as if by maintaining firmness now she was carrying out his wishes.

'I vexed him with my tears,' she said to herself. 'Ah! now I will be the very hero's daughter he bade me to be. I will be bolder than his mailed retainers. While I can get one soldier to fight for me, one warder to pace the walls, I will hold his castle ready to receive him!'

By such brave words she tried to stifle the awful

terror that assailed her secret heart that the tidings of Stephen le Hareau were indeed true.

Leaving the room hastily, she nearly fell over the fair figure of Eadgyth, who was kneeling on the threshold.

'Eadgyth! what dost thou here? Is this obeying my behests? I bade thee tend the wounded, from whom other duties called me.'

'Pardon, dear Emma! I feared lest thou shouldst need my service. I have not forgotten the day when I found thee senseless in thy chamber; and these news be so dire.'

'Faint heart!' cried Emma contemptuously, taking refuge in indignation. 'Dost thou then credit the wild stories of these runaways? How but by telling of slain leader and ruined cause could they excuse their own cowardice? The cousin of Harold Godwinsson should despise them for *nodings!*'

Her eyes blazed with the light of fierce determination, as she hissed out the word which in the ears of Saxon or Dane was the most degrading that could be applied to a warrior.

The mild-natured Eadgyth, whose courage was of the moral order, and with whom fortitude and fidelity were greater than high spirit, gazed wonderingly at her friend. She had seen Emma cry over a fawn the dogs had lacerated, or over the dead body of a pet bird, when her own eyes had been tearless, and this strange strength of Emma's made her shiver, for she fully believed that the earl was slain.

Emma looked in her startled face and laughed. 'Tend them, bonnibell, and ease the pain of their wounds; but credit them not. Let my lord deal with them when he comes back at the head of a victorious army.'

Eadgyth, like the knights, thought that the countess was going mad. Perhaps she was; but her madness saved the garrison.

Yet, to say truth, her high spirit quailed when she re-entered the spital. The draggled, blood-stained, dejected warriors who lay, and leaned, and stood around, with every variety of wound to be dressed, were no cheering sight. Nor, when she saw their pale, stern faces, grave with defeat and haggard from fatigue, did she stigmatise them in her heart, as she had stigmatised them in words, as cowards — *nodings*. Her woman's heart went out in sympathy to the suffering humanity around her. She did not pause to settle the question whether they had fled prematurely or stood by their leader— in whom was all her joy—to the last bitter gasp, as brave men should. She dared not investigate too closely, lest they should convince her that she had wronged them, and so daunt the hope that was her only comfort.

With tireless industry she busied herself in the manual labour of the leech, in such crude forms as the medical science of the day allowed. How rudimentary they were may be guessed from the story told us by old Robert of Gloucester, of the Duke of Austria in Cœur de Lion's time, some fifty years later, a patient who doubtless had at his command whatever skill the times afforded. The duke fell from his palfrey and hurt his foot, which mortified, and the doctors advised him that his only hope lay in having it taken off. Nobody, however, could be found bold enough to undertake the operation, and the poor duke at last held a keen axe with his own hands upon his ankle, and bade his chamberlain smite upon it with all his strength, the foot being severed at the third blow.

Such being the best surgical aid that a royal duke could obtain, it may be imagined that little could be done to ease the pangs of humbler men.

A stream of fugitives came straggling in before the day was done, and, alas! all told the same tale. They were mostly Bretons or Normans, for the Saxons and Anglo-Danes who had followed the earl sought refuge, not in the Norman stronghold, but in the forest retreats where their countrymen had already found shelter, and in the fastnesses of wold and fen, which were familiar to their steps.

The bride of a month before tended them with feverish assiduity, refusing rest and food, dreading that time for thought should force her to yield belief to the tidings they all brought—that she was a widow.

When evening came, Sir Alain de Gourin demanded another audience, at which he appeared alone, averring that Sir Hoël could not leave the direction of the defence at the same time as himself.

He faced the countess doggedly, with a defiant gleam in his bulging blue eyes which she did not find it pleasant to meet. His cheeks were more purple than ever, and it seemed to Emma that his red moustache almost quivered with flame, while his brawny figure was adorned with an unusual display of finery, the flashing jewels on his baldric attracting her eyes even in that moment of distress.

He urged that what had seemed a doubtful rumour in the morning had become certain news by night, since fugitive after fugitive had confirmed the tidings first brought by Stephen le Hareau, and begged her once more to think of her own safety, and allow himself and his trusty Bretons to escort her to Bretagne.

'Is it but to repeat to mine ears the idle plaints of these runaways that thou hast summoned me to solemn conclave, good knight? My answer of the morning stands.'

She broke into a laugh that was low and silvery enough, but which caused even the thick-skinned mercenary to shiver, and she would have swept from the room, but, recovering himself, De Gourin stepped forward, and, laying his mailed hand on her arm, detained her.

'By the Rood!' he exclaimed, 'thou shalt not go! Thou alone in all this castle dost refuse to believe the inevitable. I tell thee, knights of my following, whose word is sacred as my own, saw Ralph de Guader struck down by the mace of Odo of Bayeux; none could live after such a blow, were his harness sevenfold thick! Besides, the press of battle was upon the spot where he fell, and the feet of the horses must have achieved what Odo began, if his mace completed it not.'

Eadgyth, who attended the countess, uttered a scream of horror, and endeavoured to stop his speech. 'Wouldst thou kill her?' she cried.

Emma shook herself free from his grasp, and faced him with flashing eyes of scorn.

'By the mass, noble lady, pardon me! I would have spared thee these rude details, but perforce I must have thee comprehend.'

'If the earl indeed be perished,' said Emma bitterly, 'life will not be so sweet to me that I should take such care to save it. Save thyself and thy Bretons if thou wilt. If ye go, there will be less to man the walls, but fewer mouths to feed.'

The last words were uttered with a careless contempt that was absolutely sublime, and the blustering mercenary no longer ventured to detain her.

'Certes, the donzelle is mad!' he asserted, with a round oath, when she had left the chamber, for her absolute refusal to leave Blaunchcflour had thrown to the winds his plan for becoming her second husband, and becoming lord of her fair manors.

Outside the chamber door Emma turned to her loving bower-maiden like a creature of the woods at bay. Eadgyth's sympathy was more dreadful to her than the Breton's brutal frankness. 'I would be alone, Eadgyth. I am going to the oratory,' she forced her white lips to murmur, and almost fled from her side down the circling stairway.

Eadgyth followed at a distance, and, when Emma had disappeared within the sacred portal, threw herself prostrate at the threshold, like a faithful hound, as she had thrown herself at the door of the council-chamber in the morning.

Emma, alone at last, knelt before the shrine of the Virgin. She chose that rather than the one dedicated to St. Nicholas, for it seemed to her in her anguish that her husband's patron saint had forsaken his votaries in their distress.

The grief she had so long held at bay shook her from head to foot with a long quivering sob that held her speechless, and almost stopped her breath. She stretched out her arms in mute supplication to Heaven. Scalding tears formed slowly in her eyes, and rolled one by one down her bloodless cheeks.

Then a fresh gust of agony shook her like a leaf. 'Ah, *Dieu merci!*' she moaned; 'the horses! the horses! They achieved if Odo failed, he said! Oh, Christ! it cannot be! That dear head that has pillowed on my bosom!'

Quivering and shuddering, she sank upon the cold flags of the floor. The grey light of morning creeping through the narrow oriel found her still there.

. . . . . .

'Oh, countess! sweet countess! one waits without who will not deliver his message to any but thee, and *he bears the earl's signet!*'

Eadgyth was in the oratory, bending over the stiffened form of the unhappy Châtelaine of Blauncheflour.

Emma passed her hands across her brow in blank bewilderment, and Eadgyth cried to her again.

'Oh, Heaven be praised!' cried Emma, a great light of joy springing into her eyes; and, rising from her knees, 'Where is he? where is he?' she asked. 'Take me to him without delay. What manner of man is this whose advent doth so raise my hopes? The earl's signet, sayest thou?'

'He wears a Danish helm, and looks as if he had travelled over land and through water,' said Eadgyth. 'Our Lady and good St. Nicholas grant that our hopes be well founded!'

'Fetch me my golden torc, which was my wedding gift from the false Waltheof,' said Emma; 'I will meet this Dane as one who knows somewhat of his race.'

She went to her chamber to wash away the signs of her night's vigil from her cheeks, and, when her hasty toilette was made, Eadgyth saw with surprise the change in her: hope had brought back the bloom to her cheek and the elasticity to her step, and she looked well fit to be the bride of one who aspired to the third of a kingdom for his earldom.

She swept from the lodge to the great tower, and entered the council-chamber, where Sir Hoël and Sir Alain awaited her, curious enough to know the contents of the missive guarded by the fair-haired, long-limbed Dane with such jealous care, Sir Alain eyeing him as he stood before them with no very gracious countenance.

When Emma came into the room, the Dane saluted her profoundly, his tow-coloured locks almost touching his knee, and his formidable double-edged axe rattling on the floor as he bent; then he put into the hands of the countess a packet tied with a slender silken cord.

Emma started with joy, for her quick eyes noted the many joins in that silken cord, and recognised it as composed of the fringe with which Ralph's surcoat had been decked.

The Dane then drew from his finger a ring, and handed it to her, and, truly enough, it was De Guader's signet.

Emma's fingers trembled so violently that she could scarce read the superscripture, endorsed with a clerkly scroll,—

'To the fair hands of Emma de Guader,
    Castellan of our Castell of Blaunchefiour in
      Norowic.'

She drew the little *miséricorde* at her girdle and severed the silk.

'Bid the chaplain hither,' she said, for in truth she had little learning, and her literary attainments did not extend far beyond the reading of her own name; notwithstanding which, her eyes questioned eagerly the fairly illumined page before her, which was the work of the monk who has been mentioned as sitting by the hearth of Ealdred Godwinsson in his Fenland refuge, for the earl's clerkly skill was little greater than that of his wife.

Impatiently she awaited the coming of the chaplain, and, when he came, thrust the cherished parchment into his hand, and followed his reading, word by word, with hungry avidity.

'Fair and dear Lady and Countess,' said the missive, 'ill news has thy unfortunate knight wherewith to vex thine heart. The battle went against me. By little less than a miracle was my life, dear for thy sweet sake, preserved to me. A long story which some day I yet hope to relate to thee. I am sore wounded, but not dangerously'—

'The holy saints be praised!' ejaculated Sir Hoël fervently.

'Ay!—the holy saints be praised,' echoed Sir Alain, with somewhat halting zeal, for this resuscitated earl put an end to all his schemes.

'Therefore,' resumed the chaplain, continuing his reading, 'vex not thyself with fears. But for my wounds only, I had been with thee by now, but could not mount steed or *hacquenée*. The messenger will tell thee my retreat, and the plan by which I yet hope to prevail, and to win fame for thee. Defend my Castell of Blaunchefleur, sweet my Castellan, and, by the aid of good St. Nicholas, I will come back to thee at the head of such an host as will put all our foes to rout. I count the daies till I see thee again. The Blessed Virgin have thee in her keeping.

'These from thy leal and loving husband,

'RALPH DE GUADER AND MONTFORT,
'Earl of Norfolk and Suffolk.'

The missive was signed by the earl's own hand, and sealed with his wedding ring, on which was graven the cognisance of Hereford.

'Ah, fair sirs,' cried Emma exultingly, looking, however, at Sir Alain, and with contemptuous defiance in her flashing eyes, 'ye see the instinct of the true wife was more trustworthy than the eye-witness of belted knights! Let us charitably suppose that their poor heads were somewhat flustered with the hurly-burly of battle. Methinks they were over quick to believe their leader slain.'

Then, turning to the messenger, she questioned him regarding the battle and the retreat, and the manner of the earl's escape; and heard the story we already know of Grillonne's ready wit, and the refuge in the fens.

The Dane was one of those who had helped to carry the wounded earl, and had been chosen as a messenger because he was trustworthy, renowned as a swift runner, and could carry messages of importance to such Danish seamen as might be with their vessels at Norwich for trading purposes, besides his message to the countess. Dependence had not been placed on him alone; other messengers had been despatched from the Fenland camp, in case he fell into the hands of the enemy, but he had outstripped his competitors.

He said that the earl had desired to return to Norwich, but had been overpersuaded by those about him that it would be a wiser course to take ship at Wells by the sea, which he could do privily by aid of Ealdred Godwinsson, and those over whom the thegn had influence. So it was agreed that the earl should make sail for Denmark, where, without doubt, he would be nobly welcomed by King Sweyn, who had already promised him men and vessels. From thence he would go with all speed to Bretagne, and arm his retainers, and gather all help he might among the Breton nobles; and with the host thus gathered would haste to the relief of Blauncheflour, which would thus be rendered sure and certain.

The countess listened with kindling eyes and glowing cheeks.

'A device worthy of a hero!' she exclaimed. 'Let the garrison be summoned to the courtyard of the castle, and I will tell them these brave news. I would they should receive them from mine own lips. See also that this worthy messenger enjoys all hospitality the castle may afford.'

She unfastened a golden collar from her neck, and added it to the many bracelets which already glittered upon the Dane's muscular arms.

The warrior thanked her earnestly, with the frank reverence which characterised the wild sea-kings in their behaviour to women.

Half-an-hour later, the countess, arrayed in her richest robes, with steel-cap on her head, and her gorget glistening in the morning sun as it rose and fell with the swift heaving of her bosom, stood at the great east portal, with the Danish messenger at her side, and looked down upon the eager faces of the hastily assembled garrison.

A rumour had gone forth that the earl had escaped, and would yet return in triumph, and a glow of excitement lighted every eye. As Emma saw the stalwart forms and the strong determined countenances before her, a thrill of pride swelled her heart at the thought that her warrior husband should have given her command over them. The spirit of William Fitzosbern lived again in the breast of his daughter. 'I will be worthy of the honour that Ralph's choice bestowed on me,' she thought. 'If aught a woman can say or do may inspire men to gallant deeds, these men shall not fail their lord.'

Emotion brought high words to her lips and fire to her eyes. Her heart verily shouted with delight for the joyful message which she had to deliver. 'Brave knights and soldiers!' she cried, and her voice rang through the fresh morning air like the clang of a silver trumpet, 'glad news have I for loyal ears. Earl Ralph yet lives! See, this missive is signed by his own noble hand! His signet blazes on my finger!'

She held the scroll aloft in her hands, and the sunshine flashed on the ring.

'A Guader! a Guader!' shouted the assembled host;

and arms were raised and weapons clashed, while some three hundred stout throats echoed the shout, 'St. Nicholas for Guader!'

'Yesterday your countess and her counsellors were sore distressed,' Emma went on; 'for, as ye know, the unfortunate squire, Stephen le Hareau, and those who followed him, believed that the earl was slain; but we would not vex ye with our grief till doubt was changed into certainty. Doubt *is* changed into certainty;—but a certainty of life, not death!'

A roar of cheers rent the air again.

'Yes, your lord lives!' cried Emma. 'His first field is lost, but it will not be his last! He is wounded, sorely, but not dangerously. See! so the letter says! His way is open to Denmark. This gallant Dane has borne his message across field and over flood, faithfully, as he helped to carry the earl himself from the battlefield.'

She turned to the messenger beside her, who clashed his great axe upon his round wooden shield, with its strange embossing of iron nails, and shouted 'Waes hael!'

Then Emma told again the story of the earl's rescue, though she did not reveal his hiding-place, lest there should be traitors in the camp, and how he intended to take ship for Denmark to ask aid of King Sweyn, 'who,' she said, 'has already promised it. Then the earl will seek his own fair lands in Bretagne, and he will call his vassals to his standard, and come across the sea at the head of a great host to relieve his faithful garrison in

Blaunchetlour. Is any man so mean of heart that he will not vow to good St. Nicholas to do his best to keep the castle to that hour? If so, let him declare himself a *noding*, and quit the company of gallant men!'

'Not one! Not one!' rang round the castle yard, and echoed back from the high stone tower of the keep, reverberating in tumultuous thunder from base to summit.

Then old Sir Hoël de St. Brice took off his plumed barret, and waved it in the air, where he stood behind his lady, his eyes humid and his lips quivering, as he echoed, 'Not one!'

Sir Alain de Gourin, listening with a strange expression of satirical disdain on his florid countenance, rattled his sword from its sheath and waved it in the air, where he stood behind his lady, and shouted with a lusty voice, 'Not one!'

'I thank ye, friends!' cried the countess. 'To your strong arms and your loyal hearts I commit my fate and that of my lord. St. Nicholas give ye fortitude!'

Turning to a page who stood beside her with a silver tray, she took a velvet purse from it, and scattered broad pieces amongst the soldiery.

'A largesse! a largesse!' they cried; and all was joy and hilarity.

'Ye shall taste a vintage better than ever grew even in the vineyards of Hereford or Kent,' cried the countess; and she gave orders to the steward to broach a cask of

French wine which had been amongst her brother's gifts at the bride-ale; an order which called forth a fresh burst of applause.

'Drink it,' cried Emma, 'to the safe return of your lord!'

CHAPTER XVII.

HOW RALPH CAME HOME.

'SWEET nuncle, methinks some of thy wits adhered to my cap, and that, when I put the same upon thy noble skull, they found an entrance into it by that crack the worshipful bishop's mace rove therein, else thou hadst never assayed this mad journey! Why, thou hast scarce taken a step without giving a groan.'

'Have I been so weak, Grillonne?' Earl Ralph asked, a faint smile brightening his pale, worn face.

He was on horseback, but rode at a foot's pace, and bent over the neck of his *hacquenée* like an aged and decrepit man. He was dressed in a loose flowing Saxon blouse, and had not a link of mail on his person from top to toe. On his left rode Grillonne, who strove to cheer him with loving banter; on his right the young Anglo-Dane, Leofric Ealdredsson, the son of his late host in the Fenland refuge; a little behind came a small band of men-at-arms, a squire leading Ralph's Spanish destrier, and a mule bearing the earl's harness, making some score in all.

'In good sooth,' continued the earl, 'it hath not seemed to me that my path was strewn with rose-leaves, but only with the thorns stripped bare of flowers. Yet would I go through it seven times over to see my lady's face again.'

'Well-a-day, nuncle! and a pretty galliard thou art, forsooth, to figure before a gracious dame, with thy hollow cheeks and thy hawk's eyes glaring out of caverns deep eno' for pixies to bide in,' replied the privileged jester. 'Cogs bones! thou hadst done better to go to Denmark first as thou didst intend, there to have picked up a few stout followers and a little flesh to cover thy worn framework withal. The women ever love the signs of power.'

A jealous pang flushed the earl's gaunt face with a faint hue of red. What if the fool spoke truth, and Emma should turn from him in his defeat, and embitter his humiliation by fresh reproaches? She had sent him forth with a doubting heart, scarce wishing him success, in that he fought against her kinsman and suzerain, William of Normandy. All his feudal pomp and glory, at the head of the eager army he then led to battle, had failed to move the bosom of the daughter of William Fitzosbern, who, young as she was, had seen many a fair host go forth with streaming pennons and noisy clarions. How, then, would she greet the weary, wounded wight who crept back to his castle like a thief in the night, with a poor remnant of faithful followers in little better plight than himself?

Truth is seldom palatable to men in high places,

and the jester's light words had struck home too surely.

'Thou presumest, Sir Fool!' quoth the earl sharply. 'Thine office doth not establish thee a critic of mine actions!'

'Mercy, sweet nuncle! I cry you mercy! A fool's words count for nothing!' cried Grillonne, looking into his lord's face with so much love in his clear, keen eyes, that De Guader instantly forgave him.

'Thou art the best friend I have, Grillonne!' he said impulsively.

'Nay, there thou dost wrong to a thousand stout hearts, good my lord!' answered the jester, 'noble Leofric there amongst the number. But see, thy toils are well-nigh ended. Yonder rise the white walls of Norwich Castle.'

'St. Nicholas be praised!' exclaimed the earl fervently. 'Right glad shall I be to shelter my aching head within the towers. The next bosquet shall serve me for tiring-room. I will show myself in harness as befits a knight.'

Some two hours later, the warders at the great gate of Castle Blauncheflour saw a small troop of horsemen approaching the portal at a foot-pace, amongst them a knight in mail, but without cognisance, or surcoat, or shield, his countenance covered by his large round helmet, and, riding beside him, a motley-coated jester, whose well-known visage caused a thrill of excitement amongst the guards, greater than the general appearance of the group; for many a similar one had demanded and received admittance within the castle during the preceding days, since Stephen le Hareau had pioneered the fugitives.

This party had little difficulty in gaining entrance, for the faces of the men-at-arms composing it were all more or less familiar to the warders; and, after a short parley, the portcullis was raised and the drawbridge lowered to admit of their passage into the courtyard of the castle.

The news that the earl's jester had returned spread like wildfire through the garrison, with the mysterious celerity that sometimes makes it seem as if intelligence was circulated by magic.

Before the new-comers had dismounted from their horses, the countess, who was passing from the chapel to the spital, heard the rumour, and came forth into the courtyard to ascertain if it indeed were true.

Sir Alain de Gourin, who had been overlooking some target practice amongst the archers in the tilt-yard, came also to receive and examine the fugitives.

Seeing the countess and the ladies who had followed her, glad that duty gave them the opportunity to satisfy their own curiosity, he louted low, and took his place beside them.

Archers and soldiers of various arms from the guard-room, servants and others, had swarmed from all quarters, and the courtyard was well-nigh full of animated faces.

One new-comer after another was recognised, and, so to speak, 'passed' by De Gourin, and it came to the turn of the helmeted knight to declare himself—most of the others wore round steel-caps with a nasal, which left the features visible.

He doffed his steel headpiece silently, and looked around upon the throng. The gaunt, pale face woke no instant response from the many onlookers, but the countess sprang forward with outstretched arms to his saddle-bow.

'My lord!' she cried. 'Soldiers! do you not know your earl?'

'A Guader! a Guader!'

The cry resounded in the court with vigour even surpassing that of a few days before, when their Castellan's eloquence had moved them so deeply.

Ralph de Guader caught his wife's outstretched arms in his own, and looked down into the fair face he had feared never to see again; and then—not the gentle lady, but the mailed warrior swooned.

Worn out with the terrible fatigues he had undergone, while yet unhealed of his wounds, the earl reeled in his saddle, and would have fallen, if the tender arms of his wife had not caught him in their clasp.

His head sank on Emma's shoulder. The fiery Oliver turned his intelligent head and caressed her arm softly with his velvet nose, but stood without moving a limb, gazing at her with his full, bright eyes. He seemed to understand. Had he moved, the countess would have fared ill.

Emma was quickly eased of her beloved burden by the retainers around, and the insensible earl was borne within the sheltering walls of the keep, and laid upon his own broidered, carved oak bed, in his own spacious and luxurious room.

Ah! how Emma wept and prayed and joyed over him, and laughed lowly for delight that in very truth she had her warrior once more.

How she burnt sweet essences, and bathed his lips with perfumed waters, and shuddered at the print of Odo's mace that still marked his brow with a black and sullen scar.

Ralph, opening his steel-grey eyes upon that eager face, lost all fear lest his gauntness and humiliation and defeat should lessen wifely love.

'Sweetheart!' he sighed. 'Sweetheart! God be praised that I see thee again!' The memory of his desolation on the battlefield came over him with resistless force. His breast heaved with a mighty sob as he took his wife's hands again in his own and pressed them to his lips.

They brought me news of thy death, Ralph. But I knew better,' whispered Emma, as she bent over him, her quick tears falling on his face. 'I knew better! Thou couldst not have died but I had known it. My heart had been rent in twain.'

Then Ralph told her the history of his struggle, and of the long dreadful hours when he lay 'twixt life and death upon the field; and how Grillonne had schemed and saved him; and of the refuge in the Fens. A murmured story, told in a voice faint and weak with suffering, and received with many an ejaculation of sympathy and love.

'I had planned to steal away privily by Wells on the sea, and there take ship for Denmark,' De Guader said. 'But, sweetheart, the thought of thee was to me as the thought of water to the pilgrim in the desert. Thee I must see, or perish for longing. And I see thee.' He drew her to him and feasted his eyes on her face.

'And for that thou didst confront danger and difficulty and the pain of thy sore wounds?' said Emma proudly.

'In sooth the wounds were sore, but of danger there was little,' answered the earl. Then he sprang up from the couch into a sitting posture with a suddenness that startled his gentle leech. 'They deem me crushed,' he said. 'So flushed are they by their victory that they are careless to pursue it further. I found no trace of their troops as I dragged wearily to Norwich. They have gone west, I deem it, to deal with thy brother.'

'Alas, my poor Roger! I would we had news of him,' said the countess, her face drawn with pain. De Guader caught the change in her face with jealous quickness. The old haunting fear came back lest she should scorn the broken man.

'Emma, my defeat is dire! Dost thou credit how I have come back to thee,—hiding behind bush and briar, beaten, poverty-stricken, all but alone? I, who left thee at the head of a noble army, now scattered like chaff before the winds! Dost thou not spurn me?'

The daughter of William Fitzosbern looked in the face of the man she had chosen for richer, for poorer, for better, for worse.

'My knight,' she said, 'hadst thou come maimed of

a hand and foot, with thy visage marred for ever and a day by the cruel daggers of thy foes, as hath happened to thy favourite squire, Stephen le Hareau, I had but loved thee the better.'

'By the Holy Rood! has Stephen le Hareau been so foully entreated?'

'Alack, yes! Moreover, he bore a message from the king's men, that every prisoner, of whatever rank and whatever nation, they might take in this struggle, should lose his right foot.'

The earl raised himself from the couch and smote his knee with his balled fist.

'By the bones of St. Nicholas, I will avenge them! I will yet prevail.' He turned to Emma, fiercely seizing her hands again in his, this time with no very tender grip. 'Hast thou courage? Wilt thou help me now in my sore need, or is thine heart half with William? Say me sooth!'

'It is with thee!—all with thee!'

'God bless thee for that answer!' He passed his hand across his eyes, and then held his brow as if in pain. 'That accursed shaveling's mace! Sith he cracked my poor head with it, whenever I try to think I get a pang instead of a notion.'

'Strive not to think, mine own. Rest awhile. Where shouldst thou rest if not here in thine home, or when, if not after dire fatigue?'

'No, Emma! no rest for me till I have retrieved mine honour! Stephen le Hareau, thou saidest? He fought like a Paladin beside me. The smartest squire in my following, and the best born. I so loved the lad that I would have had him squire to mine own body, but that Sir Guy de Landerneau was as a father to him, and had formed him in all fitting a man-at-arms. Sir Guy dead too! Yet death is but the soldier's portion, it irks me not. 'Tis that the fiends should mutilate one of Le Hareau's gentle blood. It beggars credence! Their own leader is of such proud lineage. Ha, ha!'

Emma had moved softly to his side, and had enlaced her slender fingers round his mailed arm, striving to soothe him with mute sympathy.

'Seest thou not the menace in the insult, Emma?' They spare not rank. Had I been taken, my fate had been even as Le Hareau's.'

Emma shuddered, recalling Le Hareau's awful face as she had seen it on the day of his return. 'It bears not to think of,' she said.

'Sweet, I must go forth! I must seek Sweyn Ulfsson of Denmark in mine own person; he dallies with my messengers. I must go to him and demand fulfilment of his pledges. I must go to Wader and Montfort and assemble my vassalage. Hast thou courage to hold Blaunchefleur till my return?'

'I have courage for aught that profits thee.'

Ralph gazed in her face, his eyes aflame with joyous pride. He took her fair cheeks between his palms, and bent down and kissed her brow and lips.

'Methinks there is but little risk, my Falcon!' he said. 'They cannot turn from west to east, as the sun does, in a night. That gives me time. They will scarce attempt Blaunchefour and I not in it. If they do, it is impregnable. Ere six weeks I shall relieve thee with a fair force at my back.'

Emma looked wistfully in his eyes. Her heart ached at the thought of losing him again.

'Courage, m'amie!' he said, mistaking the cause of her hesitation.

'My courage fails not, Ralph,' she answered. 'I had held thy castle while a man would obey my orders and stand to the walls, even hadst thou been dead, as they tried to make me believe. How then should I quail to hold it for thee living? I do but mourn that we must part again.'

And again Ralph took her face between his palms and kissed it.

. . . .

Meanwhile Lanfranc, the Primate, sat writing in his closet; a satisfied smile hovered round the corners of his mobile lips and lighted up the depths of his gleaming Southern eyes. A monk stood waiting to receive the letter.

It ran thus :—

'To his lord, William, King of the English, his faithful Lanfranc sends his faithful service and faithful prayers. Gladly would we see you, as an angel of God, but we are unwilling that you should take the trouble of crossing the sea at this particular juncture. For if you were to come to put down these traitors and robbers, you would do us dishonour. Rodulph the Count, or rather the traitor, and his whole army have been routed, and ours, with a great body of Normans and Saxons, are in pursuit. Our leaders inform me that in a few days they will drive these perjured wretches into the sea, or capture them dead or alive. The details I send you by this monk, who may be trusted, as he has done fealty to me. May God Almighty bless you.'[1]

The details which Lanfranc's messenger had to give of the defeat of the Earl of East Anglia, or, as the prelate styled him, Rodulph the Count, we already know.

Turning to the monk, the archbishop said, 'Regarding the base uprising favoured and headed by our lord-king's cousin, Roger, Earl of Hereford, the tidings are of like good savour. Inform our liege that the English prelates, Bishop Wulfstan and Abbot Æthelwig, in union with Urse, Sheriff of Worcestershire, have hindered the traitor from passing the Severn, and have taken the earl himself prisoner, whereon we pray our liege heartily to make known his wishes how we may best dispose of this haught prisoner.

'Forget not to repeat likewise the stratagem by which the Count Rodulph's men deceived us, so that we made not his body secure, and know not certainly if he be dead or alive.'

'I will forget no detail, good my lord Archbishop,' replied the messenger; and Lanfranc folded his letter, and fastened it with a silken cord, and sealed it with his official seal.

[1] Lanfranc, *Opp.* i. 56, translated by Hook, *Lives of the Archbishops of Canterbury*, vol. ii. p. 136.

'Naught could be more satisfactory,' he murmured to himself, as he was performing these small offices, 'than the manner in which the Saxons have ranged themselves, in this matter, upon our liege's side. It was a bold stroke on the part of the Lady Judith to warn us of her husband's schemes, and to risk his rage and his danger. Sooth, it had been a dire struggle if the doughty son of Siward had taken his part, as the plotters did well intend. A turmoil raised for the sake of one woman, and foiled by another! Thanks to thee, Judith, the day is ours!'

But not to be ended quite so speedily as the sanguine Primate supposed. A woman was to hold his best troops at bay for a space of three long months, and then to make terms quite other than a choice between imprisonment or the bottom of the sea.

The race is not always to the swift, nor the battle to the strong!

CHAPTER XVIII.

BESIEGED.

'METHINKS, Emma, my foes will say that Ralph de Guader was a recreant knight, who fled from his devoir and left his lady to fight for him! Beshrew me, but it mislikes me to leave thee!'

So quoth the earl, when, after a few days of rest and rehabilitation at Blaunchefleur, he was making ready to go on board a Danish galley, which lay moored at Lovelly's Staithe, her brightly coloured sails flapping idly in the summer wind; the heads of the oarsmen, with their long light hair and long light moustaches, showing in even ranks along her bulwarks, and her high dragon-carved prow gleaming in the sun.

Emma, upright and determined, with the keys of the castle at her girdle, and wearing her steel-cap and mail gorget, forced back the tears that sprang to her eyes, and turned proudly to the warrior beside her, who, dressed in complete mail, with his long cross-handled sword suspended from a jewelled baldric, *looked* the perfect figure of a hero.

'Nay, my Ralph! whatever hard things they may say of thee, they will never be so mad as to accuse *thee* of aught that savours of cowardice. Thy valour has been too well proven on many a well-fought field! Did not William see thee fight at Hastings, and give thee thine earldom for thy prowess? Didst thou not defend his conquest from the Danish invaders, and win fresh honours and lands? Who could withstand thee in the tourney? Oh, it is preposterous! Rebel they may call thee, recreant never!'

Ralph de Guader, however, gauged the justice of the makers of history better than his warm-hearted countess.[1]

He looked at the waiting galley with a sigh, wondering if he should ever again be lord in his English earldom.

He had not been idle during his short stay in his capital. Without waiting for his wounds to heal, he had been up and doing as soon as a few days of rest had made it possible. He had summoned his local supporters, who—if we may judge from the number of estates entered in Domesday as '*Wasta*' later on—were numerous, to more than one council, and had done much to restore their confidence in his arms and their belief in his ultimate success.

His own heart had grown lighter as he went the round of his magnificent new castle, which William had munitioned with every improvement then known, and truly it seemed well-nigh impregnable, with its high towers and battlemented walls, and deep, sullen moats.

Preparations for the siege had been going merrily

[1] See Appendix, Note D.

forward. Fat beeves were driven up from the meadows; the bleating of sheep mingled strangely with the clangor of arms, and the large herds of swine so dear to Saxon housekeeping contributed their quota of victims, while not a little fun was caused among the laughter-loving soldiery by the exciting difficulties of persuading the squeaking porkers to cross the drawbridge, and many were the tussles and, in some cases, dire the misfortunes incurred in the sport.

Barrels of salt meat and flour and ale were rolled up the ballium by the stalwart arms of the bows and bills; arms destined, alas! to be but bare skin and bone when they should issue again from the walls of the fortress.

All was bustle and plenty. Sinews of war of every kind were there in superfluity.

De Guader saw clearly that to shut himself up in the castle was to make himself helpless; but that to leave its defence to his vassals, and go forth to collect reinforcements in Denmark and Bretagne, and take the besiegers in rear, was a plan that promised all success; and every man among his counsellors agreed with him.

Yet it was hard to leave the fair bride for whom he had risked so much, and whose noble sympathy in his misfortunes had endeared her to him a thousandfold.

No wonder that his heart failed him at the last, when the moment for parting had arrived, and the time and tide that wait for no man were ripe for departure.

'It mislikes me to leave thee!' he said.

'Sweet my lord, "he that putteth his hand to the plough must not look back,"' said Emma, meeting his wistful eyes firmly. 'An thou standest quavering for my poor sake, while yon oarsmen are broiling on their benches, I myself shall accuse thee for a recreant! Dost doubt the courage of thy Castellan?'

'No, by St. Nicholas! Thou art the true daughter of a noble sire!' said the earl. A group of knights, Saxon, Breton, and Norman, stood around him, some half-dozen in readiness to accompany him, while the rest were gathered from the neighbourhood, or formed part of the garrison; amongst these last, Sir Alain and Sir Hoël and Leofric Ealdredsson were conspicuous.

The earl turned to them: 'Obey your lady loyally, guard her zealously; and may the saints have mercy on the man who is untrue to his trust!' he cried, 'for I will have none.'

'Thy threat touches no man here, good my lord,' blustered De Gourin. 'I will warrant every soul in the garrison ready to die for that trust.'

'Ay, ay!' cried the rest; but a strange quiver of doubt ran through the bosom of the valorous Castellan, as to whether one man there was honest and leal, and the man she doubted was the Breton protester.

Then the earl mounted and rode down to the waiting galley; and soon the long oars were sweeping rhythmically through the blue water and shedding simultaneous showers of pearly drops from their glittering blades; the gay sails swelled fairly in the breeze, so that the dragon-prow moved swiftly down the shining reaches of the Yare.

But Emma did not watch it; she had slipped away to

the oratory, and knelt before the altar in speechless but passionate prayer, while the tears she had repressed so long chased each other down her cheeks.

A terrible fear was gnawing at her heart, that her husband had but left her to die in that wild Denmark, amongst the rough Norsemen, for she knew how sore and desperate were his unhealed wounds, and by what effort his high spirit forced his body into action.

She had steeled herself to serve him as he wished to be served, but it had been liefer to her woman's heart to tend and leech him into perfect health, than to command and urge his vassals to hurt others as sorely.

Meanwhile the king's forces were not so far away as Ralph supposed.

On the eve of the third day after the earl's embarkation, the warders on the battlements of Blauncheflour heard afar off the thunderous tramp of steeds and the jingle and clang of harness and arms, and, as the sun sank in a splendour of golden clouds, his last rays gilded the hastily pitched pavilions of Bishop Geoffrey of Coutances, Earl William of Warrenne, and Robert Malet, who led the investing army to the attack.

The Bishop of Bayeux, though not dead, as the fugitives supposed who had seen the combat between Odo and Earl Ralph, with its catastrophe of mutual unhorsing, was *hors-de-combat* for the time being, and unable to seek retrieval of his knightly prowess in person.

The Countess Emma, with Eadgyth and her ladies, ascended to the battlements of the keep to view the encampment of the foe, and in sooth the sight would have been gay enough if it had not borne so dire a meaning.

Groups of glittering horsemen, their long lances decked with many-coloured pennons gleaming in the golden light, their horses curveting and prancing, were riding hither and thither, directing and superintending. Long lines of bowmen and slingers were advancing in order at a quick march, wheeling and breaking into companies as they reached the camping ground. Trains of sumpter mules and squires with led horses mingled with the infantry; and shouts and laughter, the braying of trumpets and neighing of horses, mixed fitfully in the soft south wind. Sometimes even the words were audible as some man-at-arms shouted to his followers, and the blows of the mallets with which the poles of the pavilions were being driven into the ground came sharply through the air. The tents themselves were decked with richly-hued silks, and soon displayed the banners of their noble owners. As the twilight deepened, some hundreds of watchfires threw out bright flames into the dusk, and made the air fragrant with their sweet wood smoke, seeming to blaze the brighter as the curfew boomed forth from the church towers in Norwich, to bid all the inhabitants of humble rank rake out their cheerful hearths.

All 'the pomp and circumstance of glorious war,' as it was known in those days, was spread out before Blauncheflour, and, as Emma watched the doings of her foe, there rose in her spirit that wild and mysterious 'rapture of battle,' which modern Darwinians explain by tracing back our lineage to tiger forefathers,—that strange yearning to dare all and spend life itself in one great effort, which some have said is but the endeavour to satisfy our instinct to grapple with abstract evil by personifying it in the form of a human foe; but which others define, perhaps more truly, as the final efflorescence of egotism run riot, which satisfies its lust of power even at the cost of destruction to itself.

Good or bad, the feeling flooded Emma's heart. At sight of real danger, menacing and close, she who had fainted at the thought of it grew bold as any of the belted knights in the hostile host below. The blood of her hero father coursed swiftly through her veins, and the wild battle-song of Rollo, which had served her ancestors so often as a national hymn, haunted her brain.

She had ascended one of the small flights of steps at the angle of the battlements, which served to raise the sentinel above the merlons.

Eadgyth stood beside her, and the ladies and knights in attendance were all busily watching the encamping foe through the embrasures, and were out of earshot.

Emma stretched out her right hand with its small fingers tightly clenched, and shook it at the beleaguering host.

'Methinks, Eadgyth, these haught chevaliers with their baldrics and their golden spurs, and above all my Lord Bishop of Coutances, cut a sorry figure assembling their forces thus to crush a woman,' she cried, with an

Emma's first sight of the Foe.

excited laugh. 'How wrathful will they be, when the brave ger-falcon they deem to be mewed up within these towers swoops down upon them as from the skies, with a gallant army of bold Bretons, backed by some of Sweyn Ulfsson's best warriors. Do your worst, ye tools of my tyrant kinsman! I fear ye not. My lord is safe— my lord ye would fain have hindered from being mine. And I am safe also, whatever betide—my *miséricorde* assures that.'

'Holy Mary preserve thee from such a desperate safety!' exclaimed Eadgyth, whose sad, still face contrasted strongly with the flushed excitement of the impulsive Norman.

'Thou art down-hearted, Eadgyth!' said Emma, after a piercing glance into her bower-maiden's eyes. 'I know thee too well to believe that thy depression comes from vulgar fear. Tell me thy grief. We are as private here as in my bower. None can hear our speech.'

'Seest thou yon star shining between two bars of cloud, noble Emma? It reminds me of one who bore a painted star between two clouds for his cognisance. A dire doubt haunts me lest he be in the ranks of the foe; for I well remember his heart was always with the Duke of Normandy.'

'Sir Aimand de Sourdeval? Nay, surely he would not lift his hand against his lord. Besides, the earl told me that he had sent him on a long journey.'

Through Eadgyth's heart passed a quiver of pain.

'Not surely the longest journey of all,' her anxious affection whispered, but she was silent.

'Poor child, I feel for thee!' said the countess, laying her hand caressingly on the flaxen head of the Saxon, which her elevated position on the stone steps enabled her to do comfortably. She had assumed a very matronly manner since the gold ring had been slipped upon her finger by her heart's chosen, and, in truth, she felt as if years of experience had gone over her head since the day when her brother had come to her and told her 'that her broken troth should soon be mended.'

Sir Alain de Gourin approached with an obsequious air, and the countess said to him gaily, 'I hope, fair sir, the gentlemen yonder are well satisfied with the quarters they have chosen, for methinks it will be somewhat long e'er they change them for the hospitable shelter of Blaunscheflour.'

At which De Gourin laughed applaudingly, and swore that if the garrison had half the spirit of their Castellan, they would send them to bide still farther from their doors.

Then the countess led her ladies down to the chapel, where the chaplain performed a special mass, praying the protection of the heavenly powers for the beleaguered garrison and for all who fought on their side, at home or abroad, and offering prayers for the safety and success of the earl.

The tears rolled down Emma's cheeks as she repeated these last, and many of the ladies sobbed audibly, partly for the woes of their countess and partly through fears or sorrows of their own.

When the service was over, Emma dismissed her

attendants, even Eadgyth, and followed Father Pierre into his sacristy.

'I would have a mass performed, father,' she said, 'for the soul's welfare of a knight whom I regard for the sake of one who loves him well, and also in that he did always seem to me an honest wight, but of whom I know not whether he be fighting for my dear lord, or if he be in the opposing host without. There is no reason why I should make mystery of his name—Sir Aimand de Sourdeval.'

'Sir Aimand de Sourdeval!' repeated Father Pierre, gazing at the lady with startled eyes. 'Knowest thou not, noble countess, that he is a prisoner in the dungeons of this keep?'

CHAPTER XIX.

'STONE WALLS DO NOT A PRISON MAKE.'

'Sir Aimand de Sourdeval a prisoner in this castle?' repeated the countess in a tone of the most complete surprise, and her cheeks grew white with a sudden horror, for, to explain this thing, either, it seemed to her, the young knight, whose honest face and noble bearing had won her respect and the heart of her best-loved bower-maiden, must be unworthy; or—and the thought gave her a keener pang than even she had suffered from the rumour of his death—the master of the castle had made evil use of his power.

'Wherefore is this? Knowest thou his offence, father?' demanded the countess.

The young priest bowed his head. 'Daughter, if thou wilt know the truth, the offence of a too great fidelity to his suzerain, William of Normandy,' he answered in a low voice.

A spasm of pain crossed Emma's face at this objective presentment of her worst fear, and the terrible heart-searchings with which she had entered into the struggle against the Conqueror returned with renewed force.

'I would hear this prisoner's defence from his own lips, and judge for myself of his guilt,' she said, turning to Father Pierre with quick decision, and a pale, set face. 'Lead me to him.'

'Noble Emma, the dungeon in which he is chained is no seemly place for gold-embroidered slippers and ermined robes.'

'Less seemly still, then, for an innocent man, if innocent he be,' cried Emma, each syllable sounding like a challenge thrown at a foe. 'Show me the way. I will see myself to the lodgment of all under my roof.'

Then a satisfied light gleamed from Father Pierre's unworldly dark eyes, and his thin, ascetic features relaxed into a smile. 'The Holy Mother reward and sustain thee, my daughter!' he said softly. 'Come then at once!'

Emma followed him; outwardly calm, but in reality deeply moved, and not without terror at thought of entering those terrible dungeons, which, although she had passed her life in castles, had hitherto been known to her only by name.

He led her through winding passages secured by more than one heavy, clangorous portal — the vaulted walls echoing to the creak of their hinges — into the silence and the darkness of the basement.

The chaplain was free to penetrate at will into these

halls of suffering and despair in the prosecution of his sacred office, but the warders who guarded the various portals half forgot to make their reverence to the priest, as they stared with open-eyed surprise at the lady, till, on recognising her, they saluted with clumsy haste, and strove to atone for momentary negligence by quick opening of the door which formed their ward.

Emma shuddered as the torch with which Father Pierre had provided himself gleamed on the damp, massive walls. It seemed to her that imprisonment between them would of itself bring death to her, and she marvelled how any human creature should sustain life under such conditions.

'In sooth, noble Emma,' said Father Pierre, as the countess gave expression to this feeling, 'the holy saints have sent thee hither this night, because time grew pressing. A little while, and the man who is the object of thine errand of mercy would be released by a sterner liberator—death. If thou shouldst deem him worthy of his dungeon, he will not need guarding long!'

'Ah!' sighed Emma, with a sharp pang of horror, and instinctively quickening her steps, as if a moment might be fatal.

They had reached a narrow, ponderous door, studded with huge nails. Father Pierre produced a key which he had taken from a warder who stood at the end of the passage. He turned it in the lock, and, drawing back their solid bolts, pushed open the door and entered the cell into which it gave access, the countess following with shrinking steps.

The cell was small, for it was hollowed in the wall of the keep, some thirteen feet in thickness at the outside; it was, perhaps, eight feet square. The walls were running with moisture, and the air was dank and fœtid. On a stone ledge raised a little higher than the ground, the prostrate figure of a man was revealed by the fitful gleam of the torch, and Father Pierre went forward and bent over him.

'Awake, my son!' he said gently, holding the torch so that the light fell upon the slumberer's face.

Emma's hands clung together in anguish as she saw the gaunt, cadaverous features, the paled skin, and the wild matted hair and beard of the prisoner, and marked the fleshlessness of the limbs that were extended in uneasy length upon the inhospitable couch. His appearance might have moved the hardest-hearted to pity, and seemed all the more terrible in contrast with the image that was in Emma's mind, of the young knight as she had last seen him, in all the bravery of the harness of the jousting-field, neat-shaven and close-cropped as any modern English gentleman, according to the fashion of the Normans.

The unhappy knight opened his eyes with a nervous start, and sprang into a sitting posture; the rattle of chains that accompanied his movement revealing to the ruthful eyes of the countess that his ankles were loaded with heavy rings of iron, attached by chains to a stanchion in the floor

'Fear nothing, Sir Aimand,' said the priest reassuringly. 'It is I—Father Pierre; and I have brought thee hope, and at least the surety that thy case will be inquired into and sifted to the ground. See, the noble Countess Emma has herself deigned to visit thy prison. St. Michael has answered thy prayers!'

The captive stared round him with haggard eyes, which seemed almost supernaturally large and bright, and Emma quailed as they rested at length upon her, with an expression of wonder and inquiry.

'The Countess Emma?' he repeated in a faint voice, —'the bride?'

Time for him had been standing still since the day of that fatal bride-ale, which brought evil in some form to all who partook of it!

'Art thou indeed Sir Aimand de Sourdeval?' said Emma, crossing the cell and standing before the prisoner, her beautiful face full of pity, yet not all softness. 'Unhappy knight,' she added almost sternly, her clear, decisive utterance ringing round the cell, 'what crime hast thou committed against my lord, that thou art subject to such durance?'

De Sourdeval threw back his head with a gesture of indignation; then his expression changed to one of sadness, and he threw himself on his knee before the countess.

'Noble Emma,' he said, 'the only crime I have committed against thy lord and mine own liege, was that of being faithful to his suzerain and mine, nor can I believe the kind and generous De Guader knows my fate.'

'Thank God!' cried Emma, with a sudden sob.

'Thou hast been good to me always!' exclaimed De Sourdeval, with intense excitement, his breast heaving and his eyes shining as he spoke. 'Oh, gracious countess, bear my petition to thy lord, and tell him that Aimand de Sourdeval was never unfaithful to him in word or deed, and pray him to sift this matter to the bottom, for if he knoweth aught, 'tis most like that his ears have been abused by the untrue malignities of my enemies.'

'Knowest thou not that the earl is sped to Denmark, there to collect fresh forces wherewith to relieve us from the beleaguering host that now sits before the castle walls?' asked Emma, with less firmness, feeling for the first time the full weight of the responsibilities she had undertaken. 'In my hands is the ruling of the castle; tell me, therefore, the burden of thy petition.'

Then Sir Aimand related to her the story of his adventures on the night of her bridal, and how Sir Alain de Gourin had foully entreated him, a narrative broken by terrible fits of coughing, showing how deeply the chills of his prison had wrought upon his frame, and by exclamations of surprise from the countess, who was much startled to discover the conduct of the Breton knight, and in great perplexity, for she felt keenly that Sir Aimand had but acted the part of an honourable man, and that to offer him a pardon under such circumstances would be but an insult. Moreover, he seemed to ignore the earl's present position of active rebellion, and she could not gather how far he was aware of the position of affairs.

'Doubtless, Sir Knight,' she said, 'thine impulse to be faithful to thy suzerain was that of a true and loyal soul, and none can blame thee; but William of Normandy has made the land groan under his tyranny, and so haught and overbearing was he, that, for the mere delight of showing his power, he crushed his most loving peers under his heel. Thou knowest that he strove to part my lord from me, and forbade our marriage; and so wroth was he at the breach of his capricious mandate, that, in self-defence, my lord was driven to take arms. Let the past be forgotten. Thou shalt be reinstated in all knightly honour, and shall prove thy faith to the earl thy lord, by defending his lady in his absence.'

She held out her white jewelled hand to the gaunt, unkempt prisoner, looking in his face with a persuasive witchery that might have tempted a man to leave a palace for a dungeon. But De Sourdeval kept back his meagre, unwashed hand.

'Noble countess,' he exclaimed, with a long sobbing sigh, that showed how great the effort was to speak words that might close for ever his half-opened prison door, 'against whom am I to defend thee? Am I to fight men who are faithful to their knightly vows, by the side of traitors who have broken troth?'

'My son! my son!' interposed Father Pierre anxiously. The knight's bold words brought home the unvarnished truth of the situation with a startling clearness, which his own dreamy nature had enabled him to shirk facing hitherto.

Emma proved cowardly; she evaded a direct answer, and sheltered herself behind the privileges of her sex.

'Surely thy vow of chivalry binds thee to succour ladies in danger? We are in danger, myself and my ladies. Eadgyth of Norwich,'—she paused and looked in his face. De Sourdeval made a gesture of distress,—'Dame Amicia, whose age and infirmity should nerve the arm of a brave young knight and all our band, need the help of every stalwart friend who can be found. Still further, Sir Aimand, famine is our most dread foe,' she added, half smiling at the inhospitable thought. 'We can ill support idle mouths in Blancheflour.'

'Let me then starve, dear lady,' replied De Sourdeval in a low voice of desperate earnest, and avoiding her too persuasive eyes. 'I cannot lift my hand against my heart's witness to the right.'

'Fight not then, noble Sir Aimand!' exclaimed the countess, deeply moved. 'Only pass thy knightly pledge not to betray us to the foe, or to struggle to escape, and thou shalt be free! Nay, if we make a prisoner we will honourably exchange thee!'

'Not even that can I do, noble countess,' said Sir Aimand with unwavering firmness. 'I cannot pledge myself not to help the right.'

'Nay then, thou art obstinate!' cried Emma, stamping on the stones with one of the gold-embroidered slippers which Father Pierre had observed to be ill suited to dungeon floors, and turning away.

Sir Aimand bowed his head in silence, and made no effort to recall her, as she swept towards the door, though his trembling lips and clenched fingers showed the fierceness of the struggle he was making.

But Emma paused before she reached the door. 'Thou art too proud, Sir Knight,' she said coldly. 'But few can rival the Fitzosberns in that quality, and I also have my pride. I scorn to make conditions with a man circumstanced as thou art. Abuse my generosity if thou list. Thou art free!'

'Mary Mother in heaven bless thee for thy goodness, noble countess!' cried De Sourdeval, raising his head with a start of joy. 'Yet methinks I am scarce free yet!' He lifted his shackled limbs, and made the heavy irons clang upon the floor.

'Ah, good St. Nicholas, no!' cried Emma, with a fresh shock, as she realised what sufferings the prisoner must have undergone. 'But thou shalt be free before the sun is in the sky.'

'Noble countess,' interrupted a harsh voice behind her, 'what means thy presence in this cell at such an hour? By the Rood! thou dost great honour to the would-be murderer of thy husband.'

'Liar!' hissed the prisoner between his set teeth.

Emma turned with a start to face Sir Alain de Gourin, his cheeks purple with passion, and his quivering hand on the hilt of his *miséricorde*. The countess thought it politic to ignore his speech, although every word had reached her ears.

'Sir Alain!' she exclaimed, simulating pleasure at his appearance. 'Thy coming is most opportune. I was about to send a messenger to thee. Give orders forthwith that the irons be struck from the limbs of this worthy knight without delay. He hath been shrewdly misunderstood, and my will is that he be set free!'

She looked the mercenary hardily in the face as she gave him her command, and the villain quailed. He saw that he had come too late to prevent her from hearing Sir Aimand's statement of the case.

He accepted the oblivion in which she had buried his first insulting speech, and took an entirely different tone. 'Thy will is law, noble countess,' he said obsequiously, and with a low bow.

Emma did not retire to rest until she knew that the knight was comfortably lodged in the state apartments of the castle.

The Breton had been completely taken by surprise. He had imposed upon the earl with a story which the latter, in the excitement attendant upon his ambitious enterprise, had neglected to verify, and it had never entered his head that the countess would trouble herself about the matter. He supposed that the earl himself had at least spoken to her of Sir Aimand as a culprit, and that she was entirely ignorant of his presence as a prisoner in the castle; as she had been, until the strange impulse which came to her to have a mass said for him, caused her to name him to the chaplain.

Even in case of her finding the matter out and wishing to probe it, he had an ingenious story ready, wherewith to put her off the scent.

But the suddenness with which she had taken matters into her own hands, and had visited the prisoner and heard *his* version of the facts, quite overcame the somewhat clumsy wit of the Breton.

His first impulse, as usual, had been to bluster, but the firmness with which the countess confronted him had fairly cowed him for the moment, as he knew that he would have to justify himself, and to eat a good many of his words before Sir Hoël and the Norman knights of the garrison, to whom he had accounted for De Sourdeval's absence by representing that he had been sent on an embassy by the earl.

Many were the curses that he inwardly showered on the devoted head of Father Pierre, to whom he attributed the discovery of his schemes, and he also reviled himself for having forgotten him as a possible channel of communication between the prisoner and the countess.

His wits had not been the brighter for the hour at which Emma had happened on her inopportune discovery, for he had been indulging freely in his favourite spiced hippocras during the evening, and therefore it seemed best to his clumsy cunning to offer no further open opposition to the countess, and to carry out her orders himself, thus gaining time to concoct plausible excuses before Sir Hoël should know of the affair.

Emma also kept her own counsel, and did not say a

word even to Eadgyth, when the Saxon maiden, who slept in her chamber, came to help her to unrobe.

When Eadgyth ventured a question as to what had detained her to such a late hour, the countess smiled and kissed her.

'Thou shalt know all in good time, dear donzelle,' she answered. 'Ask me not to-night.'

CHAPTER XX.

À OUTRANCE.

THE morning came, and with it cares more important than the fate of the poor Knight of Sourdeval.

Before the dew was off the meadows, the shrill trumpets of the besiegers were heard at the barbican, demanding a parley, and calling for admittance in the name of the king.

The countess, holding counsel with Sir Hoël de St. Brice and Sir Alain de Gourin, and other of the knights of the garrison, replied that she would accede to the parley, and receive the messenger in person; and, accordingly, the messenger was blindfolded, admitted within the castle, and conducted to the council-chamber in the great tower.

The knight who bore the message of the king's lieutenants was sheathed in complete armour, and exceedingly stately in his mien and figure, being tall and of great personal strength. He was no other than Robert Malet, whose father, the loved and honoured William Malet, had been in bodily prowess second to none but the Conqueror himself of those who fought on the Norman side at Hastings.

As he entered the room, the rebel knights instinctively straightened themselves, and assumed such dignity of bearing as they were capable of showing; but none bore comparison with him save Leofric Ealdredsson, the stalwart Anglo-Dane, who had never bent the knee to the Norman Conqueror, and who now stood at the right hand of the countess, with the lightnings of a noble defiance gleaming in his blue eyes.

Yet Malet himself was to become a rebel before his death. When the silken kerchief with which his eyes had been covered was removed, he gazed proudly round the assembly, and bowed his tall head to the countess alone.

'In the name of William the Conqueror, King of England and Duke of Normandy,' he said in a commanding voice, 'I call upon Ralph de Guader and Montfort, heretofore Earl of East Anglia, but deprived of his earldom for that he has wrongfully taken arms against his suzerain and liege lord; and I demand that he instantly surrenders this castle, which he holds only as the Constable of the king. I demand that entrance into the said castle be at once given to the troops of his Grace the king, and that he thereby refrain from adding still further to his guilt, by contumaciously retaining it.'

'The Earl of East Anglia hath taken ship from this country, and hath devolved the duties of Castellan upon me, his countess,' replied Emma calmly.

'In that case, noble lady,—I cannot style thee countess,

for thou hast no longer right to the title,—I call upon thee, as Castellan of this castle of Blaunchefiour, to surrender it to the lieutenants of thy liege and kinsman, William of Normandy,' answered the young knight, fixing his keen blue eyes upon Emma's fair face, whose features, worn by the anxiety she had undergone, were pathetic in their pallor, and moved his heart to pity. 'I may well suppose,' he continued boldly, 'that in so doing thou wilt with pleasure disburden thy slender shoulders of so heavy and unwomanly a burden.'

Emma drew herself up with a slight gesture of disdain for such misbestowed sympathy. The knight responded by adding hastily, 'Moreover, I would appeal to thy gentleness and natural instincts of mercy to prevent the useless shedding of blood which the holding of this castle must cause, by prolonging a struggle which can only end one way.'

Emma's delicate nostrils quivered, and the fine firm lips set fiercely.

'The Countess of East Anglia desires to know the terms on which she is asked to yield up her faithful garrison to the tender mercies of the men who mutilated Stephen le Hareau,' she said, still calmly, but with flashing eyes, and due emphasis on her title. 'The race is not always to the swift, nor the battle to the strong, and methinks her gentleness and love of mercy are more nearly concerned in preventing her faithful defenders from encountering such a fate as his.'

'To the Castellan of Blaunchefiour I reply, that the

surrender must be without conditions,' answered the knight.

'In that case,' answered Emma, 'the Countess of East Anglia replies, that her garrison will win their own terms by their swords.'

Leofric Ealdredsson burst out with a loud 'Ahoi!' in the exuberance of his approbation, and clashed his heavy axe upon the floor, his many bracelets jingling like small bells. 'Well said!' exclaimed the venerable Sir Hoël de St. Brice, looking at the young countess with an expression of reverent affection, and from one and all the representatives of the garrison who stood around her chair broke various expressions of approval.

The countess turned to her knights with sparkling eyes. 'I have ye with me, then, in this reply, fair sirs?' she asked, and the tumult of assent with which they answered hindered Robert Malet, for some moments, from further speech.

In truth the enthusiasm was contagious, and the royal envoy's own eyes flashed. The chivalrous spirit of Fitzosbern's daughter jumped well with his humour. He had been a sorry Norman else; no true heritor of the wild sea-kings. It cost him some effort to resist his impulse to join in the applause, but he controlled himself, and said gravely, 'I pray thee, noble lady, to consider well before coming to so direful a decision; involving, as it doth, no less an issue than the adding of high treason on thine own part to the heavy guilt of the man thou hast wedded against the express mandate of thy suzerain. The daughter of William Fitzosbern should be slow to draw the sword against William of Normandy.'

'The decision is final, Sir Knight,' replied Emma curtly; thinking to herself that William of Normandy had not scrupled to insult the son and daughter of William Fitzosbern. She added to those in attendance, 'Let this brave gentleman be reconducted to the gate without delay.'

The envoy bowed in silence, and, allowing the silken kerchief to be again bound over his eyes, he marched with stately grace from the apartment.

So Emma de Guader cast down her gauntlet beside that of her husband, and dared the power of her great cousin.

Before the sun was midway in the heavens, a fierce struggle had begun between the besiegers and the besieged for possession of the barbican. This was not a strong construction of masonry as in the Norman castles of the twelfth century, but a deep and wide fosse or moat, with a high vallum strengthened with stout palisading on its inner side, of a semicircular or horse-shoe form, the horns nearly touching the present ditch. The causeway that passed between the horns and the present ditch, by which access was given to the castle, was amply protected by the towers of the gate-house and the walls of the castle itself, from whence arrows and quarrels would easily reach assailants. The similar fosse and palisaded vallum surrounding the castle meadow afforded additional protection to the eastern extremity of the causeway; the portion of the semicircle to the south-west being most open to attack.

Spearmen and javelin-throwers lined the palisades, and from their cover repelled the onslaught of the assaulting men-at-arms, who had further to withstand a whizzing shower of arrows from bowmen hiding in the wooden stalls of the market.

The king's men were endeavouring to throw a wooden bridge across the ditch. One end was furnished with wheels, the other with huge grappling-irons, which they strove to make fast in the vallum.

Watching them stood Leofric Ealdredsson, who, on the night before, when Sir Alain de Gourin had been sneering at the primitive Saxon earthworks, had said, with a laugh and a fierce gleam in his eyes, 'Let me defend them; I am used to the rude English fashions.' A band of his terrible house-carles, armed with their great battle-axes, and long of hair and large of limb, waited his orders with the air of bloodhounds in a leash straining at their collars.

From a loophole on the southern side of the keep, lighting the gallery which runs within the walls on a level with the great entrance, the countess and her bower-maiden Eadgyth watched the strife.

Eadgyth had been present in the council-chamber during the audience of Robert Malet. 'Thou wast grand, Emma,' she was saying to her lady and friend. 'Thou wast so strong and courageous, while, to say sooth, my own heart was beating like an armourer's hammer.'

'Thou art a strange child, my Eadgyth,' said Emma

affectionately, well pleased with the admission of the English maiden.

A wilder shout from the besiegers than any preceding broke their converse, and for some moments each watched the progress of the fight in breathless silence.

For the assailants had established their bridge against the vallum, and over it the attacking knights charged in a body, led by Robert Malet in person, his high crest topping them all, and by sheer weight of horse and harness they drave down the barricades and pressed in, hewing in sunder all before them.

Eadgyth gave a shrill scream and threw her arms wildly round the countess, who stood motionless, with eyes dilated and heaving breast.

Then rang out the wild Norse war-cry, 'Ahoi! ahoi!' And Leofric and his fierce carles sprang forward like tigers; and the flash and crash of their great axes smote eye and ear, while more than one knightly saddle was emptied, more than one riderless destrier ran neighing around the enclosure; more than one mailed warrior, impervious to arrows and quarrels, was cloven through his helm and lay lifeless on the ground.

The Anglo-Danes laughed in their yellow beards, and vigorously improved their advantage, so that in a few moments the knights were forced back beyond the line of the barricades, some getting back across the bridge, some falling into the water.

'See, foolish child! thy cousin has driven them back!' cried Emma. For Leofric was akin to Harold on the mother's side, and so akin to Eadgyth. She stroked the cheek of the frightened girl as a mother who comforts an infant. 'And had he not, there are stout walls and strong arms betwixt them and thee.'

'I know it! I know it! But it is all so terrible! I have not thy nerves of steel! Oh, Emma, in pity watch no longer! I cannot bear it!'

'Faint heart!' cried Emma lovingly. 'The clash of arms doth but spur my courage. I have always loved it from my cradle. Methinks I had made a doughty knight! It is not danger that quells me.'

Her face grew sad, for the bitter pang of an uneasy conscience gnawed her soul. Danger did not quell her, but her doubting heart tormented her.

Let me then starve, dear lady; I cannot lift my hand against my heart's witness to the right.

The sentence sprang into her mind and seemed to glow before her eyes as if it had been seared upon her brain with red-hot irons.

She drew her breath with a long shuddering sigh. In the rapid crowding of events that morning, the man who had spoken it in such despairing earnest had been forgotten, though she had thought of nothing else through the long watches of the night.

She turned to Eadgyth, and bade her go to the chapel, and offer prayers for the earl, and the garrison, and the souls of the fallen. 'Thou wilt feel safe within the holy precincts,' she said; 'and Dame Amicia shall attend me. She is short of sight, and the shouts of yonder madmen will scarce penetrate her ears; she will prove more courageous than art thou.'

When the aged lady-in-waiting came to her, in obedience to the message Eadgyth had conveyed, the countess left the loophole through which so stirring a drama was visible, and advanced to meet her. 'I need the support of thy reverend presence, dear dame,' she said, and told her how she had found one of her lord's knights imprisoned, as she believed, on a misunderstanding, and that she wished to question him again, having taken it upon her to free him.

The old lady could hear each syllable of Emma's clear, soft voice, though she was untroubled by the shouts of the combatants below, and she nodded her stately head with its crown of snow-white hair, tastefully draped with a broidered veil of Cyprian crape.

'A good lad, a good lad, and ever courteous,' answered Dame Amicia. 'Thou dost well to probe the matter. I thought he had gone to Bretagne.'

'It seems he was in durance in this castle,' said Emma. 'But we knew it not; or, if my lord knew it, he had no time to sift the charges against him. Methinks, if he have somewhat erred, he has been punished enough, and I may grant him pardon.'

'Ay; if we forgive not the trespasses of others, how can we pray with a clean heart that our own may be forgiven?' replied the old lady, nodding again. 'We must practise forgiveness, or our paternosters are but a mockery.'

No further words were spoken till they reached the apartment to which, according to the orders of the countess, Sir Aimand had been conveyed.

De Gourin had taken the precaution to place a stout warder at the door, who announced the visit of the countess to the knight.

When Emma entered the chamber, Sir Aimand threw himself on his knee before her, with an expression of deep homage, and bowed to her and to her venerable attendant.

'Noble countess,' he exclaimed, 'I scarce know how to form my gratitude in words!'

Emma was freshly shocked when she saw his face and form. Shaven and close-clipped as became a Norman knight, and clad in tunic and hose, the ravages of two months of misery were but the more conspicuous, as they owed no adventitious aid to wild elf-locks and shaggy beard. His cheeks were sunken, and his eyes unnaturally bright with fever, and the bones of his thin hands and limbs were pitiful to see. His voice also was hoarse and hollow. Emma felt that the revelations of the morning moved her more, not less, than the doleful horrors of the preceding night.

'I fear me thou hast greatly suffered,' she said involuntarily. 'Rise, Sir Aimand, and be seated; thou art not fit to stand.'

And Sir Aimand was forced to obey her, for, as he rose to his feet, he tottered and clutched at a stool for support, and Emma recalled some fears that had crossed her mind during the night, with pathetic amusement, for she had been haunted with the idea that she had perhaps let loose a very dangerous champion in the castle. The poor knight looked little able to fight either for her cause or against it.

'I had come hither to question thee more closely as to the circumstances of thy imprisonment,' the countess said, 'and to see if thy proud spirit be at all softened by my bounty, but methinks the best thing I can do is to send thee a good leech.'

'Noble countess, thy generosity hath not left me unmoved,' said Sir Aimand eagerly. 'I give thee my parole, neither to attempt escape, nor in any way to communicate with, aid, or abet the besiegers, if indeed thou wilt be gracious enough to accept it so ungraciously and tardily given.'

'I will accept it,' replied the countess, with a gratified smile; and Dame Amicia smiled also, seeing that her lady was well pleased, although her deafness prevented her from knowing very clearly her reasons for satisfaction.

The countess had felt that the old dame's infirmity might be convenient, for the chief object of her visit was to question the knight more closely regarding the circumstances of his imprisonment, and she cared not to trust his indictment of Sir Alain to any of her gossip-loving ladies.

'I would that Sir Alain bore not so important a position in the garrison,' she said, after listening again to De Sourdeval's story. 'The Bretons make the most part of our strength, and, save one or two, who are vassals to my lord, he hath them all under his command.'

'Lady,' answered De Sourdeval, 'strive not to see me righted to the detriment of thy welfare. It may well be that De Gourin will serve thee faithfully, though he satisfied a private vengeance against me. Let him not know that I accuse him; say only that thou dost grant me pardon. But be on thy guard against him.'

'It must be so,' answered the countess, '*for the present.*'

So saying, she took her leave, the knight following her with grateful eyes.

When Emma regained her bower, she summoned Eadgyth to her.

'I have news to comfort thy courage,' she said. 'A doughty champion is in the castle. Does not thy heart tell thee his name?'

Eadgyth opened her blue eyes in vague surprise, then cried, with a start of joy,—

'Ah, Emma, dear Emma! hath the earl so soon returned?'

'Fie, maiden! wouldst make me jealous? Doth *thy heart* suggest the name of my lord?'

'What meanest thou, Emma? Jest not, I pray thee. These days are too terrible for jesting,' said Eadgyth, with distressed mien and paling cheeks.

Emma took both her slender wrists in hers and looked lovingly in her face. 'Nay, we must jest to keep our blood from curdling, Eadgyth. But I will not tease thee. Sweet, 'tis Sir Aimand de Sourdeval of whom I speak.'

Eadgyth said nothing, but met Emma's gaze with eyes in which joy and surprise, and doubt of herself that was almost terror, were struggling for mastery.

Emma drew her gently upon the seat beside her. 'Surely thou art glad to know that he is safe, if thou joyest not that he is near?'

'Ah yes! I am glad—glad indeed of his safety!' replied Eadgyth in a low, thrilling voice, and her hand sought the bracelet which she wore as ever.

'And not of his nearness?'

'I know not! I know not! It means but fresh struggle and misery!' The tears rolled down her cheeks.

'Why struggle, Eadgyth? Fate has united you when all pointed to separation. Eadgyth, he needs thee. I told thee sooth when I said he was in safety. But he has suffered much. He is ill. Be thou his leech. Dame Amicia will attend thee—her motherly heart warms towards the youth.'

'Ill?' Eadgyth looked in the countess's eyes with almost fierce questioning.

'Ill,' repeated Emma, smiling. 'Not dying; not in danger; I said "safe." It is a long story, Eadgyth, but I must tell it thee.'

Then she told the history we already know; and how, after Eadgyth's remark about him on the battlements, it had entered her heart to have a mass said for him; how it had led to his discovery, and how she had visited him in his dungeon.

When she came to that point, and narrated her visit, describing his sorrowful aspect with unconscious pathos, Eadgyth sprang up and clasped her hands above her head. 'Oh, the terrible injustice of it!' she groaned, and afterwards she paced backwards and forwards, unable to control her emotion.

'But thy hero was shrewdly saucy, Eadgyth. Woe-begone and desperate as he was,—I almost wish I had let thee see the figure he cut, with his unkempt beard and tangled locks, as long as those of thy Saxon champions,—natheless he would make no terms. I might free him, or leave him chained by the leg like a hobbled steed, as I found him. One might have thought he had passed a pleasant time down there in the dark. He would not even give me his parole not to help our besiegers if I gave him the chance.'

Eadgyth's eyes lighted up with a proud joy. 'That was noble,' she said under her breath.

Emma laughed. 'He had come to a better mind this morning,' she said; 'I found means whereby to tame his proud spirit.'

Eadgyth turned to her with a start, and wild visions of racks and thumbscrews, and other fashionable instruments of the time, passed through her mind. Her spirit was so torn with the terror of the day, and the excitement she had undergone, that she did not pause to consider probabilities. 'Emma! thou hadst not heart to crush one so unhappy?'

'I had!' said Emma.

Eadgyth's eyes looked dumb reproach more eloquent than words.

'Yes,' said Emma; 'I hold not the office of Castellan of Blauncheflour by halves! I made use of my power.'

'What didst thou do?' asked Eadgyth in a scarcely audible voice.

'I gave him his liberty without conditions, and had him lodged in one of the best apartments of the castle. *That* touched my knight's pride; he would not have me outdo him in generosity, so he capitulated this morning, and offered me his parole without further asking!' and the countess broke into a silvery peal of laughter.

'Oh, Emma, that was like thy dear self!' cried Eadgyth, running to the countess, throwing herself on her knees before her, and hiding her head in Emma's robes like a repentant child.

Emma kissed her. 'Now, maiden, thy part must be done. The knight has promised neither to help the enemy nor to attempt escape. Be it for thee to persuade him to buckle on his harness and fight for us. He can scarce see thy sweet face, and know thou art in danger, and not lift his hand to help thee!'

'*I* persuade him!—to break his knightly vows and fight against his lawful liege? Never!' cried Eadgyth, raising her head and throwing it back proudly. 'Strange,' she continued, more to herself than to the countess, indeed, scarce knowing that she spoke aloud, 'how thy haught courage and noble generosity are allied with so little sense of moral right!'

A flash of pain and some indignation crossed the countess's brow. 'I deny thy right to judge me,' she said coldly. 'There are some who strain after such high ideals, they fail to see the duties that lie near; gratitude, for instance, and the welfare of their friends!'

Eadgyth was silent, for she felt that Emma was unjust; she would have given her life to serve her, though she would not go a step against her conscience.

'Sir Aimand has suffered much,' said the countess gently, after a pause. 'He is out of health and out of hope. A little happiness would serve him in better stead than an armful of herbs and simples. Go to him, Eadgyth! Encourage his contumacy if thou wilt, but go to him.'

And Eadgyth went.

CHAPTER XXI.

THE ORDEAL BY FIRE.

At the close of the day the barbican still remained in the keeping of the besieged.

It had not been retained without the loss of many a stout soldier, and the spital was crowded with patients, who occupied all the healing talents of the countess and her ladies.

When Emma at last retired to her chamber, with her Saxon bower-maiden in attendance, she was so weary and worn with the excitement and strain of the day, that she threw herself upon the bed, without even taking off her jewels, and fell asleep almost immediately; while Eadgyth, after softly laying a warm coverlet over her, lay down beside her.

But not to sleep. Her brain was full of dire and disturbing images, and even the face of Sourdeval, which it had been so great a joy to her to behold once more, came to her as she had seen it, wan and melancholy, when he turned to her as she entered his apartment, before it flashed with brightness on recognising who had come to him. The change in him had shocked her, and in her nervous and depressed mood she thought of him as one whom death had marked for his own, and his image was but as a pale spectre, round which the manifold forms of wounded and dying and tortured men, whom she had beheld during the day, grouped as a central point.

Her ears were full of the wild shouts of the besiegers and the shrieks of the injured, the awful clash of seax on helm, and hurtle and whiz of arrows. Again and again she woke from a fitful doze, thinking to hear the thunder of charging knights and the fierce 'Aoi!' of Leofric Ealdredsson and his carles, as they leaped forth from the cover of the palisades upon the foe.

At last from such an awakening she sprang from the bed; better, she thought, to wake all night than suffer such awful dreams.

But the awakening did not silence the cries. They were no dreams, those screams of terror, those head-rending shrieks for help, they were dreadful realities; and, rushing to the window, she gazed out with a beating heart at the western sky, which flickered and flared with strange and ghostly gleams.

She ran back to the sleeping countess, and by the lurid light saw that she was smiling in her sleep.

'Wake! wake! Oh, Emma! dear countess! this is no night for sleep. Methinks the dawn is like to bring the last dread day! Alas! she sleeps like a young infant that knows not danger or woe. Wake, Emma! Thy life may hang on it!'

Then the countess, opening her eyes dreamily, murmured, 'Thou hast brought good succour, Ralph!' The next moment she started up. 'Mary Mother! what is it, child?'

'There is murder in the air, Emma! See, the very sky is full of tokens. Listen! listen! Oh, saints in heaven! how they scream!'

They did indeed! The countess sprang from the bed and rushed to the window also.

'They have fired the town!' she cried; 'they have fired the town!—the Saxon quarter! Sir Hoël said they would!'

'The Saxon quarter! Oh, my home, my home!' cried Eadgyth, and, pressing her hands to her ears in a vain effort to shut out the shrieks of the sufferers, she cowered, with closed eyes, upon the floor.

'Let us go to the great portal of the keep, whence we can see it,' said the countess.

'See it!' cried Eadgyth. 'Ah, Emma, no! I could not look! It would kill me.'

But Emma went forth boldly, intent to know if anything could be done to rescue the victims.

Norwich in those days was an open town. The walls and towers, of which portions still remain to gladden the eyes of archæologists, were not built till some fifty years later, so that it was not possible to defend the town itself. Moreover, although the earl had found supporters amongst the Saxon and Anglo-Danish inhabitants of the older quarters, numbering more than one relative of Harold Godwinsson, the majority of the Norman denizens of the New Burg around the Chapel-in-the-Field remained loyal to William, and were ready to give all help to the besiegers. For this reason was it that the western sky had but flickered with the reflections of flames. It was the Saxon quarter by the river, the wooden tenements in King Street, which provided fuel for the bonfire.

Looking east from the portal of the great tower, a grand and terrible spectacle confronted the beholders.

Crackling flames shot up against the dark midnight sky, dancing like living demons of fiery destruction, and sinking only to lick the doomed houses with their scorching tongues and spring up higher than ever. Every now and again some beam or stone would burst with a sharp report, throwing blazing fragments into the air; and the volumes of smoke rolled far into the night, lurid with the red glare of the flames. Moats and marshes and river gleamed and sparkled weirdly with the light of destruction, so that the ground was broken by inverted images of fiery tongues; and it seemed, indeed, as if the nether world—so ardently believed in by those who were watching as a material hell of fire and brimstone—had broken bounds, and was let loose to destroy the world.

But most awful was it to see the small black figures that every now and again raised wild arms against the flare of the fire; most awful was it to here the screams that every now and again rose above the dull roar and crackle and hiss of the destroying element.

When such figures were seen, and such sounds heard,

curses and execrations burst from the white lips of the soldiers who were crowding the eastern walls of Blaunchefour, and the knights who had assembled before the portal of the keep.

As the countess came down amongst them, she could not repress an exclamation of horror, for never in her life had she beheld anything so awful.

Sir Hoël de St. Brice came instantly to her side.

'Alas, dear lady! this is no scene for thee. Return to thy bower. There is no danger for the castle.'

'My place is here, Sir Hoël,' said Emma firmly. 'I am Castellan of this castle. The battle is not always to the strong. See, yonder flames hissing through the air are more terrible than a hundred mailed warriors! The flame of wit is given to woman as well as to man!'

'William's men are doing thee homage, noble countess,' said De Gourin, with a sneer. 'These are finer bonfires than the good people of Norwich lighted on the night of thy arrival in their town!'

Emma turned from him with a shudder of disgust.

'How hath this been accomplished, Sir Hoël?' she asked of the older knight. 'By what means hath the fire been enkindled?'

'The king's men are provided with mighty engines,' answered Sir Hoël. 'Never have I seen mangonel or balista that carried so far. They are throwing red-hot stones and balls of lead from them, and the old houses yonder have been so well dried by the sun of late, that they burn like tinder. See,' he added, pointing out some glowing stars in the south-east, which Emma had not before distinguished from the burning fragments tossed aloft by the action of the flame, 'their fiery hail continues even now. They have got possession of the Cyning Ford, and are flinging their missiles from across the river.'

'And are we to stand here and gape at them, and do nought to stop them?' demanded the countess eagerly. 'Good St. Nicholas! how the cattle bellow in the castle meadow! Are the poor beasts in danger?'

'The fire frightens them, and no wonder!' answered Sir Hoël. 'But they are in safety, unless, perhaps, some fragment, here and there, may be carried from the fire, and somewhat scorch their hides. As for thy former question, I see not that anything can be done. Having possession of the ford, I know not how we can dislodge them.'

'It would be but throwing away good lives to attempt it,' said De Gourin, who cared little whether a few Saxons more or less were burned on their own hearthstones.

'Eadgyth!' exclaimed the countess impetuously to her bower-maiden, who had followed her, notwithstanding her terror, 'hast thou not told me there was a way through the marshes, that Harold used against the Vikings?'

Eadgyth, with wild eyes and teeth chattering in the extremity of her horror, gazed at the countess as if her fear had taken away her reason.

The countess repeated her question, and Eadgyth, with an effort, forced herself to attend.

'Ay, that is so. My kinsman Leofric would be

familiar with it. He has fought every inch of this ground against the Danes under your lord!' she said.

'Where is this Leofric? Let him be summoned,' commanded the countess.

'He is yonder helping his countrymen to save their skins from the fire,' said Sir Alain contemptuously.

Again the countess commanded, 'Let him be summoned!'

And when, not long after, Leofric Ealdredsson stood before her, still breathing hard after his exertions, his face begrimed with dust and smoke, and the wild firelight gleaming on his torc and mail corselet and bracelets, she asked him if he knew of any way by which he could steal unperceived through the marshes, and take the artillerymen of the foe by surprise.

'By Asgaard! yes!' exclaimed Leofric, turning to De Gourin. 'And so I told this fair sir an hour ago, and offered to show him how he might take them in flank, and stuff their accursed red-hot balls down their own throats; or I would have taken a band under my own order, twenty of my house-carles, if he would add twenty stout men from the garrison. But he would hear none of it.'

'We shall be the safer that the buildings yonder are burned,' said De Gourin. 'Why throw away good lives to stop it?'

'Why was I not told of this suggestion?' asked Sir Hoël, frowning. 'Thou takest over much upon thyself, Sir Alain!'

'Grant me the men now, countess!' said Leofric eagerly.

'My lord owed his life to thee, Leofric Ealdredsson!' answered the countess. 'I know I may trust thee! Take thy stout carles, and twenty men beside.'

'Ahoi! By Freya! thou art a pearl among women!' cried the wild Leofric, who was much of a Viking himself.

'Ah, kinsman Leofric, leave those heathen names alone!' said Eadgyth. 'Thou hast a better symbol in the hilt of thy sword!'

But he had not stopped to listen to her. He had gone off to call his carles together, and to choose his twenty men from the garrison.

And some forty of them, for the most part Anglo-Danes or Saxons, left the castle a few minutes later, leaving by the western horn of the barbican, and making their way by the streets north of the castle, by Tombland, to the river; slipping along through the fire-lighted night with a panther-like trot on their silent shoes of untanned leather, their trusty seaxes in their right hands, and their round red shields on their left arms.

Arrived at the river, they possessed themselves of boats without particularly asking the leave of the owners, and crossed over to the marshes on the eastern bank, leaving a man in each boat to guard it. They crept through the rushes, as only men who had grown up amid the fens could have done, and fell upon the unsuspecting Normans like thunderbolts; knocked their balistas to fragments, served a good many of their men likewise, and returned as they came to the west bank of the river.

Then they added their strength to that of the townsfolk to fight the flames, and, by means of clearing large spaces to windward of the burning houses, stopped the fire from spreading its ravages indefinitely. But five less returned through the castle gate than had left it.

So went the first day and the first night of the siege.

When day broke, the attack on the barbican began again, and so it was for five days afterward; but at the end of the sixth the barricades were almost battered down, and strong bridges were established across the ditch, so that the defenders thought it wise to abandon it to the enemy, as scarcely worth the lives it would cost to maintain possession of it. But this meant no very great advantage to the besiegers.

They stood before the great gate of the castle, the actual entrance to which looked like a mere mouse-hole between the sheer strong walls of its two flanking towers. They well knew the make of such gateways: their folding-doors of solid oak, strengthened with bars and bolts of iron, and studded with huge nails to prevent the cutting out of a panel or staving in of the same; the strong portcullis behind them, a harrow-shaped iron grating, to be let up and down in a moment by means of pulleys from the inside; above the doors a row of chimney-like apertures, called machicolations, through which the defenders could pour scalding water, molten lead, or any other deadly matter, upon the devoted heads of the assaulting column, who were exposed also to a cross fire of quarrels, stones, and other missiles from the flanking towers.

Truly, to assault such a portal was no child's play, even with such aid as could be given by the rude artillery of the times: petronels and agerons for throwing stones and leaden pellets, catapultas for shooting arrows, and the trebuchettum, or warrewolf, specially designed for the smashing in of gates and walls; all these, and more of their kind, the king's men were well provided with.

Stout Earl Warrenne, and the astute Bishop of Coutances, and the accomplished lance, Robert Malet, held many a consultation as they rode round the invested fortress, and scanned it eagerly to see if haply they might discover some weak point which should give them advantage in the attack.

But they decided that they must become masters of the great gate, and so of the ditch, before they could make any assault on the castle itself.

A month had passed away before they were so masters; but being so, they had their opponents in a veritable trap. The besieged knew well that a harder struggle than ever lay before them in their awful isolation, cut off from communion with their fellow-creatures by a wall of human fury as effectually as if they had been wrecked on some desert island in that vast ocean of the west, the opposite shores of which were all unknown to them, though its great eastern rollers dashed in spray upon the Breton and Norman coasts.

Through all this weary time of fear and suspense, with its harassing duties and oppressive sorrows, the Countess Emma found comfort in two dumb friends: Oliver, the earl's Spanish destrier, who had been left in the fortress when De Guader embarked for Denmark; and the brave tassel-gentle, that had been Ralph's gift to her upon the day on which she had promised to share his fortunes, good or ill.

Oliver had been restored to his master, after he had been struck down by Odo's mace, by one of those strange accidents which seem to have the finger of fate in them. Some of the old thegn Ealdred's men had visited the battle-field several days after the fight, to see how the land lay and what the king's men were doing. They were attacked by a band of Norman soldiers, headed by a knight who was mounted on a splendid destrier. The animal was full of strength and courage, but the rider being, as they afterwards found, one Stephen Main-de-fer, a parvenu who had made his fortune out of the woes of England, like so many of his countrymen, and who had won his spurs without having learned to ride, instead of profiting by the noble booty that had fallen to his share, was brought to his ruin thereby; for the fiery barb, unused to such handling as he gave it, and doubtless wondering, like Johnny Gilpin's steed, 'what thing upon his back had got,' became unmanageable in the excitement of the fray, and threw his clumsy new master heavily to the earth. There he lay sprawling, as little versed in carrying his armour as in managing his horse, and Ealdred's men did not lose their opportunity of despatching him. After a short struggle, his followers beat their retreat, and the destrier fell into the hands of the Anglo-Danes, who took him back with them to their refuge in the Fens, where he was immediately recognised with much jubilation by Grillonne, and restored to his master.

So it came to pass that Ralph de Guader had been able to ride back into Blaucheflour on his trusty Oliver.

Since the earl had quitted the castle, Emma had visited the barb morning and night, and had taken him many a dainty wastel cake or sugary comfit such as horses love; and, stroking his satin neck with many an endearment, longed for the time when she should see his master on his back again. A time which would never come!

At such moments she would often have the tassel-gentle on her wrist, and the bird seemed almost human, so intelligent and tame was he.

She needed some comfort, for she had one great sorrow. The gentle and loving Dame Amicia de Reviers, who had watched over her from her cradle, was stricken down by paralysis, and a few days later died. It was really but the natural end of a long and happy life; but Emma, in the mood for self-torture, blamed herself for having dragged the aged dame into tumult and terror, and shed tears that were beyond the usual bitterness of grief. She was buried in the holy precincts of St. Martin at Bayle, which stood before the castle gate, the besiegers granting a truce for the occasion, with that chivalrous courtesy that was so oddly mixed with the ferocity of the times.

So the king's men and the earl's met in friendly sympathy one day, and prepared for bitter contest on the morrow, when the besiegers planned to make assault upon the walls themselves.

Within the castle all was bustle and business. Harness was mended and bullets were moulded, bows restrung and arrows feathered, axes and swords whirred on the grindstone, huge cauldrons were prepared wherein to heat water to pour upon besiegers' heads; and even the countess and her ladies helped to carry stones with their own fair hands, and pile them ready for the use of the slingers.

Meanwhile the swallows wheeled and twittered overhead as they wheel and twitter now; and down in the woods the merles and mavises sang on undisturbed by the tumult, while swans were marshalling green-grey cygnets across the pools in the marshes of the Cowholme.

CHAPTER XXII.

A SUBTERRANEAN CONFLICT.

THE besiegers on their part had not been idle. They had established quite a *menagery* of mechanical contrivances, rejoicing in the zoological names of tortoises, sows, and cats, to protect their approaches to the white walls of Blaunchefolur, and under cover of these they had cut a channel to the castle ditch and drained the water from it, so that it was as dry as at present, though, instead of growing fair greenery of bushes and flowers, it showed a bottom of parched, fœtid mud under the hot summer sun.

They had thrown up large mounds of earth at intervals around the ballium, and upon these had built up towers of wood overtopping the walls. These were furnished with drawbridges which could be let down at pleasure upon the merlons of the battlements, so to give ingress to their men-at-arms; their upper storeys serving to shelter archers and slingers, while from the lower, battering-rams were sturdily plied, and the warrewolves flung their stones and balls of lead.

These towers had cost them many good lives, for not one had been established without a fierce struggle. Sally after sally had been made from the castle, but, in the end, numbers prevailed, and at last their impertinent wooden crests were reared above the Caen stone of Blaunchefiour.

Those within were, however, more troubled by the mines which their assailants had run from the bottom of the moat beneath the foundations of the castle; for although these had been met by countermines, and many a furious combat had taken place in these uncanny lists, each mine meant a point to be guarded with jealous care, and was a source of weakness and anxiety; demanding exhausting sentry duty from the already overburdened garrison.

The countess found her office of Castellan no sinecure. The motley garrison were anything but homogeneous. All manner of petty jealousies, personal and national, raged among them. The Normans were jealous of the Bretons, and the Bretons blustered about independence, boasting that they were 'no man's men;' while the Saxons hated them both, and regarded their refinements as dandyisms and their courtesies as cant; and the Normans and the Bretons both looked down upon the Saxons as savages, and gibed at their priest-bestowed knighthood; so that, on the whole, they were as much inclined to fight against each other as against the king's forces outside the walls, and sometimes actually came to blows.

However, the countess set her woman's wit to weigh

these quarrelsome gentlemen against each other, and managed to do it, owing to the three-sidedness of the situation.

After all, their want of unity had its advantages, as they never 'went solid' in any direction, except under the self-evident necessity of defending their lives and the castle.

Still, at times, Emma grew very weary, and almost failed under the burden she had taken upon her slender shoulders, feeling terribly feeble and lonely and out of her depth.

Sir Hoël de St. Brice was her chiefest comfort and principal counsellor. The old knight had come to regard her with absolute veneration and the deepest affection, and in him she felt that she had a true and sincere friend.

His zeal for the earl's cause nearly equalled her own. To say that he would have given his life for it would express little, for all in the garrison were formally pledged to do that; but he had no other object in life.

Emma had sought the earliest opportunity to tell him the circumstances under which she had discovered the imprisonment of Sir Aimand de Sourdeval, and to repeat his account of the foul treatment he had met with from De Gourin.

'Unknightly!' he had said,—'from first to last unknightly. But what would you have? Can a man who sells his lance to the first bidder, without inquiry into the justice of his cause, be a true knight?' Altogether he gave evidence of shrewd indignation, but no keen surprise.

'I love not the mercenary,' he answered, 'and wish that he had not so high a command in the garrison. I know well that he had no great liking for the young Norman *prudhomme*, whose boyish enthusiasms were stronger than his prudence, and led him to throw taunts at Sir Alain's thick head, all the more galling that they were barbed with truth.'

But he agreed that, under the circumstances, it was best to let matters stand; De Gourin was evidently of the same opinion, and, save for a few veiled gibes at the magnanimity of the countess, made no reference to the freeing of the young knight.

Sir Aimand, for his part, had a dismal time of it, and almost wished himself back in his dungeon, securely chained by the leg.

As soon as his health began to mend, which was speedily enough, under the combined influences of good food, good air, and the sight of his lady's face, Eadgyth withdrew that last and sweetest influence.

For she was determined by no word or look of hers to tempt him to be untrue to his high standard of honour, and she felt on her own part more Saxon than ever, and judged the gulf between them impassable, save by the wreckage of the ideals of both; and therefore she deemed that to bestow her company upon him would be but cruel kindness.

So the poor knight mooned about in solitary meditation, and his returning strength made inaction a veritable purgatory to him. To hear blows going, and have no hand in giving or taking them, was truly about the cruellest torture that could have been invented for one of his order and temper in those days when Christians still thirsted for the Valhalla of the old Norsemen, wherein the immortal heroes were healed of their wounds at night that they might slay each other over again in the morning.

Again and again he was on the point of throwing his scruples to the wind, and buckling on sword and helm in defence of the generous dame who had given him his freedom so unconditionally. Again and again he restrained himself, and did penance by fasting and prayer, wishing the while that she had left him in durance, so he had escaped such doubting and searching of heart.

Nor did he find much peace in Hall. Norman, Breton, and Saxon were all against him. Gibes and jeers were his portion. They called him the 'ladies' tame tiercel,' the 'gamecock without spurs,' the 'dancing bear,' and a hundred other names suggestive of carpet-knight-errantry. Then his fists would ball and his clear-cut, high-bred face grow white with anger, though he never made reply, as he felt it an evident point of honour that, being a prisoner on parole, he might neither risk his own person, which carried value for ransom, nor seek to injure any of the garrison.

But on the eve of the assault, when the countess was holding council with Sir Hoël de St. Brice, attended only by Eadgyth, the young Norman prayed audience of her, and on its being granted strode into the chamber with curiously flashing eyes.

'I beseech thee, noble Emma, to furnish me with an helm and an hauberk, and the sharpest sword thou canst spare out of thine armoury, and I will put them to a good use in thy service,' he said, with speech that was rather too hasty to be clear.

'Hast found thy senses at last, brave sir?' demanded Sir Hoël, smiling indulgently, for he had always liked the young knight.

But Eadgyth noticed his flushed cheek and excited mien with a chill dread at her heart. Was he about to be false to the noble ideals for which he had endured so much, or—saints in Heaven forfend!—did his exaggerated love to his suzerain lead him to contemplate a baser falseness still, and so confuse his mind that he should fancy it would be virtue to betray the castle? Her cousin Leofric had said more than once, that only a woman playing Castellan would be so imprudent as to allow one holding so invidious a position as did De Sourdeval, to be free of the castle and aware of all its secrets; and though at the time she had cried shame on his mean suspicions, the words had rested in her mind with the burr-like persistency characteristic of such suggestions of evil.

The countess, however, looked at him with her frank glad eyes, and rejoiced, for she had always hoped that the time would come when he would repay her generosity with complete allegiance, and she was about to reply unconditionally, 'Ay, that will I.'

But before she could speak, Sir Aimand continued, 'I ask thee more. I want not only arms for myself, but twenty men to back me.'

Sir Hoël looked grave, and lifted his bushy white eyebrows high in astonishment.

'Pick men of whose fidelity you are assured,' Sir Aimand cried. 'Let Leofric Ealdredsson go with me. Thou knowest he has no liking for me, and is in no way in collusion with me, sith there is race hatred between us and rivalry in love.'

'Rivalry in love!' exclaimed Emma, turning quickly to Eadgyth, and the cheeks of the Saxon maiden burned scarlet under her gaze, but not more redly than those of the knight, who had exposed his jealousy unawares.

'I should not have said rivalry,' he amended hastily, 'sith I have no claim.'

Eadgyth was in a difficult position. If she made the protest her heart urged, that Leofric was her cousin and nothing more, and never could be more, she would give Sir Aimand an encouragement which was cruel. If she did not make it, she let that be believed which she imagined had no foundation in fact.

Emma saved her from need of reply.

'Upon the honour of Leofric Ealdredsson I can rely,' she said, 'whether he have cause to like or mislike thy person, fair knight. What more hast thou to ask?'

'That he, with twenty of his stout Anglo-Danes, may be put under my guidance, with instructions to hew me in sunder if I in any way show token of treachery. I can serve thee best if none know of this matter, nor the end in view, save Leofric alone. But this I will say in explanation, there is a traitor in thy camp, and I would fain foil him. I cannot fight under thy banner, noble countess, but it accords with my vow of chivalry to save thee from foul betrayal.'

'Let Leofric Ealdredsson be summoned, Sir Hoël,' said the countess.

And in the end De Sourdeval obtained his boon.

Knowing what had been granted to the Norman, and that Leofric and his stout carles would not have accepted service under him unless with some prospect of stiff work to follow, Sir Hoël was somewhat surprised to see the Anglo-Danes linger later than usual over the wassail bowl in Hall that even, seeing too that on the morrow it was certain that shrewd blows would be going, and all heads wanted clear.

Sir Alain de Gourin thought fit to rebuke them. 'For as thick skulls as your battle-axes there may boast, Childe Leofric,' he said, 'they had best have wakeful wits under them by dawn.' And he set a worthy example by leaving the revel.

His most important followers slipped after, first one and then another, but still the Vikings drank on, and Sir Hoël began to have queer doubts of the wisdom of granting the whimsical De Sourdeval control over such a crew, and determined to watch them out.

Presently in came Sir Aimand, wrapped in a long cloak, with a hood over his head, and whispered to Leofric,—

"The big rat was gone into the hole!"

'The big rat has gone into his hole.'

And Leofric wagged his yellow beard approvingly, and rose up, tall and strong, with a rattle of mail and bracelets, and took his great two-handed axe and strode with De Sourdeval out of the hall; and Sir Hoël saw that under De Sourdeval's cloak was a mail hauberk and steel headpiece.

Then one after another the Anglo-Danes picked themselves out of the rushes, whither they had subsided to save the trouble of falling, and went out also, with strange steadiness for tipsy men.

And De Sourdeval led Leofric to a mine that had been run to meet one dug by the enemy on the north-west side of the castle, near the chiefest of the wall towers, and two dozen good men and true were at their back.

They went down into the darkness, dimly lighted with rude lanterns, and they found the watch were one and all Breton mercenaries. These one after another they stealthily seized, gagged before they could make outcry, bound, and carried up into the outer air, setting their own men in their stead. Then they crouched down and waited at the extremity of the mine, where it met the Norman parallels.

And after a while they heard sounds approaching. The clink and chink of weapons and mail and the muffled beat of creeping footsteps.

'Remember—Sir Alain to me,' hissed De Sourdeval in a hoarse whisper,—'Sir Alain and his traitors. I strike no blow against the king's true men.'

'By Odin! all's fish that comes to my net. Breton or Norman, what have they to do in Harold's Norwich?' returned Leofric savagely. 'But I'll not poach on thy manors. Sir Alain to thee.'

Two minutes later, the Breton mercenary, leading the foe with whom he had traitorously compounded to save his own skin, was startled to meet the fierce white face of Sir Aimand instead of the friendly countenance of one of his own ruffians.

'Ha! caught in thine own burrow, despicable rat!' shouted the Norman, and the next moment they were hewing at each other with the fury of a long hatred.

De Gourin had the disadvantage of surprise, and he lost his head and struck wildly. De Sourdeval got within his guard, and the next moment the Breton rolled heavily to earth.

Over his dead body waged a fierce battle, but it was not maintained for long. The besiegers, expecting to be led straight into the heart of the castle, were not prepared for the determined resistance they met with thus at the outset, and credited the Bretons with decoying them into a trap. The latter were therefore the chief combatants, for their case was desperate. They were between two foes, and scarce one of them escaped alive; nor did Sir Aimand find any great difficulty in keeping his vow to deal with them alone.

So Sir Aimand slew his enemy in the bowels of the earth; the man through whose treachery he had been forced to live for so many long days as deeply buried from the free air and cheerful light of day. Yet the personal quarrel was merged in a greater cause, and in revenging his own wrong he was saving the brave Countess Emma and the lady of his love, with all the womanhood in the castle, from the horrors of a sudden sack.

When the garrison heard of this feat which 'the ladies' tame tiercel' and 'the Danish wolf' had carried through between them, the enthusiasm knew no bounds, and the curses and maledictions that were poured on the senseless head of the treacherous Breton knew no bounds either, till Sir Aimand said,—

'The greater his sins, the greater need we pray for him,' and ordered masses for the dead man's soul at his own expense, so putting bitter tongues to shame.

The countess came down into the great hall and met the heroes of the hour with shining eyes and heartfelt thanks; but, to say truth, they were both more anxious for kind glances and sweet praise from her Saxon bower-maiden, and their eyes went round the hall in search of her. But she was not there; she had slipped away to ask the chaplain to set her penances for having entertained suspicions of an innocent person.

Perhaps none felt deeper indignation against the foiled traitor than those of the Breton mercenaries whom he had not included in his band of deserters. If his plot had been successful, they would probably have suffered most of all in the garrison, for mercenaries are rolling stones who make enemies wherever they go, and whose services being paid for in cash and plunder, win no gratitude even from those they defend. They knew well that if the besiegers got the upper hand, it would go hard with them.

Therefore they stood aghast when they heard of the treachery of their leader and of those of their comrades who had been with him, feeling that treachery to be in a manner twofold towards themselves. They gathered round De Sourdeval asking eager questions.

'How had he discovered the plot? Had he known it long? What proofs had he to support his assertion?'

To which he made reply that he had not known it long, only an hour or two before his counterplot was framed and executed, and it had come to his knowledge in this wise. A certain soldier in De Gourin's band had been Sir Aimand's warder during his imprisonment in the dungeons of the castle, and it seemed that the man had conceived a great affection for him. Being one of the sentries whose duty it was to guard the mine, he had received instructions from De Gourin to admit the king's troops, and was perforce made privy to the nefarious designs of the leader.

Believing De Sourdeval to be hostile to the garrison, and wishing to do him a good turn, he had told him of the scheme on hand, and had undertaken to procure a disguise for him, so that he might pass out amid De Gourin's band. The man would tell them the story himself; he now lay bound in the courtyard of the castle with the rest of the Breton sentries.

The next day Sir Aimand returned to the countess the arms with which she had provided him from the castle armoury, holding fast to his resolution not to bear them against the king's forces.

CHAPTER XXIII.

HOW OLIVER DIED.

But there was little time for asking questions and making inquiries, or for celebrating the exploits of heroes, Norman or Anglo-Dane.

The morning light was creeping up the east, and the chirp and twitter of wakening sparrows was the signal for the battering-rams and pickers to commence their ominous clatter.

The attack was made at several points simultaneously; and all the strength of the garrison, weakened as it was by the losses of a month of strife, was needed on the walls.

From every loophole the archers and slingers aimed whizzing arrows and hurtling stones upon the columns of the assailants, and from between the merlons great sacks of wool and horsehair were suspended to protect the walls from the battering-rams, while huge logs of timber were hurled upon the pickers. Molten lead and boiling water was poured down upon the heads of the besiegers like a veritable hell-rain.

But for all their efforts the assault made progress. In two distinct places the walls were so battered that horsemen could have ridden through the breach.

The garrison did their best to throw up earthworks inside the broken walls, and fought valiantly to defend them, sallying forth at intervals with the impetus of men who felt their case desperate.

But the besiegers fought with fury also. They were weary of dallying week after week before the walls of a castle which was under the command of a woman, and were determined to get the mastery, if energy and valour could accomplish it.

The countess, mounting the battlements of the keep one day, that she might see for herself the working of the mighty engines which were plied against her stronghold, had seen Earl William de Warrenne and Robert Malet standing together in one of the wooden towers already described. As she bent forward to look below, a stone from a petronel struck the wall not far beneath her, and the fragments and dust flew into her face and upon the wall on which her hand had rested.

Her noble adversaries, who were watching her, could not repress an exclamation of dismay at this; but Emma, without blenching, took her kerchief from her gipsire and nonchalantly dusted the walls with it.

'You do well to fight a housewife with dust, fair sirs!' she cried, sending a mocking peal of silvery laughter to follow her words.

Such taunts were not unheeded or forgiven. They helped to nerve the leaders who led the attack; and they were men who were accustomed to lead their men to victory. On this day the chequered shield of Earl Warrenne pressed forward as if it were possessed of magic powers, which made it proof against every blow, and wherever it went it had eager followers; while young Robert Malet showed himself the worthy son of his great father. As for the Bishop of Coutances, he contented himself with blessing the column before it started, and reminding the soldiers that the brother of the Countess Emma was an excommunicated man.

Earl Warrenne strained every nerve to make the assault a success. He led his men in person to the breach; and his strong voice dominated the tumult with trumpet tones, as he cried, 'Dex aie! For William the Norman!'

'A Warrenne! a Warrenne!' responded his men, as they struggled forward over the counter-scarp, under a pelting hail of arrows and javelins from the battlements.

Within the breach stood Leofric Ealdredsson, holding his great double-edged axe in his hand, with his men arranged in a Saxon wedge, the front row kneeling, with shield touching shield, and a forest of spears bristling out above them, like the spines of a porcupine. They answered the Norman battle-cry with a wild shout that made the walls ring again, and echoed up the sides of the keep behind them, 'Ahoi! ahoi! A Guader! a Guader!' otherwise they were motionless as statues.

A Warrenne! A Warrenne! For William the Norman!

Earl Warrenne had won experience of that formation at Hastings, and he well knew how invulnerable it was, and how the terrible seaxes could crash through helm and hauberk. He knew how stratagem alone had prevailed over it; how pretended flight had cheated the Saxons into pursuit, and how they had so foregone their advantage; and he determined to employ the same device again.

So he leapt his horse in over the shattered wall, and his men-at-arms followed him, but spent their force in vain on the living rampart before them; more than one reeled with cleft helmet from the saddle, and Warrenne himself wavered and turned.

Seeing their leader give way, the band broke and pressed tumultuously back over the temporary draw-bridge thrown across the waterless moat for their use; and Leofric and his men sprang forward to pursue them.

Then Warrenne turned again with a fierce rallying cry, and his knights, used to strict discipline, and instantly understanding his aim, turned with him, and, as at Hastings, the advantage was won. It was a hazardous experiment, but it had succeeded.

Man to man the battleaxes and spearmen were no match for the mailed and mounted Normans. The struggle was bitter. Horses and knights, Normans and English, fell cursing and kicking from the bridge into the moat. But Earl Warrenne, with a bevy of knights at his heels, made their way through the breach, penetrating into the courtyard of the castle;

while Leofric lay senseless on the bridge, with his yellow curls dangling over the edge, streaked with crimson, and dripping red drops into the gulf below.

So the king's men had made their way within the walls of Blaunchefleur, after two months of strong endeavour; and the sight of Warrenne's chequered banner inside the defences they had held so manfully brought terror into the hearts of the besieged. Their unnerved arms struck feeble blows; and the king's knights rode them down, driving them to the very stairway of the great entrance to the donjon keep.

All at once, from above their heads came a clear voice like a clarion,—

'St. Nicholas for Guader! A Guader! a Guader! Shall your lord come back, and find his castle lost?'

There, on the platform before the grand entrance, stood a white-robed figure, with uplifted arms and a wildly shining face, which set the half-pagan Anglo-Danes thinking of Valkyries and Norns, and the Bretons and Normans of angels and saints; but when they recognised the face of Emma the countess, they shouted a mighty shout, and the blood came back into their hearts with a great glow of determination, and they rushed once more fiercely against their assailants.

'I am here to see how bravely you maintain his cause in his absence!' cried Emma from the portal.

Then the knights mixed in the wild *mêlée* at her feet; while the king's archers shot their whizzing shafts from the wooden towers, and the king's slingers hurled their leaden balls and stones, fighting the men who upheld the East Anglian banners on the walls. Whether or no every arrow had its billet, as it is said every bullet has in modern days, many an arrow flew far beyond the men at whom it was aimed, and whistled down into the courtyard.

As the besieged knights looked for inspiration to their beloved Châtelaine, brimming over with the strong desire to distinguish themselves before her eyes, they saw a cloth-yard shaft fly straight to her white figure, and strike the tender form they were burning to protect, marring it with a crimson streak. A great howl of rage rose up against the sky, and the passion of vengeance nerved their arms with furious force.

They sprang at the foe, who had also seen the arrow strike its mark, and had paused a moment in chivalrous horror, and so were unprepared to meet the onslaught. Thus the tide of battle turned once more, and Earl Warrenne and his followers were driven out through the breach by which they had entered.

Then, when the knights of the garrison rode back in grievous haste to satisfy their anxiety for their lord's bride, the countess still sood before the portal, laughing, though the arrow stuck in her arm.

'See!' she said, 'it is nothing! Only a flesh-wound. I have leeched a hundred worse.'

The Normans and the Bretons and the Saxons

all joined in tumultuous cheers, and vowed to save their countess and their castle if they died to the last man.

'*Merci!* brave hearts!' cried the countess. 'That was well spoken! Holy Mary grant my lord may relieve us ere many days are past!'

Then they entreated her to have her wound looked to; and she swept away to the spital, and there had the arrow cut out of her white arm, so all her wounded warriors might see; and the legend of her unflinching courage spread like wildfire through the garrison, and even into the camp of the besiegers without.

'By St. Michael!' cried Robert Malet, 'these rebels seem to have the knack of coining heroines. Thou and my father, Earl Warrenne, had shrewd experience of Hereward's witch of a wife in the Fenlands by Ely,—how she wound up the wild galliards her husband got to follow him with her sorceries and incantations till they were at the point of madness! Sooth, methinks we have to deal with such another.'

Then Leofric Ealdredsson, who had been carried into the camp, and lay within earshot, raised himself up and swore mightily.

'No witch was Torfrida,' he cried in anger, 'but as true and noble a woman as ever God made! So truly is De Guader's countess, Norman though she be!'

At which the king's captains laughed, and turned to Leofric.

'Ay! thou wast one of that pestilent Hereward's most saucy upholders, I well remember; and now thou art leader in this hornet's nest also, I trow!' said Earl William. 'Dost thou know the mark we are bid to set on all our prisoners in this affair, to the end that we may recognise them again when we meet them?'

'Do your worst, usurping cowards!' answered the furious Anglo-Dane. 'When Sweyn Ulfsson follows De Guader home, and claims his own, and drives the tanner's grandson from the throne he has stolen, he will put *his* mark on *you* in return, I warrant me!'

Malet's face grew dark; for William himself and William's followers resented no insult so deeply as any allusion to the honest fell-monger of Falaise.

But Earl Warrenne was too wise to quarrel with a wounded man, and said good-humouredly,—

''Twould be a pity to lop a limb from so fine a warrior as thyself, noble Leofric. Perhaps some exception can be made in this case. We are told that Sir Aimand de Sourdeval is detained in Blaunchefleur against his will, and that he is faithful to the king. If that be so, an exchange might be effected.'

Leofric, who did not relish the prospect of having his right foot hewed off, courageous as he was, gasped for joy at this proposition. It meant even more to him than escape from cripplehood for life; it meant that he would regain entrance into Blaunchefleur, and be near the fair cousin who had become dear to his heart, and that his rival would be parted from her.

'That is true,' he said eagerly. 'The knight is there, and has refused to strike a blow against the king's troops.'

Meanwhile the sun was sinking in the sky, and with night came partial cessation of hostilities. The besieged were holding council as to what step should next be taken, but the counsellors had dwindled in number. Sir Alain de Gourin was no longer there with his purple face and blatant ways, but he could be better spared than Leofric, and than several others who had fallen during the month.

'We cannot hold the walls another day,' said Sir Hoël sadly; 'there is nothing for it but to retire into the keep. It will take them some time to dislodge us from thence; the masonry is solid as the earth.'

'And time is all we need!' exclaimed the countess eagerly. She was very pale, and had her arm in bandages, but her eyes were bright with fever and determination, and she insisted on taking her part in the discussion. 'My lord must soon be here.'

'We may hold the keep for months,' said a knight.

'Yes, if manna would fall from heaven,' suggested another jestingly; 'else I fear we must needs eat each other ere many moons had waned.'

'Gentlemen,' said Sir Hoël gravely, 'there is a means by which we may increase our supplies a shade less desperate than that.'

The countess turned to him with anxious curiosity. Sir Hoel continued,—

'We cannot stable all our horses in the keep, some must be sacrificed; better we kill them with our own good swords, and salt their flesh, than let the king's men have them. Horse-flesh may not be palatable, but at least it would be better fare than picking each other's bones. Relief may come before we need fall back on such provender. Still, it will be there.'

A sick shudder of horror passed through Emma's heart. Was famine indeed so near?

The faces of the knights grew serious. No man stood forward to proffer his own steed for the sacrifice. More than one gave evidence, by trembling lip and quickened breathing, of the hardness of the trial. For those mailed warriors were a centaur race. Their steeds were almost a part of themselves. Their lives were constantly hanging on the qualities of their mounts. A hard mouth or a nervous temper might bring them their death any day, and docility and nimble limbs be their safeguard. The horse became a trusted friend, and a champion's destrier was often as celebrated as himself.

The countess's lip trembled also, and her cheeks grew even paler than before, while her heart throbbed in cruel doubt.

For was not Oliver, the earl's noble Spanish war-horse, in the castle? Had she not visited him morning and night, and seen with her own eyes that he had his due ration of corn, and that his satin skin was sleek as grooming could make it? Had she not patted his splendid neck morn and night, and plaited his thick mane, and had his velvet nose thrust into her soft palms for an apple or a wastel cake? She knew how the earl loved the creature, and had misliked leaving him behind, and she herself loved him both for his master's sake and for his own. He seemed to her half human as she thought of his intelligent eyes, and the clear, soft neigh, musical as the whistle of a blackbird, with which he was wont to greet her, and a sob caught her breath as she thought of condemning him to death. She knew also that he was worth his weight in gold.

Yet to sacrifice him seemed to her a clear duty, as she looked round the circle of reluctant men about her. They would never ask it, she knew. Some few horses would be kept, and the earl's destrier amongst them, as a matter of course; but she remembered how she had heard it told of William the Conqueror, that when, on his march on Chester, his men, weary with labour and cold, begged him to let them go back, he dismounted and went afoot to encourage them, and shared all their hardships. Was her lord a less generous knight than William? A thousand times no! If he were in Blauncheflour, he would be the first to lead the sacrifice. As he was absent, she must do it for him. These thoughts flashed through her mind in a moment, though they are long to write.

'Thou art right, Sir Hoël,' she said in a steady voice. ''Tis like killing a child for a knight to kill his steed, I well understand. Yet it is but wisdom as we are circumstanced, and I make no doubt if my lord were here, he would be the first to make the sacrifice. Therefore I beg thee, dear Sir Hoël,'—she laid her left hand on his arm, and would have put the other with it, had it not been stiffened with bandages, and looked into his face with her clear, brave eyes, very pathetic now, with heavy rings of blue round them, and thin, wan cheeks beneath, —'I beg thee, dear Sir Hoël, despatch my lord's destrier with thine own blade, and see that he suffer no needless pain.'

A chorus of protests burst from the knights; not a man but offered his steed to save Oliver; but the countess said hastily, 'Attend to my behest, I pray thee, Sir Hoël!' and hurried from the room.

She went to her bower, where Eadgyth was awaiting her. She had not trusted any of her ladies to attend her in her council-chamber, lest their courage should give way, and so weaken her influence over the knights. Now, when she met Eadgyth's look of tender inquiry, and felt her caressing arms round her, she was overcome herself. She dropped her poor weary head on Eadgyth's shoulder and wept—wept as she had never done in her life before—no, not even in the chapel through that long sad night when she believed herself a widow; for her fresh young strength was in its prime then, and now she was weakened physically by the strain of continued anxiety and the acute pain of her wounded arm.

The storm of sobs was so long and violent, that Eadgyth, who had scarcely ever seen her cry, was sore afraid. She dreaded that some fell disaster had befallen.

But she was a good comforter; she did not tease with questions, she only pressed her friend fondly to her, and kissed and caressed her till she grew calmer.

'Oh, Eadgyth,' said the countess at length, 'they are going to kill the horses, and Ralph's destrier must die. The dear Oliver!'

To Eadgyth this reason for such excessive grief seemed almost absurd, and her blue eyes opened widely.

'Oh, I am a poor weak fool!' said Emma, drawing away, 'to break down so utterly. But my arm aches shrewdly, Eadgyth, and I am not used to pain.'

She threw herself upon the embroidered bed, tears rolling silently down her cheeks.

'Poor sweet!' said Eadgyth. 'I do not marvel that even thy wonderful spirit should yield to nature. This day has been fearful indeed.'

'Why does not Ralph come? Why does he not come?' exclaimed Emma, covering her face with her slender hands, which had grown so thin that she could scarce keep on her wedding ring. 'My heart is full of fears, Eadgyth. I dreamt of him last night, ill and sorrowful, tossing on a bed of fever. He was ill when he went away, his wounds half-healed. It is all doubt and dread—and horror!'

'Ah, Christ have mercy upon us!' said Eadgyth, who was kneeling beside the bed.

'I dare not ask for mercy,' said Emma piteously. 'I am fighting in a wrong cause! Thy Sir Aimand said it. I have brought all this woe and suffering on the man who loved me, and on those who love him and follow him, like leal knights and true!'

'Oh, do not torment yourself with such thoughts, sweet heart! Surely it was no wrong cause to strive with the oppressor of this wretched land,—he whose minions were killing the heart out of his victims with every species of wrong and outrage!'

The tears were running swiftly enough down Eadgyth's cheeks now.

'Alas!' said Emma, 'I fear we thought less of that than of our own revenge and ambition.'

'But how couldst thou have helped it?'

'I might have helped it. I might have refused to marry against the king's command, and gone into a convent, and then the bride-ale would never have been, nor its direful following.'

'Perchance it had been better,' said Eadgyth thoughtfully.

'No, it would not have been better!' cried Emma, starting up, impatient at Eadgyth's acquiescence; she had given her scruples voice that they might be combated, not confirmed. 'I would go through it all again and more to be Ralph's wife, and I am a contemptible coward, a *noding*, to be puling here because my roses are not thornless, when I might be helping to keep my hero's castle for him!'

She sprang from the bed, and insisted on going to the spital to leech the day's wounded, though Eadgyth told her that she needed leeching far more sorely herself.

Yet in all her self-abandonment she had spared Eadgyth, and had not told her that they were to be imprisoned in the keep from that day forth, nor that her cousin Leofric Ealdredsson was dead or in the hands of the enemy.

CHAPTER XXIV.

FAMINE.

WHEN the besiegers attacked the walls of Blaunche-flour on the morning following, they found them undefended, and took possession with shouts and jubilation.

The besieged, sheltered behind the strong ramparts of the keep, felt much as shipwrecked mariners, who, from the present safety of some rocky islet, watch the rising of the tide, knowing that their lives depend upon the height to which the shining water will attain,—unless indeed some friendly vessel come to the rescue and carry them off.

The hope of the imprisoned garrison was in the coming of the earl, and as Earl Warrenne and Robert Malet rode round the keep, and saw how strong and flawless was the masonry, they had a shrewd fear that De Guader would yet bring the Danes and Bretons upon them before they had time to complete their victory, and that, after all their hard fighting and expenditure of lives and time and money, the quarry would escape them.

So they determined to call a parley, and endeavour to cajole the countess into resigning the fortress.

Needless to say, their summons was eagerly responded to by the garrison.

Emma trembled with hope that was almost pain, as she inquired what terms the envoy was empowered to grant.

'Safe-conduct to herself, her ladies, and a reasonable escort, if she would give her parole to leave the country within a month—no more.'

She realised then that her hope had been despair; that she had not had courage to hope at all.

'Safe-conduct for myself, my ladies, and every soul in the garrison,' replied the countess proudly. 'I will yield for no less.'

The envoy was not empowered to grant it.

'Dear lady, it were better to accept the terms. We cannot insure the safety even of thyself and thy ladies in the end,' advised Sir Hoël privately. 'Nought lies before us but quick starvation; the provisions are very short.'

'Desert you and all who have fought so nobly for us, and braved every peril for us, to insure our own safety? Never! Remember Stephen le Hareau! They would deal with you likewise,' cried Emma. 'I have given my answer. Convey it to thy lords!' she told the envoy.

Then the messenger said there was a further matter. It was understood that a loyal knight, Sir Aimand de Sourdeval, was in the castle, a prisoner, and, the gallant Childe Leofric Ealdredsson having fallen into their hands on the previous day, they proposed an exchange.

This was, of course, accepted, and Sir Aimand was sent for.

Eadgyth had begged to attend the countess to the council-chamber, and Emma turned to her. 'I am glad, Eadgyth. I feared a worse fate for thy kinsman.' The poor girl turned to her with a white face, well knowing that the words were spoken to cover her agitation. She tried to smile.

'It is a happy thing for him,' she said.

'Thy presence here is no longer needed,' said the countess. 'Let Sir Aimand wait upon me in my bower before he goes.'

'Poor child, thou shalt have a comfortable leave-taking at least!' she said, as Eadgyth followed to her private chamber. 'It is good for him to go, donzelle; he is eating his heart out in misery here.'

'Good for him to go that he may be free to slay my people!' cried Eadgyth bitterly. 'Ah, wretched me! that I should love my country's foe!'

Emma had no time to answer, for De Sourdeval's mailed step was clanking up the passage. A moment later he entered the bower. His eyes were shining and his cheeks flushed. He threw himself on his knee before the countess.

'Ah, noble lady,' he exclaimed, 'would that thy cause were one with that of my liege-lord William, so I might fight for thee, and show my gratitude for all thy kindness and generosity! I will seek service far from here; my sword shall not be against thee!'

'The generosity has not been all on my side, Sir Knight!' replied the countess, with moistening eyes. 'I would indeed that my cause were one with that of William of Normandy; that all this turmoil was at an end, and that no more brave lives were to be sacrificed for me and mine.' A deep, quivering sigh followed her speech.

'Lady Eadgyth,' said Sir Aimand, with a voice not quite so steady as before, as he turned to the Saxon maiden, 'I am glad thy kinsman profits by my freedom. It will comfort me that if I cannot myself labour in thy defence, my poor life has served to restore one who can to the garrison—far more valiantly and worthily than I.'

He forced out the words. He himself tried to believe that he was glad, but, in truth, the bitterest sting of parting lay for him in the thought that the man whom he regarded as his rival should be in the castle, favoured by daily and hourly intercourse under circumstances that must needs draw the hardest-hearted together. He remembered with renewed anguish all the tortures of Tantalus he had endured during his enforced inactivity; burning to distinguish himself before his lady's eyes, and forced to remain a drone in the hive, while Leofric had been free to show himself the hero he was, and would now have still fairer opportunity.

His eyes sought hers, therefore, full of a sadness which belied his words.

Eadgyth longed to tear a favour from her dress, and bid him wear it in his helm against all comers, for that no other knight, stranger or kin, should ever carry it. But she thought, 'Who knows that we shall ever meet again? Why should I bind him?' So she answered, bowing her head to hide the springing tears, 'Mary Mother have thee in her keeping!'

She gave him her hand, which he kissed reverently, and so departed, and half-an-hour later Leofric Ealdredsson was borne into the keep on a litter.

When Eadgyth saw her kinsman, her heart smote her that his fate had moved her so little; for his brow was damp with pain, and his brawny arms dropped feebly by his side, and all his strength was fled from him. She pansed and bound his wounds with tender care, and washed the clotted blood from his long yellow curls, wondering if indeed it were true that he was Sir Aimand's rival, or if it were only a figment of love's self-torturing jealousy.

From time to time Leofric moaned as she ministered to him, but scarcely opened his eyes. Did he know who it was, she wondered, or, if he knew, did he care?

When the last bandage was fastened, and she stood for a moment to see if aught more could be done for her patient, Leofric raised his weary head and looked in her face.

He did not speak, he had scarce strength for that;

his eyes were full of gratitude, and spoke his thanks, but they told her something more.

Then Eadgyth knew that Sir Aimand had said sooth, and her heart smote her, and her breath caught with an inward sob.

Leofric lifted his hand feebly and held it for hers. Had she given it, he would have pressed it to his lips; she could not,—but an hour before Aimand de Sourdeval had kissed it!

Leofric let his great nerveless hand fall listlessly beside him again.

'Thou art the best leech in the world, cousin,' he murmured, and closed his eyes again.

Eadgyth hurried away to the bower.

The days that followed were like an evil dream for all in the castle. The deadly monotony let them note clearly how, hour by hour, death was creeping nearer.

The mangonels and warrewolves were busy at their work, and the din of their projectiles was ever in the ears of the besieged. But these were not what they feared. These could but splinter a fragment off a stone here and there, but could make no dangerous breach in walls thirteen feet thick; besides, wooden galleries had been projected from the battlements, through which the defenders poured scalding rain of boiling water and molten lead upon the engineers, and so prevented any lengthened attack upon a given spot.

No; the enemy they feared was *Famine!* She stared

them in the face. Day by day more nearly her awful ghoulish eyes came nearer, and the grip of her bony hands was at their throats.

And still the warders scanned the horizon vainly, in hope to see the glimmer of friendly armour, still vainly watched the river for the flash of friendly oars.

Day after day dragged its slow length along, and yet the position remained unchanged, save that the assailants had almost given up effort, and quietly surrounded them, biding their time, knowing well that it must come if only no relief appeared.

The garrison had long been reduced to the barest rations on which it was possible to sustain life, and the few poor horses which had been taken into the keep, in the hope of some happy chance making their services available, had shared the fate of their brethren.

Gaunt faces and spectre forms dragged wearily from post to post, and strange thoughts flitted across hungry brains when slain men had to be buried in the donjon vaults. If one were to eat a body now, what would happen at the last day? Would it be more difficult for the soul that needed it again than for those whose flesh had been food for worms in the usual way? Would the men who had partaken of the flesh, and incorporated it into their own bodies, have to give it up again when the time of resurrection had arrived, and go scant themselves? Then they shuddered and crossed themselves, and muttered an ave or a paternoster, shunning the hungry eyes of their neighbour, lest he should guess their thoughts, or be thinking like horribleness himself, while they buckled their belts tighter to stay their pangs.

The countess, worn to a shadow, with her arm still bandaged, — for the worry and care she had undergone had hurt her health and kept her wound from healing, — was ever among them, consoling, entreating, commanding, inventing all manner of comforts for their souls and their bodies. She it was who prompted the cooks to make dainty dishes out of most unlikely materials; who sang the song of Rollo as she passed on her way, and kept up their hearts with gay jests.

One day an archer had the good fortune to shoot a heron that was flapping with evenly beating wings across the sky, so that it fell fluttering upon the roof of the keep, and was soon killed and presented by the lucky marksman to the countess, as a fit tribute to her private table, the fare on which, as all knew, had been poor enough for some time past.

She thanked the stout bowman heartily, but bade him follow her, and led the way to the great kitchen. Then she bade the scullions pluck the noble bird; and, after that was done, put it with her own white hands into the great cauldron which was cooking for the men.

'Share and share alike,' she said; and the soldiers cheered her, so that the king's men heard it outside the walls, and wondered what good luck could have come to their prisoners.

One morning Eadgyth met her kinsman, Leofric Ealdredsson, who had so far recovered from his wounds as to be able to keep watch and ward, and to see that the sentinels did their duty. His face bore traces of violent agitation.

'Well met, coosine,' cried he; 'I wanted to see thee. Keep thy lady off the battlements to-day, and go not thither thyself.'

Eadgyth looked in his face, and trembled. 'Thou hast bad news. I will heed thy warning. But wherefore? Is aught more terrible than we daily witness to be seen?'

'By Odin and Thor, yes! It bears not the telling.'

'Oh, Leofric, invoke not those dreadful pagan names in such an hour! Pray rather to the holy saints.'

'If thou wouldst take me in hand, a good man might perchance be made of me, coosine,' said the wild Leofric, with a laugh half tender and half bitter.

Eadgyth shook her head.

'But thou hast sorely alarmed me, Leofric. I would rather know the worst.'

'Well, the countess must know some time; perhaps it were better told through thee. This, then, is the sight to be seen from the battlements, and it is ugly as sin.' The veins on his forehead swelled, and his strong throat gathered into knots, while his fingers clenched on the hilt of his dagger. 'A tall gallows, right close under our noses, and three men hanged thereon; with an inscription over them, "The traitor Breton's traitor messengers."'

Eadgyth clasped her hands. 'The earl has sent, and they have caught his men!'

'That's it;' and Leofric murmured a few wishes regarding the king's men that at the least were uncharitable. 'Further, one of the men is the poor fool Grillonne—a quick-witted rascal as ever was called wise—he who saved his master so cleverly after the battle.'

'Grillonne! What! Grillonne so entreated?' exclaimed Eadgyth, with a shudder. 'But that will be a sore blow to the earl when he comes to know it. Art thou sure?'

'Ay; the knave's face was one not easily mistaken,' said Leofric.

Eadgyth hurried to the bower, and told the countess what she had heard.

'But it is good news, it is great news!' cried Emma, with sparkling eyes. 'Ralph is alive, and trying to help us! Alacke! I grieve for the poor envoys and Grillonne. Ah, 'tis sad such a fate has befallen him, the poor honest fool! his quick wits have not saved him after all.'

Emma was right, it proved to be good news, for Earl Warrenne and his colleagues, before hanging the messengers, had extracted from them the intelligence that Ralph de Guader had collected a great force in Bretagne and amongst the Danes, and that he was coming to the relief of his beleaguered castle. A day or two later they called a parley, and offered safe-conduct to the whole garrison, without exception, on condition that they left England within forty days, counting from the day on which they surrendered the castle.

Emma would fain have held out still, hoping that the earl was on his way to relieve them; but she had no certain knowledge of his movements, and the famine was so direful that even the fire-eating Leofric was obliged to counsel her to accept the terms.

'It is a victory!' exclaimed Sir Hoël, moved almost to tears; 'and we owe it to thy haught spirit and determined courage, noble countess. Thy name shall be famous in days to come.'

So the garrison were called together into the great hall, and told how that their lives were saved, and that they were to march out of Castle Blaunche-flour with banners flying, and all the honours of war, instead of having their feet cut off like poor Stephen le Hareau and the other prisoners the king's men had taken; and the men, who had looked forward to certain ill-fortune for themselves, whatever might betide their superiors, thought it a victory also.

How the hall rang with cheers, and congratulations, and praise of the countess! Norman and Breton, Saxon and Dane, raised what voices hunger had left them, and verily they shouted lustily, notwithstanding a light breakfast.

The countess stood amongst them, sobbing like a child.

'No praise is due to me; it is all to you, my gallant defenders.'

So the answer went back to Earl William de Warrenne that the keys of Castle Blauncheflour should be surrendered on the morrow.

Then all the garrison attended a 'Te Deum' in the chapel of St. Nicholas.

Afterwards, when the knights had again assembled in the great hall, the countess said,—

'Leofric Ealdredsson, these gentlemen, thy comrades in arms, shame themselves that they should wear the belt and spurs while one who has fought so knightly should not claim them. We well know thou hast them not solely because thou wert too careless to claim them, but I would not have thee leave Blauncheflour undubbed.'

Leofric's pale hunger-eaten cheeks turned red with pleasure.

'If the men who have fought with me here esteem me peer, I will not reject the honour,' he answered; at which the hall rang with cheers.

Then said the countess, smiling, 'Wilt thou have thine accolade in our Norman fashion, from the hands of a knight, and take Sir Hoël de St. Brice for thy sponsor, or, in the way of thine own people, at the hands of Father Pierre?'

'Nay,' quoth the turbulent hero, 'there is a better way than either. Many a good man has taken his knighthood from the hands of a maiden. Let my fair kinswoman, thy bower-maiden, stand sponsor to me;' and he turned appealingly to Eadgyth.

'A truce to thy jests, Leofric Ealdredsson, this is no time for them!' answered Eadgyth sharply, fingering the bracelet she always wore upon her arm.

'By the Rood, I mean no jest, coosine! Jourdain took his knighthood from the hands of his lady; why not I from thee?'

'Keep to the old Saxon custom, Leofric; take it from the hands of Father Pierre.'

And so he did; and his last night within the walls of Blaunchcflour was spent in vigil and prayer before the altar of the chapel, whereon lay his armour.

On the morrow, the brave defenders of Norwich Castle marched forth from its sheltering walls, with all the honours of war; carrying their arms, and fully equipped, with flags flying and banners waving.

The leaders of the royal forces sent palfreys for the countess and her ladies, and came in state to meet the woman who had held them all at bay so long, armed *cap-à-pie*, their horses prancing and curveting, and plumes dancing in the breeze. Many a courtly compliment they paid to their fair foe, and Earl Warrenne took the keys himself from her white hands.

Then Bishop Geoffrey, and Earl Warrenne, and Robert Malet took possession of Castle Blaunchcflour formally, and threw into it a garrison of three hundred men-at-arms, and a body of *balistarii* and other engineers.

And Archbishop Lanfranc wrote to King William, in terms more forcible than polite, 'Glory be to God on high! your kingdom is at last purged from the filth of these Bretons.'

CHAPTER XXV.

BRETAGNE.

THE days that followed seemed like an evil dream to the countess and her ladies.

Several of the Breton knights who were amongst the garrison had manors in the neighbourhood; these were, of course, under confiscation; still, for the forty days allowed them to get away from England, they retained the lordship of their estates, and were able to offer hospitality to Emma.

On their way to a temporary retreat thus provided for them, the newly-dubbed knight, Sir Leofric Ealdredsson, reined in the somewhat sorry jade he had managed to procure, to the side of his kinswoman Eadgyth, as on a happier occasion Sir Aimand de Sourdeval had reined in a nobler steed.

'Alack, coosine! the Norman fell-monger is safe in his seat now. Our last chance is over and done. We have nought left but to submit with the best grace we can muster,' he said sadly.

Eadgyth turned to him with an unfathomable regret in her limpid eyes. 'Yes, it is too true; the Normans have conquered.'

'But not us, coosine! We shall never be conquered in spirit, you and I! We are Angles to the backbone, and always shall be. In the fat Fenland we may yet live a life of our own, doing homage to no man, and defying fate. Share my island home amongst the meres, Eadgyth. I have strength to protect thee.'

Then Eadgyth shook her head sadly, her voice was scarcely audible as she answered,—

'I am not so staunch as you think me, kinsman. I fear I am conquered, body and soul. Day by day it hath been borne in upon me more strongly that the Normans have won because they deserved to win.'

Leofric opened his blue eyes at this announcement, and rounded his mouth for an oath, but recollected himself and checked it, and tugged his yellow beard instead.

'I say it advisedly, Leofric Ealdredsson: we English have lost because we were selfish and lazy; sunk in enjoyment; turbulent, and unwilling to submit to discipline. Hast thou not thyself told me how the Normans spent the night before Senlac in prayer and vigil, while the English feasted and drank it away?'

'Ah, Eadgyth, well for thee thou art a woman!' answered Leofric, grinding his teeth, his cheeks flushed with anger. Then he burst out laughing in his light-hearted, merry way, though there was a taint of bitterness in his mirth.

'By Asgaard and Odin! I believe thou art bewitched by that pale, shaven-faced Norman *prudhomme*, as they call it—Aimand de Sourdeval. My unclerkly tongue and downright ways doubtless bear ill the contrast with such a "parfait knight"!' He brought down his strong hand on his thigh with a force that made all his bracelets jingle. 'Say frankly now, kinswoman, thou thinkest him the better man of us twain?'

He dreaded the answer, though he braved it. But Eadgyth, looking steadily in his face, replied,—

'I should not speak sooth, Leofric Ealdredsson, if I denied it. I do think him the better man. Thou thyself hast said he was thine equal in the *mêlée*; and, certes, he is more gentle in hall.'

Leofric turned away and hung his head, only for a moment. Then he faced Eadgyth with a bright smile, the indomitable spirit of the man meeting the heart-wound as it would have met one of the flesh.

'But I am here, and he is absent,' he said; 'a live dog, they say, is better than a dead lion. And he is of the conquerors, and I of the conquered, so all thy generosity should be thrown into my side of the balance. Beside,' he added seriously, 'the blood of thy countrymen is on his blade, whilst I am of thy people.'

Eadgyth shuddered, and clutched the pommel of her saddle; the quick tears started from her eyes, and rolled one after another down her cheeks.

Leofric leaned over and laid his broad palm upon her little trembling hand.

'Go not away from thy country in the train of the foreign woman, Eadgyth,—though God forbid that I should say aught against her, for she is brave and beautiful,—but come thou over into the Fenlands, and share my risks, and comfort my poor old father, and tame me. Rough as I am, I would always be gentle to *thee*, Eadgyth.'

'Wouldst thou wed me with another man's image in my heart, Leofric?' asked Eadgyth, with a trembling voice.

'I would drive out that image by my own,' avowed Leofric.

'That thou wilt never do, coosine!' said Eadgyth firmly. 'No, do not dream it. I can never be his, neither can I wed any other. Nor can I leave my lady now in her sore distress and sorrow. No, Leofric, I cannot go with thee; ask me no more, it is but pain to both.'

Then Leofric saw she was in earnest, and desisted. Affecting to see some dangerous object that required investigation, he struck spurs into his *hacquenée*, and dashed off into the brushwood that bordered the road; and when he joined the cavalcade again, he took care not to choose the neighbourhood of his cousin's palfrey.

About a fortnight later, the countess and her ladies, amongst whom was the faithful Eadgyth, went on board a long-bodied, high-prowed galley at Lovelly's Staithe. It was propelled by twenty-five oars on each side, and flaunted gaudy embroidered sails to the wind, the main-mast being surrounded by a gallery round which a sentinel could walk. The garrison of Blauncheflour embarked on board a small flotilla of similar vessels.

We may imagine how they suffered as they made

tedious progress down the rough east coast, passing Dunwich and Ipswich, and the low-lying estuaries of Maldon and the Thames; and farther south, Sandwich and the high white cliffs of Dover, famous then, although no Shakespeare had sung them. How they raised their weary heads and strained their sad eyes to look at the castles which William the Norman had built at Hastings and Lewes and Arundel; and how Eadgyth wept to see them, because they reminded her of slain Harold Godwinsson, and were proof of the downfall of her nation. Emma was sorrowful too, because they witnessed to the valour and success of the greatest captain of the age, whom her father, stout William Fitzosbern, had loved and honoured, and against whom she was in rebellion.

They slipped as quickly as might be past the rough Norman coast, keeping as far out to sea as possible, lest Norman vessels should come down on them and harry them, and bear off the precious charge they guarded, to be kept in durance vile till ransom was extorted, which was far from improbable, notwithstanding the forty days' safe-conduct given them by William's officers.

Standing out so far to sea, they got a rough tossing on Atlantic rollers, and many a baptism of Atlantic spray. With what joy they hailed the first glimpse of the Breton rocks! How glad they were when they made the Ille, and floated under the staithes of Dinan!

Then all was question and curiosity, one side as eager to hear as the other. The countess and her *meinie* asking news of Ralph de Guader and Montfort; the

Brittany folks as anxious to learn how she had fared, and how escaped.

The countess learned with joy that Ralph was at Montfort, scarce forty miles away, preparing with might and main an expedition for the relief of Blaunchefleur. 'Had she not seen the warships in the harbour?' they asked.

We may guess how quickly messengers were sent off to Montfort, and how Ralph mounted in hot haste as soon as they told him that his countess had come, with all her gallant garrison, and how he galloped to meet them as fast as his steed could gallop. No doubt he sighed that he had not Oliver under him then.

Emma and her following got what horses they could, and started for Montfort.

The August sun shone hotly from the blue continental sky, and the apples were turning yellow and red in the orchards along the road. As noon came on, the travellers, having ridden some fifteen miles on very sorry beasts, were fain to rest them at a wayside hostel.

The countess and her ladies ascended the ladder that served for a staircase to the upper chamber, and, while food was preparing below, lay down upon the rushes to rest their weary limbs.

The countess occupied a low pallet bed that stood in a corner of the room, and so utterly weary and broken down was she, that she could not even rejoice at thought of seeing her husband speedily. She soon fell into a heavy slumber, broken by dreams of the dreadful past more terrible even than the reality.

She heard again the din of the warrewolves and mangonels, and the crash of the stones flung by them as they struck the walls, the clash of swords and clangor of armour; and the terror and woe of it overcame her. She awoke with a scream. Throwing out her arms wildly, her hands came in contact with a man's mailed gauntlets, and she sprang up, crying, 'Blaunchcflour is taken! To the rescue! to the rescue!'

'Dost thou not know me, my wife, mine own?' answered Ralph's voice, broken with sobs. 'Would to God I had never left thee!'

Emma burst into hysterical laughter, and threw herself upon her husband's breast, sobbing for joy. 'I was dreaming, Ralph! Would all bad dreams might end as happily.'

Then they sat down side by side upon the bed, and looked in each other's faces. They were alone, for Emma's ladies had delicately withdrawn when the earl entered, knowing that they would rather be in private.

'How pale thou art and thin, my sweet,' said Ralph, reproaching himself more and more bitterly that he had left her to struggle alone.

'I fear my poor face has lost its fairness, Ralph,' with an anxiety of tone that was all of love and naught of vanity.

'Thou art ten times fairer to me than ever before, my heroine!' answered De Guader fondly. 'But let me make excuse e'er I question thee. This is how I came not to thine aid. I went, as thou knowest, to Denmark, and sought Sweyn Ulfsson, and begged him bear out his promises and assist me with men, telling him that he might yet hoist William from the English throne. And Sweyn swore by the head of Sleipnir, Odin's horse, which thou knowest is a mighty oath amongst these Danish heathens, that he would support me. But then my wounds, being half healed, broke out afresh; and my head being still sore through Odo's blow, I fell into a fever, and lost my mind for six weeks. Meanwhile Sweyn had made no move, and when I came to myself I was still weak and powerless. As soon as I got strength enough, I came over here to collect my vassals, and call to me whoever would put his hands between mine and be my man; and I sent off messengers to comfort thee'—

'Whom William's men caught, and hanged on a gallows as high as the donjon keep,' interposed Emma.

Ralph gnashed his teeth.

'Ah! was it so? My faithful Grillonne, was this the reward of thy long service? I have brought evil on all who loved me! I had all in readiness, and should have started in a day, but, the blessed saints be praised! thou art here in safety, and there is no need. None can tell how I have suffered thinking of thee.'

'*Thy* cheeks are hollow enough, in truth; thou canst not crow over me,' said Emma, with a flash of her old gaiety. And then she told him the long story of the siege of Blaunscheflour.

Ralph listened as one spellbound, and when she had ended her tale he slipped on his knee at her feet.

'Let me do thee homage,' he said, with a proud, fond

glance in her eyes. 'What am I that thou shouldst have so suffered for my sake? It humbles me unspeakably.'

Ever after it seemed to Emma that the poor garret of that wayside inn was the noblest, fairest, and most beautiful apartment into which she had ever set foot.[1]

[1] See Appendix, Note E.

CONCLUSION.

WHOEVER will, may find no small part of the ensuing chapter in the pages of grave historians; but in no sober leaf of history will they find recorded how it fared with Eadgyth of Norwich and Sir Aimand de Sourdeval.

Ralph and Emma, like an orthodox hero and heroine, lived happily together to the end of their days; though they had to fight a good many more battles. De Guader had made himself a mighty enemy in William the Conqueror, King of England and Duke of Normandy; one who, in his latter capacity, had no mind to have Ralph rampant on the borders of his dukedom. So he invaded Brittany, and strove to run De Guader to earth in his own country; he invested Dol, but had to raise the siege somewhat ignominiously, owing to the help rendered to the besieged by Alan Fergant, son of the reigning Count Howel of Brittany, and Philip of France, who was always delighted to supply aid against William.

Sweyn Ulfsson, King of Denmark, carried out his promises to Ralph, and sent his son Cnut with Hakon Jarl to invade England; and they appeared on the east coast with a fleet of two hundred ships, and actually put into the Humber, though rather too late to serve the purposes of the ambitious earl.

William, whether really frightened, or moved by the lust of power which was rapidly gaining upon him, and which clouded his later years with hate and misery, made the descent of the Danes a pretext for the worst crime of his reign—the judicial murder of Waltheof; —for it must be noted that, with this exception, his conduct to the English princes was generous and mild.

When the son of Siward had carried to William the news of the plot in which he had taken part, the Conqueror had received him graciously, and had pardoned him freely for his own share of the mischief. But he kept him at his side, although he did not call him a prisoner; and, soon after landing in England, arrested him on a charge of complicity with the Danes, who had been his old comrades. William had that excuse for thinking him dangerous.

Then came Judith's opportunity. She hated the husband she had been forced to marry for State purposes, and stood forth as his accuser, pouring her poison into the ears of her royal uncle. Unfortunately William listened, and cast the son of Siward into prison at Winchester, where he languished for months, while a mock trial was going on, which many hungry Normans, who wanted his estates, were determined should end to their liking. Ivo Taillebois, who had been one of Hereward's most venomous foes, and whose lands adjoined those of Waltheof, was amongst the most clamorous for his destruction; and the Primate Lanfranc his best advocate and almost sole friend, recognising perhaps that it was by his persuasion that Waltheof had been induced to place himself in the power of the Conqueror.

Early one morning, while the good folks of Winchester were asleep in their beds, the Normans led the Saxon chief without the walls of the town. Waltheof walked to the place of execution clothed in his earl's apparel, which he distributed among some priests, or gave to some poor people who had followed him, and whom the Normans permitted to approach on account of their small numbers and entirely peaceful appearance. Having reached a hill at a short distance from the walls, the soldiers halted, and the Saxon, prostrating himself, prayed aloud for a few moments; but the Normans, fearing that too long a delay would cause a rumour of the intended execution to be spread in the town, and that the citizens would rise to save their fellow-countryman, exclaimed with impatience to Waltheof, 'Arise, that we may fulfil our orders.' He asked, as a last favour, that they would wait only until he had once more repeated, for them and for himself, the Lord's Prayer. They allowed him to do so; and Waltheof, rising from the ground, but remaining on his knees, began aloud, 'Our Father who art in Heaven;' but at the verse, 'and lead us not into temptation,' the executioner, seeing perhaps that daylight was beginning to appear, would wait no longer, but, suddenly drawing his large sword, struck off the Saxon's head at one blow. The body was thrown into a hole, dug between two roads, and hastily covered with earth.[1] But the monks of Crowland, to whom he had made rich gifts in his lifetime, and who had been staunch throughout to the English cause, got the body up again a fortnight later, and averred that it was still unchanged and the blood fresh (sixteen years later they pronounced that it was still as fresh, and that the head had grown on to the body again!); and they bore it away to 'Holland,' to St. Guthlac's in the Fens, and erected a tomb in the abbey, with William's permission, whereat great miracles took place. When his traitress wife Judith, the 'foreign woman,' as the chroniclers style her, went to cover this monument to her husband with a rich pall of silk, which she had prepared for it, the martyred hero refused her hypocritical gift, and the offering was snatched away and thrown to a distance by an invisible hand.

So the Saxon monks made a holy martyr of the wavering Waltheof, whose fate, and the fate of England with it, might have been very different if he had possessed as much moral as physical courage.

The Norman ecclesiastics accused the Saxons as idolaters, and found the occasion good for deposing and dishonouring Abbot Wulfketel, and putting Norman Toustain in his stead; which only made the English

[1] Thierry, *Norman Conquest*, p. 113. Almost literal translation of Orderic Vitalis.

more keen to honour their dead hero, and they rushed in crowds to his tomb.

Judith thought herself very lucky to have all the money and lands that had belonged to Waltheof, and to be free of him, and made up her mind to have a second husband according to her own taste. But she wished him alive again when William made a present of her, possessions and all, to one Simon de Senlis, a brave, but lame and deformed knight.

She refused to carry out the bargain, so William consoled De Senlis with her daughter instead, together with all the lands and money; and the Saxon chroniclers gloat over Judith's subsequent poverty and sorrows. But we, looking back, now the years have rolled away, may pity her, and see that the crime lay with those who treated a woman as a chattel, and 'gave' her away to this man and that, without consulting her welfare or her happiness, rather than with the woman so treated.

And Emma's brother, the son of William's staunchest vassal, how fared he?

When the Conqueror passed the Straits after his attempt to reduce De Guader at Dol, he called a great council of Norman barons to pass judgment on the authors of the recent conspiracy. Ralph de Guader they dispossessed of all his English property as absent and contumacious; and Roger of Hereford, being a prisoner, was brought before them, and condemned to lose all his lands, and to pass the rest of his days in prison.

But William seems still to have had a soft place in his heart for the son of his old friend, and sent him one Easter, according to the custom of the Norman court, a complete suit of precious stuffs, a silk tunic and mantle, and a close coat trimmed with foreign furs.

But Roger was full of pride and bitterness, and he took the rich present and threw it on the fire.

When William heard how his gift had been received, he flew into a mighty rage.

'The man is too proud who does such scorn to me,' he cried. 'He shall never come out of my prison in my days, *par le splendeur Dex!*'

Nor did he; neither in the days of William Rufus. He died in prison. But, in the reign of Henry I., his two sons won back a portion of their father's possessions.

The lesser accomplices of the three great earls fared even worse.

At the council before mentioned, 'Man foredoomed all the Bretons that were at the bride-ale at Norowic, some were blinded, some were driven from the land, and some were put to shame. So were the king's traitors brought low,' say the chronicles.

Truly a disastrous bridal!

Yet the bride and bridegroom, who risked so much for each other and involved so many in ruin, were the most fortunate of those who attended it.

Though Ralph lost his English estates, he had broad lands in his mother's country, and lived with his hard-won consort in his castles of Guader and Montfort. A son and a daughter were born to them. The son succeeded to his father's Breton possessions, and the daughter, whom one chronicler names Amicia, another Itta, married Earl Robert of Leicester, and became a great English lady.

A little over twenty years had Emma and Ralph lived together, the stream of their true love having found peaceful channel after the rapids and whirlpools that followed on the first joining of their courses twain in one. Grey hairs had begun to muster in Ralph's dark locks, though his sturdy figure was as strong and active as ever and his hawk eyes as keen; motherhood had softened the high-spirited Emma, and had brought soft dimples into her cheeks and a lovelight to her brow. Happy in her home, she did not give much heed to the signs of the times, or note the strong new spirit that was stirring in the air.

But one day De Guader came into her bower in full harness, wearing helm and hauberk, with his great two-handed sword by his side.

He came up to her, and stood before her, and looked in her face, and took her soft mother's hand between his two big palms.

'See'st thou?' he asked, and he guided her eyes with his own towards his arm, whereon was bound the cross of the Crusaders.

'Ah, Ralph!' she cried, 'not thou!'

'Sweet,' he said gently, 'When I lay on the field of

De Guader dons the Cross.

my greatest fight, in sore distress and despair, with the choughs and ravens waiting to feed on mine eyes, and the thought of thee as of one I should never see again till the sounding of the last trump, I vowed that if life were spared me, I would one day make pilgrimage to the Holy Sepulchre. Now the time has come, my lady. Life has given me more than I had dared to hope for, but it is passing; we are no longer young, you and I, old wife! Let me join the men who have responded to Pope Urban's call. Robert Curthose is moving. I will put my hands between his and be his man, and march under his banner to join Godfrey de Bouillon.'

'Whom all men honour!' said Emma under her breath.

'Wilt thou give me thy blessing and thy leave, my lady?'

'Thou art sudden! Let me be alone and think,' said Emma; and she left him for a space. When she came back to him, her face was very pale, but she met his eyes with a steady smile, and, in turn, guided them to *her* arm, on which was bound the cross of the Crusaders. 'Wilt thou give me thy blessing and thy leave, my knight?' she asked.

Then Ralph caught her in his arms and kissed her, as if the fatal bride-ale had been but the day before.

So it came to pass that Ralph de Guader, with many of his vassals, joined the standard of the Duke of Normandy, and took his lady with him. With them went also Eadgyth of Norwich, faithful in all things, and unmarried still, having met no champion who could compass that in which her kinsman Leofric Ealdredsson had failed; her fair face still winsome, with its frame of soft yellow hair, and her blue eyes pathetic and serious.

In August 1096, De Guader led his knights to swell the great army of Crusaders then assembling on the banks of the Moselle, with Godfrey de Bouillon at its head, that 'very parfit gentil knight' and mirror of chivalry, whom all historians agree to praise, not only for spotless morals and untarnished honour and the high ideal he upheld before the face of the world, but for the 'consummate skill and patient perseverance, self-possession and presence of mind,' by which alone such a host of turbulent and independent chiefs as that which he commanded could have been led to victory.

As De Guader and his lady rode into the great camp beside the blue Moselle, a knight came forward to conduct them to the quarters which had been assigned to them. He had a worn ascetic face, seamed with scars and lighted by the large sombre eyes of a dreamer of day-dreams, his spare figure witnessing to a life of hard service and activity.

He met De Guader's lady with a sweet smile of reverence and recognition; but when he saw her companion, Eadgyth of Norwich, a flush passed over his bronzed cheeks and up into his forehead as far as it could be seen under his helm.

'Sir Aimand de Sourdeval!' cried Emma, with a quick movement of delight. 'Welcome the sight of thy brave, true face amidst this host of God.' Then she called back her husband, that he might pardon and be pardoned for what had happened in the old, sad days, and Ralph did so with the free, candid generosity of the times, which were saturated with the spirit we strive to keep alive in our public schools to this day—free fight and no malice borne.

Sir Aimand was one of Messire Godfrey's most trusted knights, whom the commander held in close attendance on his person; heart and soul in the Holy War, full of joy that so great a thing was going forward.

'You leave not wife or child by a lone hearthstone, Sir Knight?' asked Emma, feeling sure that the answer would be 'Nay.'

And 'Nay' it was. 'The lady of my choice would not have me, noble dame,' he answered in a low voice, scarcely daring to look at Eadgyth; 'a leal knight loves not twice.'

'But she will have thee now,' said Emma, and, taking Eadgyth's hand, she laid it in his. Nor did Eadgyth withdraw it.

Before the host of the Crusaders had moved from the Moselle, the Norman and the Saxon had vowed to be one.

Did they see the Holy City together with the eyes of the flesh? Did De Guader and his faithful consort see it? History answers not; it tells us only that

Ralph and Emma died together somewhere near Jerusalem.

Whatever their faults, whatever their sins, at least they were true to each other, and died fulfilling what the judgment of the time esteemed the holiest of duties.

APPENDIX.

NOTE A. THE MARRIAGE OF RALPH DE GUADER.

THE bridal of Ralph de Guader to Emma Fitzosbern is very fully described by the chroniclers, and I have endeavoured to keep as closely as possible to history. But though I have searched at least half-a-score authorities, ancient and modern, every one of whom states that many abbots and bishops were among the company, in no case is the name of any ecclesiastic recorded. I have therefore taken a liberty with the Abbot of St. Albans, of whom Freeman says: 'All that certain history has to say about Frithric is, that he was Abbot of St. Albans, and that he died or was deposed some time between 1075 and 1077.' These dates would make it not impossible that he attended the bridal, and tradition represents him as a very active worker in the patriotic cause of the Saxon Church, and the untiring opponent of Lanfranc.

NOTE B. NORWICH CASTLE.

Harrod, *Castles and Convents*, p. 145. Some later archæologists are of opinion that the castle built by William the Conqueror was so injured in the siege that it had to be rebuilt, and the chronicler, Henry de Knyghton, under date 1100, ascribes its erection to William Rufus. All agree that a fine Norman castle was built on the old Saxon earthworks by the Conqueror, though they differ as to whether the existing keep is the one then erected.

Note C. De Guader's Defeat.

It is to be remarked that none of the chroniclers, Norman or English, say anything of this encounter of Odo and Ralph. Nor do they notice Ralph's wound. What they do say is that De Guader was defeated at a place called Fagaduna. Lingard suggests that this name is probably a translation of Beacham, in Norfolk, and the theory is rendered more probable by the fact that Beachamwell St. Mary was anciently divided into two parishes, Beacham and Welle. But eight miles from this is the village of Fouldon, which name, according to Blomefield, is a corruption of its old Saxon cognomen. 'At the Great Survey, this town occurs by the name of Fulgaduna, Fulendon and Phuldon, and takes its name from the plenty of wild fowl which frequented it, it being seated in the midst of fens and morasses. *Fugol*, in Saxon, signifies wild fowl, and in some antique writings 'tis wrote Fugeldune.' What a slight misunderstanding of a strange name, or slip of the pen, might change this word into Fagaduna!

Note D. De Guader and Waltheof.

The chroniclers called Ralph's embarkation from Norwich a flight; while modern historians accuse the stout earl of not *daring* to stand the siege in his own person, and of leaving the bride for whom he had risked so much to sustain dangers he feared to face.

Ralph was unfortunate in offending all parties. Chroniclers of Norman sympathies hated him for his rebellion against William; Saxons for fighting against his people at Senlac: neither had any motive to say a good word for him, while they canonized Waltheof as a saint, — Waltheof, who surely earned the name of traitor as richly as ever did Ralph, since he entered in the conspiracy against William, after having voluntarily accepted the hand of the Conqueror's niece in marriage, and binding himself under a solemn form of fealty; then, to shield himself, acted the ever-hateful part of an informer.

Hugh and Roger Bigod, Ralph's successors in the earldom of Norfolk, are spoken of as worthy bearers of the title. Yet Hugh rebelled, first against King Stephen, and afterwards against Henry II.; and Roger wrested a charter from Richard I., in which the inhabitants of Norwich were first recognised as citizens, and afterwards joined the barons against King John, being one of the foremost of those who forced him to sign Magna Charta. It may be said that the treasons of the Bigods were justified by their ends, to obtain liberty for the people; but it must not be forgotten that Ralph de Guader alleged as his motive the intolerable oppression of the Saxons under the *régime* of William's subordinates.

Victor Hugo, writing of the good service done to English liberty by the jealous watch kept by the barons on the crown, and by their determined resistance of all royal encroachments, says: 'Dès 1075 les barons se font sentir au roi. Et à quel roi! A Guillaume le Conquérant!' The date thus given is that of the rebellion of De Guader and Hereford.

Note E. The Siege of Norwich Castle.

All that certain history has to tell of this siege of Norwich Castle, is that De Guader left it in the hands of his countess and knights, the names of the latter not being given; that they were attacked by the king's forces under the leaders named in the text, armed with all the mechanical inventions of the day; that the countess held it for three months, and gave it up on the terms related through lack of provisions; and that she rejoined her husband in Brittany. Why he had not appeared to relieve his castle is not recorded.

These details may be found in Orderic Vitalis, Matthew Paris, Florence of Worcester, the Chronicles of Worcester and Peterborough, and in all modern historians who deal with the period, perhaps the best account being that of Freeman in the fourth volume of his *Norman Conquest*, a work abounding in interest and spirited description.

MORRISON AND GIBB, PRINTERS, EDINBURGH.

RECENTLY PUBLISHED.

ST. DUNSTAN'S CLOCK. A Story of 1666. By E. WARD. With Eight Illustrations. Price 5s. cloth.

A PAIR OF ORIGINALS. A Story by E. WARD. With Eight Illustrations. Price 5s. cloth.

'A fresh and pretty story.'—*Daily Telegraph.*
'Is sure to be popular.'—*Record.*

FRESH FROM THE FENS. A Story of Three Lincolnshire Lasses. By E. WARD. With Eight Illustrations. Price 5s. cloth.

'The distinct but delicate characterisation of two little girls. They are realised for us with a force that is really admirable.'—*Spectator.*

CAEDWALLA. The Saxons in the Isle of Wight. By FRANK COWPER. With Illustrations. Second Edition. Crown 8vo, cloth, price 5s.

'The author has accomplished the difficult task of giving life and interest to his picture, and a perusal of the book will give boys a truer idea of the manners and customs of their rough forefathers than any other with which we are acquainted.'—*Standard.*

THE CAPTAIN OF THE WIGHT. A Romance of Carisbrooke Castle. By FRANK COWPER. With Illustrations. Third Edition. Crown 8vo, cloth, price 5s.

'Mr. Cowper has produced a very attractive story, and one which deserves, and will doubtless secure, many readers.'—*Spectator.*

BELT AND SPUR: Stories of the Knights of Old. With Coloured Illustrations. Fifth Thousand. Crown 8vo, price 5s.

'A very high-class gift-book of the spirit-stirring kind.'—*Spectator.*
'A sort of boy Froissart with admirable Illustrations.'—*Pall Mall Gazette.*

BORDER LANCES: A Romance of the Northern Marches in the time of Edward II. By the Author of 'Belt and Spur.' With Coloured Illustrations. Crown 8vo, cloth, price 5s.

'The book is a good one ... the illustrations are excellent.'—*Spectator.*

FOREST OUTLAWS; or, ST. HUGH AND THE KING. A Tale of the time of Henry II. By the Rev. E. GILLIAT. With Sixteen Illustrations. Crown 8vo, cloth, price 6s.

'Distinctly one of the very best books of the season.'—*Standard.*

JOHN STANDISH. The Rising of Wat Tyler. By the Rev. E. GILLIAT. With Illustrations. Crown 8vo, cloth, price 5s.

'The author, Mr. E. Gilliat, is well known as a successful writer of semi-historical fiction, and in this little book is quite up to his usual standard.'—*Guardian.*

SEELEY AND CO. LIMITED, ESSEX STREET, STRAND.

TALES BY M. E. WINCHESTER.

ADRIFT IN A GREAT CITY. Price 5s. cloth.

PEARL OF THE SEA. Third Thousand. Price 5s. cloth.
  'A charming conception.'—*Saturday Review.*

A CRIPPLED ROBIN. Third Edition. Price 5s. cloth.
  'A pretty story, and there is fun as well as feeling in many of the chapters.'—*Times.*

A CITY VIOLET. Fifth Edition. Price 5s. cloth.
  'Miss Winchester, whose power of delineating character is giving her an honourable place among the writers of serious fiction, has never done anything better than this.'—*Spectator.*

A NEST OF SPARROWS. Eighth Edition. Price 5s. cloth.
  'Miss Winchester not only writes with skill, but writes from the heart, and with full knowledge of her subject. Her story is most genuine, pathetic, without being sad.'—*Pall Mall Gazette.*

UNDER THE SHIELD. A Tale. Sixth Edition. Price 5s. cloth.
  'We wish all religious stories were written in the same simple and natural way. We can conceive no more healthy reading for children.'—*Academy.*
  'We welcome with real pleasure another book by the author of "A Nest of Sparrows." "Under the Shield" is to be noted for its purity of tone and high aspirations. . . . There is true fun in the book, too.'—*Athenæum.*

THE CABIN ON THE BEACH. A Tale. Fourth Thousand. Price 5s. cloth.
  'This tender story cannot fail to charm and delight the young.'—*Guardian.*

THE WAYSIDE SNOWDROP. A Tale. Fourth Edition. Price 3s. 6d. cloth.
  'A bright flower indeed. With all her tenderness and grace Miss Winchester narrates one of those pathetic stories of a poor London waif that at once arouse the loving sympathy of children.'—*Guardian.*

CHIRPS FOR THE CHICKS. With Thirty-one Illustrations. Price 2s. 6d. cloth.
  'The book is worthy to be a nursery favourite.'—*Guardian.*
  'The merriest, most amusing, and infinitely the most rhythmical book of poetry for young people produced this season. . . . Others besides children may read the "Chirps" with pleasure and amusement. The illustrations are very happy.'—*Standard.*

SEELEY AND CO. LIMITED, ESSEX STREET, STRAND.

A LIST OF BOOKS PUBLISHED BY
SEELEY & CO. LIMITED

46, 47 & 48, ESSEX STREET, STRAND, W.C.

PUBLISHERS OF THE PORTFOLIO, *an Artistic Periodical.*

EDITED BY

P. G. HAMERTON.

A NEW SERIES WAS COMMENCED IN 1890.

Each Number has Three Plates. Published Monthly. Price 2s. 6d.

The Volume, which is Published at the end of the Year, contains 36 Plates and 150 Minor Illustrations. Cloth, 35s.; half morocco, 2l. 2s.

LIFE AND LETTERS OF SAMUEL PALMER, PAINTER AND ETCHER. Edited by A. H. PALMER. With One Etching and Eight other Plates on Copper. Cloth, 21s.

Large-paper Copies, 42s.

AN ENGLISH VERSION OF THE ECLOGUES OF VIRGIL. By the late SAMUEL PALMER. With Illustrations by the Author. Fourteen Copper-plates. Price 21s. cloth.

MILTON'S MINOR POEMS. With Twelve Copper-plates, after SAMUEL PALMER. Price 21s. cloth.

'One of the choicest publications of our time.'—*Athenæum.*

THE BRITISH SEAS. By W. CLARK RUSSELL. With Chapters by P. G. HAMERTON, A. J. CHURCH, JAMES PURVES, and CHARLES CAGNEY. Illustrated with Etchings and Engravings and many Vignettes after J. C. HOOK, R.A., HENRY MOORE, A.RA., COLIN HUNTER, A.R.A., HAMILTON MACALLUM, and many other Marine Painters. Cloth, with gilt edges, 21s.

Large-paper Copies (100 only), 42s. net.

THE GRAPHIC ARTS: A Treatise on the Varieties of Drawing, Painting, and Engraving. By PHILIP GILBERT HAMERTON. With Fifty-four Illustrations.

'This massive and authoritative treatise on the technical part of almost every branch of art. ... It is the masterpiece of Mr. Hamerton. ... A beautiful work of lasting value.'—*Saturday Review.*

THE PRESENT STATE OF THE FINE ARTS IN FRANCE. By P. G. HAMERTON. With Etchings and other Illustrations. Cloth, gilt edges, 21s. Large Paper, 42s.

IMAGINATION IN LANDSCAPE PAINTING. By P. G. HAMERTON. With Fourteen Copper-plates and many Vignettes. Price 21s. cloth, gilt edges.

THE SAÔNE: a Summer Voyage. By P. G. HAMERTON. With 152 Illustrations by J. PENNELL and the Author. 4to. price 21s. cloth.

Large-paper Copies (250 only), price 2l. 2l. half bound.

PICTURESQUE ARCHITECTURE. Twenty Plates by ERNEST GEORGE, LALANNE, LHERMITTE, &c. &c. Imp. 4to. price 21s. cloth.

THE AVON FROM NASEBY TO TEWKESBURY. Twenty-one Etchings by HEYWOOD SUMNER. Price 1l. 11s. 6d. Large-paper Copies, with Proofs of the Plates, 5l. 5s.

THE ITCHEN VALLEY FROM TICHBORNE TO SOUTHAMPTON. Twenty-two Etchings by HEYWOOD SUMNER. Price 1l. 11s. 6d.

'We heartily commend it to artists.'—*Athenæum.*

EIGHTEEN ETCHINGS BY ENGLISH, FRENCH, AND GERMAN ARTISTS. Notes by P. G. HAMERTON. Imperial 4to. 31s. 6d.

THE ABBEY CHURCH OF ST. ALBANS. By J. W. COMYNS CARR. Illustrated by Five Etchings by ERNEST GEORGE and KENT THOMAS, and many smaller Illustrations, 18s.

LANDSCAPE. By PHILIP GILBERT HAMERTON, Author of 'Etching and Etchers,' 'The Graphic Arts,' &c. Columbier 8vo. with Fifty Illustrations, 5l. 5s.

Large-paper Copies, with Proofs of the Engravings, 10l. 10s.

'The superb volume before us may be said to represent, so far as this country is concerned, illustration, decoration, typography, and taste in binding at their best.'—*Athenæum.*

THE INNS OF COURT. By W. J. LOFTIE. With
Twelve Engravings and many other Illustrations, chiefly by
HERBERT RAILTON. Cloth, 21s.
Large-paper Copies (100 only), 42s.

SCOTTISH PAINTERS. By WALTER ARMSTRONG.
With Copper-plates and many Vignettes. Price 21s. cloth.
Large-paper Copies (50 only), price 4l. 4s., half morocco

SCHOOLS OF MODERN ART IN GERMANY.
By J. BEAVINGTON ATKINSON. With Fifteen Etchings and
numerous Woodcuts. Price 1l. 11s. 6d. Large-paper Copies,
with Plates on India paper, price 3l. 3s.
'In every respect worthy of its subject.'—*Athenæum.*

Specimen of Minor Illustrations in 'Isis and Thamesis.'

ISIS AND THAMESIS: Hours on the River from
Oxford to Henley. By Professor A. J. CHURCH. With
Twelve Plates and many Vignettes. Cloth, gilt edges, 16s.
Large-paper Edition, with Proofs of the Plates, 42s.
A Cheap Edition of this work, under the title of 'Summer
Days on the Thames,' has been published. Sewed, 1s.; cl. 1s. 6d.

LANCASHIRE. By LEO H. GRINDON. With Fourteen Etchings and numerous Vignettes. Price 1l. 1s. Large-paper Copies, with Proofs of the Plates, 3l. 3s.
Also a Cheap Edition. Cloth, 6s.
'Cannot fail to delight those who admire good artistic work.'—*Liverpool Daily Post.*

FINE-ART BOOKS.

STRATFORD-ON-AVON, from the Earliest Times to the Death of Shakespeare. By SIDNEY LEE. With Fourteen Plates and Thirty-one Vignettes by E. HULL. Price 21s. cloth, gilt edges. Large-paper Copies, price 4l. 4s. vellum.
Also a Cheap Edition. Crown 8vo. price 6s. cloth.

Specimen of Minor Illustrations in 'Ruined Abbeys of Yorkshire.'

THE RUINED ABBEYS OF YORKSHIRE. By W. CHAMBERS LEFROY. With Twelve Etchings and numerous Vignettes. Price 1l. 1s.
'A very charming volume.'—*Leeds Mercury.*
Also a Cheap Edition. Crown 8vo. price 6s. cloth.

WESTMINSTER ABBEY. By W. J. LOFTIE. With Twelve Plates and many Minor Illustrations, chiefly by HERBERT RAILTON. Price 21s. Large-paper Copies, 4l. 4s.
'The volume is likely to be one of the most popular of the many books that have been written dealing with the great Abbey.'—*Guardian.*
Also a Cheap Edition. Large crown 8vo. price 7s. 6d. cloth.

ETCHINGS FROM THE NATIONAL GALLERY. Eighteen Plates by Flameng, Rajon, Le Rat, &c. With Notes by R. N. WORNUM. Large 4to. 1*l*. 11*s*. 6*d*. cloth, gilt edges.

ETCHINGS FROM THE NATIONAL GALLERY. Second Series. Eighteen Plates. Text by R. N. WORNUM. 1*l*. 11*s*. 6*d*.

LIFE OF ALBERT DÜRER. By Mrs. CHARLES HEATON. New Edition. With Portrait and Sixteen Illustrations. Price 10*s*. 6*d*.

'In its present form Mrs. Heaton's work deserves high commendation.'—*Guardian*.

THE EARLIER ENGLISH WATER-COLOUR PAINTERS. By COSMO MONKHOUSE. With Fourteen Copper-plates and many other Illustrations. Price 21*s*.

EARLY FLEMISH ARTISTS, AND THEIR PREDECESSORS ON THE LOWER RHINE. By W. M. CONWAY. With Twenty-nine Illustrations. Price 7*s*. 6*d*. cloth.

MICHEL ANGELO, LIONARDO DA VINCI, AND RAPHAEL. By CHARLES CLEMENT. With Eight Illustrations on Copper. Price 10*s*. 6*d*.

THE LIFE OF HENRY DAWSON: The Landscape Painter. By his SON. With Fourteen Copper-plates. Price 21*s*.

Large-paper Copies, 2*l*. 12*s*. 6*d*.

FLAXMAN'S CLASSICAL OUTLINES. Cheap Edition for the Use of Schools of Design. With Notes by J. C. L. SPARKES, Head Master of the National Art Training Schools, South Kensington. 14*s*. complete, cloth.

THE SYLVAN YEAR: Leaves from the Note-Book of Raoul Dubois. By P. G. HAMERTON. With Twenty Etchings, by the Author and other Artists. 8vo. 12*s*. 6*d*. cloth.

Also a Cheap Edition, with Eight Etchings. Price 5*s*.

CHAPTERS ON ANIMALS. By P. G. HAMERTON. With Twenty Etchings. Post 8vo. 12*s*. 6*d*. cloth.

Also a Cheap Edition, with Eight Etchings. Price 5*s*.

THE GREY RIVER. The Thames from Greenwich to Chelsea. By JUSTIN M'CARTHY and Mrs. CAMPBELL PRAED. With Twelve Original Etchings by MORTIMER MENPES. (200 only printed.) Price 5*l*. 5*s*.

'Mr. Justin M'Carthy, Mrs. Campbell Praed and Mr. Mortimer Menpes have made among them a delightful volume. They have called it 'The Grey River,' and Messrs. Seeley and Co. have published it for them with a luxury of type and binding that will make it one of the most exquisite gift-books of the season.'—*Daily News*.

FINE-ART BOOKS.

OXFORD. Chapters by A. LANG. With Ten Etchings by A. Brunet-Debaines, A. Toussaint, and R. Kent Thomas, and several Vignettes. Price 1*l.* 1*s.*

'Told in Mr. Lang's best style, and beautifully illustrated.'—*Literary Churchman.*

Also a Cheap Edition. Crown 8vo, price 6*s.* cloth.

CAMBRIDGE. By J. W. CLARK, M.A. With Etchings and Vignettes by Brunet-Debaines and Toussaint. 1*l.* 1*s.*

'A thoroughly artistic work of topographical description and illustration.'—*Illustrated London News.*

Also a Cheap Edition. Crown 8vo. price 6*s.* cloth.

CHARING CROSS TO ST. PAUL'S. By JUSTIN M'CARTHY. With Twelve Copper-plates and many Minor Illustrations by JOSEPH PENNELL. Price 21*s.*

Large-paper Copies, with Proofs, 2*l.* 12*s.* 6*d.*

'The topography of a practised writer like Mr. M'Carthy, whose notes on the life of the streets, the theatres, and so forth, are written in an animated style, forms an agreeable accompaniment to Mr. Pennell's clever etchings. The artist's skill in pen-and-ink drawing is never more strikingly shown than in his treatment of city life and open-air impressions of the bustle of streets and street architecture.'—*Saturday Review.*

Also a Cheap Edition. Cloth, 6*s.*

Specimen of Minor Illustrations in 'The Laureate's Country.'

THE LAUREATE'S COUNTRY. Sketches of Places connected with the Life of Alfred Lord Tennyson. By A. J. CHURCH. With Fifteen Copper-plates and many other Illustrations by EDWARD HULL. Price 21*s.*

Large-paper Copies, bound in vellum, 3*l.* 3*s.*

'There can be no better gift for the lover of Lord Tennyson's poems. *Guardian.*

EVENTS OF OUR OWN TIME.

A New Series of Volumes dealing with the more important events of the last half-century. Published at 5s. With Portraits on Copper or many Illustrations. Library Edition, with Proofs of the Plates, in roxburgh, 10s. 6d.

THE REFOUNDING OF THE GERMAN EMPIRE. By COLONEL MALLESON, C.S.I. With Portraits on Copper of the Emperors William I. and Frederic, Prince Bismarck and Count von Moltke, and with Maps and Plans.

THE WAR IN THE CRIMEA. By Sir EDWARD HAMLEY K.C.B. With Portraits on Copper of Lord Raglan, General Todleben, General Pelissier, Omar Pasha, and the Emperor Nicholas; and with Maps and Plans.

'A well-written historical narrative, written by a competent critic and well-informed observer of the scenes and events it describes.'—*Times.*

THE INDIAN MUTINY OF 1857. By Colonel MALLESON, C.S.I. With Portraits on Copper of Sir Colin Campbell, Sir Henry Havelock, Sir Henry Lawrence, and Sir James Outram; and with Maps and Plans.

'Battles, sieges, and rapid marches are described in a style spirited and concise.'—*Saturday Review.*

*ACHIEVEMENTS IN ENGINEERING. By L. F. VERNON HARCOURT. With many Illustrations.

'We hope this book will find its way into the hands of all young engineers. All the information has been carefully gathered from all the best sources, and is therefore perfectly accurate.'—*Engineering Review.*

THE AFGHAN WARS OF 1839-42 AND 1878-80. By ARCHIBALD FORBES. With Portraits on Copper of Lord Roberts, Sir George Pollock, Sir Louis Cavagnari and Sirdars, and the Ameer Abdurrahman; and with Maps and Plans.

*THE DEVELOPMENT OF NAVIES DURING THE LAST HALF-CENTURY. By Captain S. EARDLEY WILMOT, R.N. With many Illustrations.

Among the other Volumes to follow are—

THE LIBERATION OF ITALY.
*THE OPENING OF JAPAN.
DISCOVERIES IN AFRICA.
THE AMERICAN CIVIL WAR.

Of Volumes so * marked there will be no Library Edition.

AMYOT BROUGH. By E. VINCENT BRITON. With Illustrations. Price 5s. cloth.

'With national pride we dwell on a beautiful English historical novel ... this sweet unpretending story, with its pretty engravings.'—*Academy.*

AN ITALIAN PILGRIMAGE. By Mrs. PENNELL. With many Illustrations by J. PENNELL. Price 6s. cloth.

'The extremely clever and artistic sketches with which the book is fully illustrated add a charm and zest to these most pleasant pages.'
Literary World.

HOLIDAY PLEASURES. Twelve Etchings by RUDOLF GEISSLER. Cloth, 5s.

REYNOLDS AND GAINSBOROUGH. By W. M. CONWAY. With Sixteen Illustrations. Cloth, 5s.

'Mr. Conway's essays are sound examples of the art of exposition, penetrative in criticism, happy in expression, and delightfully unconventional in method.'—*Saturday Review.*

STUDIES IN MODERN MUSIC. Berlioz, Schumann, and Wagner. By W. H. HADOW, M.A. With Five Portraits on Copper. Cloth, 5s.

GLIMPSES OF ITALIAN SOCIETY IN THE EIGHTEENTH CENTURY. From the Journey of Mrs. PIOZZI. With an Introduction by the Countess MARTINENGO CESARESCO, and Sixteen Illustrations.

CHAPTERS ON ANIMALS. By P. G. HAMERTON. With Eight Etchings. Published in cloth, demy, at 12s. 6d., and crown at 5s.

BOTH SIDES OF THE RIVER. A Tale for Girls. By CECILIA LOWNDES. Cloth, 5s.

'A charming little story of English life, very gracefully told, and perfectly natural.'—*Lady.*

EDINBURGH. PICTURESQUE NOTES. By R. L. STEPHENSON. With many Illustrations. Crown 8vo. cloth, 3s. 6d.; roxburgh, 5s.

'Daintily and deliciously illustrated and charmingly written, they form a volume which may be described, without exaggeration, as a literary gem of the first water.'—*St. James's Gazette.*

WINDSOR. By the Rev. W. J. LOFTIE. With Sixty-seven Illustrations. Cloth, price 6s.

PARIS IN OLD AND PRESENT TIMES, with Especial Reference to Changes in its Architecture and Topography. By P. G. HAMERTON. With Seventy Illu trations Cloth, 6s.
A few Copies of the Original Edition still remain, vellum, 4l. 4s.

Specimen of Minor Illustrations in Hamerton's 'Paris.'

ROUND MY HOUSE. Notes of Rural Life in France in Peace and War. By P. G. HAMERTON. Cloth, 5s.

JAMES HANNINGTON: First Bishop of Eastern Equatorial Africa. A Memoir. By the Rev. E. C. DAWSON, M.A. With Portrait, and Illustrations after the Bishop's own Sketches. Price 2s. 6d. paper boards, or 3s. 6d. cloth.

'We doubt whether a nobler or more pathetic story has ever been told in biography.'—*Athenæum.*

THE DRAGON OF THE NORTH. A Tale of the Normans in Italy. By E. J. OSWALD, Author of 'Studies in Iceland,' &c. With Illustrations. Price 5s. cloth.

SINTRAM AND HIS COMPANIONS. By DE LA MOTTE FOUQUE. A New Translation. With numerous Illustrations by Heywood Sumner. Cloth, price 5s.

THE CAPTAIN OF THE WIGHT. By FRANK COWPER. With Illustrations by the Author. Price 5s. cloth.

A CANTERBURY PILGRIMAGE. Ridden, Written, and Illustrated by JOSEPH & ELIZABETH PENNELL. Price 1s.; cloth, gilt edges, 2s. 6d.

'The most wonderful shillingsworth that modern literature has to offer.'
Daily News

Specimen of Illustrations in 'A Canterbury Pilgrimage.'

FLATLAND A Romance of Many Dimensions. By A. SQUARE. Price 2s. 6d.

'This book is at once a popular scientific treatise of great value, and a fairy tale worthy to rank with "The Water Babies" and "Alice in Wonderland."'—*Oxford Magazine.*

CÆDWALLA; OR, THE SAXONS IN THE ISLE OF WIGHT. By FRANK COWPER, M.A. With Illustrations by the Author. Price 5s. cloth.

BOOKS FOR PRIZES AND PRESENTS.

THE YORKSHIRE COAST AND THE CLEVELAND HILLS AND DALES. By JOHN LEYLAND. With Map, Etchings, and other Illustrations by ALFRED DAWSON and LANCELOT SPEED. Crown 8vo. cloth, 7s. 6d. Large-paper (250 only), roxburgh, 12s. 6d.

THE PEAK OF DERBYSHIRE By JOHN LEYLAND. With Map, Etchings, and other Illustrations, by HERBERT RAILTON and ALFRED DAWSON. Crown 8vo. cloth, price 7s. 6d. ; roxburgh, 12s. 6d. (250 only printed).

Specimen of Minor Illustrations in the 'Peak of Derbyshire.'

AN EXPLORATION OF DARTMOOR. By J. LL. W. PAGE. With Map, Etchings, and other Illustrations. Second edition. Crown 8vo. cloth, price 7s. 6d.

'The book is well written, and abounds in practical descriptions and old-world traditions.'—*Western Antiquary.*

AN EXPLORATION OF EXMOOR. By J. LL. W. PAGE. With Map, Etchings, and other Illustrations. Second Edition. Crown 8vo. cloth, price 7s. 6d.

'Mr. Page has evidently got up his subject with the care that comes of affection, and the result is that he has produced a book full of pleasant reading.'—*Graphic.*

A SHORT HISTORY OF NAPOLEON THE FIRST.
By Professor J. R. SEELEY. With Portrait. Price 5s. cloth.

'Within the limits which the author has set himself the essay seems to us one of singular force and brilliancy.'—*Guardian.*

THE ARAB AND THE AFRICAN.
Sketches of Life in Eastern Equatorial Africa. By S. TRISTRAM PRUEN, M.D., F.R.G.S. With Portrait of Sir Charles Euan-Smith, and other Illustrations. Crown 8vo. cloth, price 6s.

Specimen of Minor Illustrations in 'New China and Old.'

NEW CHINA AND OLD.
Notes and Observations on the Country and People, made during a Residence of Thirty Years. By Ven. A. E. MOULE, Archdeacon in Mid-China. With 31 Illustrations. Crown 8vo. cloth, price 7s. 6d.

'Archdeacon Moule deals with topics of great interest, and speaks of them with the authority due to wide personal experience.'—*Times.*

THE PHARAOHS AND THEIR LAND: Scenes of Old Egyptian Life and History.
By E. BERKLEY. With Coloured Illustrations. Cloth, price 5s.

'An account of that wonderful land which is not only interesting but valuable.'—*Leeds Mercury.*

DEAN SWIFT AND HIS WRITINGS. By G. P. MORIARTY, Balliol College, Oxford. With Nine Portraits on Copper. Cloth, 7s. 6d.
Large-paper Copies (150 only) 21s.

LADY MARY WORTLEY MONTAGU. Extracts from her Letters. Edited by A. R. ROPES, late Fellow of King's College, Cambridge. With Nine Portraits on Copper. Cloth, 7s. 6d. Large-paper Copies, 21s.

HORACE WALPOLE AND HIS WORLD. Select Passages from his Letters. Edited by L. B. SEELEY. With Eight Portraits on Copper. Cloth, price 6s.

FANNY BURNEY AND HER FRIENDS. Select Passages from her Diary. Edited by L. B. SEELEY, M.A., late Fellow of Trinity College, Cambridge. With Nine Portraits on Copper. Third Edition. Cloth, price 7s. 6d.
'The charm of the volume is heightened by nine illustrations of some of the masterpieces of English art, and it would not be possible to find a more captivating present for any one beginning to appreciate the characters of the last century.'—*Academy.*

MRS. THRALE, AFTERWARDS MRS. PIOZZI. By L. B. SEELEY, M.A., late Fellow of Trinity College, Cambridge. With Nine Portraits on Copper. Cloth, price 7s. 6d.
'Mr. Seeley had excellent material to write upon, and he has turned it to the best advantage.'—*Pall Mall Gazette.*

FOREST OUTLAWS; OR, ST. HUGH AND THE KING. By the Rev. E. GILLIAT. With Sixteen Illustrations. Price 6s. cloth.
'Distinctly one of the very best books of the season.'—*Standard.*

JOHN STANDISH; or, The Harrowing of London. A Story of Wat Tyler's Rebellion. By Rev. E. GILLIAT. With Illustrations. Price 5s.

BORDER LANCES. By the Author of 'Belt and Spur.' With Coloured Illustrations. Price 5s.

BELT AND SPUR. Stories of the Knights of Old. By the same Author. With Sixteen Illuminations. Cloth, price 5s.
'A sort of boys' Froissart, with admirable illustrations.'—*Pall Mall Gazette.*

THE CITY IN THE SEA. Stories of the Old Venetians. By the Author of 'Belt and Spur.' With Coloured Illustrations. Cloth, price 5s.

STORIES OF THE ITALIAN ARTISTS FROM VASARI. By the Author of 'Belt and Spur.' With Coloured Illustrations. Price 5s. cloth.

Specimen of Illustrations in 'Greek Gulliver.'

THE GREEK GULLIVER.   Stories from Lucian.
By Rev. A. J. CHURCH.   With Illustrations.   New Edition.
Crown 8vo. cloth, price 1s. 6d. ; 1s. sewed.

'Every lover of literature must be pleased to have Lucian's good-natured mockery and reckless fancy in such an admirable English dress.'
Saturday Review.

PROFESSOR CHURCH'S WORKS.

Stories from the Greek Comedians. 5s.
The Story of the Iliad. 5s.
The Story of the Odyssey. 5s.
The Burning of Rome. 5s.
Stories from Homer. 5s.
Stories from Virgil. 5s.
Stories from the Greek Tragedians. 5s.
Stories from the East from Herodotus. 5s.
The Story of the Persian War. 5s.
Roman Life in the Days of Cicero. 5s.
Stories from Livy. 5s.
The Count of the Saxon Shore. 5s.
With the King at Oxford. 5s.
The Chantry Priest. 5s.
Stories from the Magicians. 5s.
The Young Macedonian. 5s.
The Story of the Last Days of Jerusalem. 3s. 6d.
To the Lions. 3s. 6d.
Heroes and Kings. 1s. 6d.
Stories from the Iliad and Aeneid. Sewed, 1s.; cl. 1s. 6d.

VOLUMES OF POPULAR SCIENCE.
With Illustrations.

THE GREAT WORLD'S FARM. Some Account of Nature's Crops. By SELINA GAZE. 5s.
THE OCEAN OF AIR. Meteorology for Beginners. By AGNES GIBERNE. 5s.
SUN, MOON, AND STARS. Astronomy for Beginners. By AGNES GIBERNE. 5s.
THE WORLD'S FOUNDATIONS. Geology for Beginners. By AGNES GIBERNE. 5s.
THE STORY OF THE HILLS. By Rev. H. N. HUTCHINSON. 5s.

WORKS by MRS. MARSHALL.
At 5s.

Rachel, Lady Russell.
Winifrede's Journal.
Winchester Meads.
Under Salisbury Spire.
In the City of Flowers.
Mrs. Willoughby's Octave.
The Mistress of Tayne Court.
Constantia Carew.
Dame Alicia Chamberlayne.
Joanna's Inheritance.
Under the Mendips.
In Four Reigns.
On the Banks of the Ouse.
In the East Country.
In Colston's Days.
Life's Aftermath.
Edward's Wife.

At 3s. 6d.

Violet Douglas.
Christabel Kingscote.
Helen's Diary.
Brothers and Sisters.
Millicent Leigh.
Mrs. Mainwaring's Journal.
Lady Alice.
Heights and Valleys.
A Lily among Thorns.
Dorothy's Daughter.

WORKS by MRS. MARSHALL—*Continued.*
At 1s. sewed; 1s. 6d. cloth.

ROMANCE OF THE UNDERCLIFF.	BRISTOL BELLS.
BRISTOL DIAMONDS.	UP AND DOWN THE PANTILES.
THE TOWER ON THE CLIFF.	HER SEASON IN BATH.
THE OLD GATEWAY.	THE TWO SWORDS.

MRS. BROCK'S WORKS.

CHURCH ECHOES: a Tale illustrative of the Daily Service of the Prayer-book. Price 5*s*. cloth.

    'Will be found very useful in leading thoughtful young people to an intelligent use of their Prayer-book.'—*Guardian.*

CHURCH ECHOES, II. A Tale illustrative of the Special Services of the Prayer-book. Cloth, 5*s*.

CHANGES AND CHANCES. 5*s*.	CHILDREN AT HOME. 5*s*.
WORKING AND WAITING. 5*s*.	THE RECTORY AND THE MANOR. 5*s*.
MARGARET'S SECRET. 5*s*.	HOME MEMORIES. 5*s*.
CHARITY HELSTONE. 5*s*.	THE VIOLETS OF MONTMARTRE. 5*s*.
MICHELINE. 5*s*.	
MY FATHER'S HAND. 2*s*.	DAME WYNTON'S HOME. 3*s*. 6*d*.

SUNDAY ECHOES IN WEEKDAY HOURS. A Series of Illustrative Tales. Eight Vols. 5*s*. each.

    1. The Collects.
    2. The Church Catechism.
    3. Journey of the Israelites.
    4. Scripture Characters.
    5. The Epistles and Gospels.
    6. The Parables.
    7. The Miracles.
    8. The Example of Christ.

TALES by MISS CHARLESWORTH.

MINISTERING CHILDREN. 5*s*., 2*s*. 6*d*., 1*s*., or 6*d*.	THE OLD LOOKING-GLASS. 1*s*.
A SEQUEL TO 'MINISTERING CHILDREN.' 2*s*. 6*d*.	THE BROKEN LOOKING-GLASS. 1*s*.
SUNDAY AFTERNOONS IN THE NURSERY. 2*s*. 6*d*.	OLIVER OF THE MILL. 2*s*. 6*d*.
	ENGLAND'S YEOMEN. 2*s*. 6*d*.

TALES by MISS WINCHESTER.

ADRIFT IN A GREAT CITY. 5*s*.	UNDER THE SHIELD. 5*s*.
A NEST OF SPARROWS. 5*s*.	THE CABIN ON THE BEACH. 5*s*.
A WAYSIDE SNOWDROP. 3*s*. 6*d*.	A CITY VIOLET, 5*s*.
CHIRP WITH THE CHICKS. 2*s*. 6*d*.	
A CRIPPLED ROBIN. 5*s*.	A SEA PEARL. 5*s*.

London: Printed by STRANGEWAYS & SONS, Tower Street, Cambridge Circus, W.C.

www.ingramcontent.com/pod-product-compliance
Lightning Source LLC
Chambersburg PA
CBHW032024220426
43664CB00006B/362